WE
ALL
FALL
DOWN

by Nic Sheff

LITTLE, BROWN AND COMPANY
New York · Boston

We All Fall Down

Living with Addiction

Little, Brown and Company

Hachette Book Group
237 Park Avenue, New York, NY 10017
Visit our website at www.lb-teens.com

Little, Brown and Company is a division of Hachette Book Group, Inc.
The Little, Brown name and logo are trademarks of Hachette Book Group, Inc.

First Edition: April 2011

Excerpt from "Hold On" © 1970 Lenono Music. Written by John Lennon.

The publisher does not have control over and does not assume any responsibility for the
author or third-party websites or their content.

Library of Congress Cataloging-in-Publication Data
Sheff, Nic.
We all fall down : living with addiction / by Nic Sheff. — 1st ed.
p. cm.
ISBN 978-0-316-08082-8
1. Sheff, Nic. 2. Drug addicts—California—Biography—Juvenile literature. 3. Drug
addicts—Rehabilitation—California—Juvenile literature. 4. Methamphetamine abuse—
California—Biography—Juvenile literature. I. Title.
HV5805.S52A32 2011   362.29'9—dc22   [B]   2010038831

10 9 8 7 6 5 4 3 2 1

RRD-C

Printed in the United States of America

For my family.

For my mom and Karen and

my dad and Jasper and Daisy.

And Charles Wallace.

And Quimby and Ramona.

Hold on, John.

John, hold on.

It's gonna be all right.

—JOHN LENNON

NOTE TO READERS

This work is a memoir. It reflects
the author's present recollections of
his experiences over a period of years.
Certain names, locations, and identifying
characteristics have been changed.

Dialogue and events have been re-created
from memory and, in some cases, have
been compressed to convey the substance
of what was said or what occurred.

INTRODUCTION

2002
20 YEARS OLD

Akira lived in the basement apartment of his mom's house.

Actually, I didn't even know he'd be there, but I knocked a couple times, and then his voice came through — soft, always calming.

"Yeah?"

The bathroom window was still broken more than a year later. I could see the reflection, turned upside down, of the tall grass and the eucalyptus trees silhouetted against the darkening sky. The Presidio stretched out all the way to the beach behind me. Just forest and Army housing. Akira lived at the very edge of the city. I'd always loved that.

"Hey, Akira, man, it's Nic."

He became suddenly visible behind the dirty glass garden side door.

Long dreads all tied together behind his head. Eyes soft and lined and smudged with black underneath. Skinny, skinny like me.

"Holy shit, Nic, what the hell?"

He opened the door and I stepped forward, giving him a hug. He smelled like pot and incense and something else familiar.

"I always knew you'd show up like this," he said, keeping an arm over my shoulder. "I just had a feelin'. So, what's going on? How you been doin'?"

My eyes looked down beneath a shadow covering the base of the door and cobwebs and things.

"Great" was what I told him.

I followed him inside. I mean, I knew the goddamn way.

I'd been using again for about five months at that point. I was enrolled at Hampshire College, but I'd pretty much done nothing my last semester there except teach myself how to shoot drugs and finally make it through all of the original Legend of Zelda. No one knew I'd relapsed, though. Not even my girlfriend.

But coming home for summer break, back to San Francisco, well, I was pretty much ready to self-destruct good and proper. As much as I'd tried, I couldn't find crystal meth in Western Massachusetts. Heroin, though, was everywhere, so I'd gotten pretty sick on that shit. Actually, when I went to see Akira, I was trying to wean myself off opiates with a whole bunch of Vicodin I'd stolen.

Opiates weren't ever really my thing, though.

I mean, crystal was the drug I'd fallen in love with.

It was Akira who'd given it to me the first time. But, look, I was gonna find it one way or the other. I was searching. Akira just helped me find it. I woulda done the same for him. He's one of the most incredible people I've ever known. I sensed that about him the first time we met.

So here I am, being led back to his room, where I see the same bed and couch and Björk poster and record player and, actually, a drawing of mine that I'd done more than a year ago and forgotten.

Since then I'd been in two rehabs. At one point, I'd been sober and going to meetings for over six months. As it was, it had been more than a year since I'd done crystal. I mean, I hadn't done it since the last time I saw Akira.

We sat down on the bed together, and we talked and laughed and smoked a bowl.

Then I asked him, all casual-like. "You still talk to D ever?"

Akira looked at me, and then looked at me again.

"Ha-ha, man. What you thinkin' 'bout?"

"You know, if the factory's still on, or what?"

He lit a cigarette—a True.

He offered me one.

"Yeah," he said. "I think it's goin'. But D ain't there no more. She went crazy, man, so Gavin's running the place now."

"Crazy?"

"Uh-huh, all paranoid 'n' shit. You wanna see if Gavin's around?"

"Sure," I said, not wanting to sound too, uh, desperate or something.

So Akira called and, yeah, the factory was still operational.

We got in the car together—my dad's car. We both lit cigarettes and drove listening to a mix tape I'd made. The afternoon light was turning dull and gray as the fog slowly stretched out across the bay. The Bay Bridge kept going on for way too long, spilling out onto the different East Bay freeways like veins running in every direction.

The cookie factory was a series of warehouses with trucks coming in and out. There was a smell of cooking dough always—hot butter and sugar. There was a code Akira had to enter to get in the big electronic gate, and then we drove around back, to the offices that'd been converted into a sort of live/work space. The work being selling drugs.

I always loved how the place just looked like straight outta some movie or something. It was like magic, exciting, full of possibilities. Of course, it also looked like the kinda place the cops would straight raid. I could see the helicopters circling, the flashing sirens, the guns being drawn. Really, the place was a perfect setup.

But not that night, I told myself. That night was protected— sacred—my night. I willed everything to be okay.

We climbed up the concrete-block stairs and then around to D's, or, uh, Gavin's door.

Akira knocked.

It was a good couple minutes before we finally heard something click. Then the door opened very slowly, and the arc of a crossbow was pushed out, the arrow sticking right over Akira's head.

"Who's with you?" asked Gavin.

Akira sort of crouched down lower. "What? No one. What're you talking about?"

Gavin panned the crossbow slowly above our heads.

"All right," he said. "Come in."

We went quickly through the door, both of us trying to maybe duck down a little.

Gavin locked everything and then let the crossbow hang down. He still hadn't dropped it, though.

"Akira, Nic, it's been forever, right?"

His eyes were very wide. He had a dirty trucker hat covering a bald spot, with long hair still trying to hang down in back. He had on loose shorts and a T-shirt and big ol' construction boots. His hand was bandaged, which he quickly pointed out.

"Nearly cut it off with a hacksaw. Good thing I jerk off with my left hand, huh?"

What I did was, uh, laugh awkwardly. That's what I can give myself credit for.

The factory was set up like this, right? A waiting room with a big-screen TV and couches. Gavin's office is in the back, and normally you wait in the waiting room while they fill your orders. But that night Gavin led us back to the office.

Basically, the office was a bed and four computer screens all playing different porns. There was a swivel chair, where Gavin sat. There was also a table in the corner with a woman sitting at it—hunched over, her cheap-looking, stringy, overgrown black weave hanging long down her sharply protruding backbone. She said absolutely nothing to us as we entered the room, and Gavin didn't acknowledge her. She was too busy with a big pile of cocaine on the table. She was like a precision machine, the way she was going about cutting and doin' those lines.

Cut a line.

Do a line.

Cut a line.

Do a line.

It was fucking crazy.

But, anyway, Gavin asked us the question that made me love the cookie factory more than any place in the whole world.

"So, y'all wanna line of coke, or, no, meth, right?"

"Awesome," we both say together.

"Meth?"

"Yeah." I answered that one.

I'll tell you what, when he handed over that plate with the two generous lines of crystal cut there, man, it was like they almost looked evil to me. I could see it right there, in the color and smell and texture. It was sinister. It was like being in the presence of death.

But, fuck, I did the goddamn line, now, didn't I?

Akira did his line.

I counted.

It wasn't very long before the rush of it exploded in me like thousands of Cupid's arrows shot up and down my whole body.

I breathed out long, long, and slow.

There was no turning back, right?

Motherfucker.

And then that girl cutting lines sat up and spoke suddenly. Her eyes were crazy open, and her words were hard to understand. Her accent sounded Jamaican maybe.

"Earthquake," she said.

We all looked at each other.

"What?" asked Gavin.

"Earthquake," she said again.

And then it hit.

The whole place, like, lurched on its foundation and then just started shaking, shaking, shaking. The sound of metal and concrete grinding came through deafening.

Growing up in San Francisco, I'd been in the big '89 earthquake, when part of the Bay Bridge collapsed, but I'd never felt the world shaking around me like that night at the cookie factory.

Akira and I got in the doorway—force of habit from countless earthquake drills at school.

The shaking went on.

And then it stopped.

"Holy shit," Gavin almost yelled. "What the fuck?"

"Man, a fucking earthquake" was my brilliant observation.

"Yeah, and she sensed it, man," said Gavin, pointing at the girl. "That bitch sensed it—like a goddamn animal."

The woman didn't respond. She went back to her whole line cutting/doing thing.

In my stomach I knew.

There was a tightness there, a knotting and twisting.

That earthquake was the start.

It always worked out that way.

I start using, and the whole world just closes down on me. There are never new opportunities, no callbacks ever come. My car gets towed, and I end up losing everything all over again.

The world shuts.

I always know it's gonna come, but I try to tell myself it'll be better next time.

And maybe the earthquake wasn't a sign, didn't mean anything.

But a week later I'd been kicked outta my house and would eventually find myself living in the park behind Fort Mason.

So you tell me.

'Cause it goes the other way, too.

The longer I stay clean, the more the world just opens up with possibilities and hope.

But it's so hard to remember that shit.

And I guess that's the problem.

So today I wanna remember.

Let me tell you what happens:

It

all

falls

down.

Just like that.

Every fucking time.

Part 1

Ch.1

2005
23 YEARS OLD

She hasn't called.

I mean, I haven't called her either, but still—she hasn't called and I know it's over.

I know she's not gonna wait for me.

I know it.

She hasn't called.

The only reason I can figure is that she's afraid of telling me—afraid of what I'll do.

But I haven't called her either.

At least this way I can still pretend it's my choice.

Besides, I know leaving her is the only option I have. Practically all the therapists in this whole goddamn place have made it their personal mission to convince me she's nothing but poison for me—that what we have together isn't really love—that she's been using me—that I've been using her.

I fought it at first.

I fought it real hard.

But I can't deny it anymore.

I know the truth.

Even if I still can't give her up.

Even if I'm not sure I'll ever be able to.

Being with her is the only thing that's ever made me feel good about myself.

The fact that she chose me. I mean, Christ, she could've had anybody—fucking anybody.

And who am I?

Nothing.

Nobody.

She's everything that I'm not—everything I've always wanted to be.

She's just so cool, you know?

So fucking cool.

The way she talks, dresses, carries herself—her experiences—her beauty—how much older she is than me—how goddamn funny she is.

I admire everything that she is. Her famous ex-husband. Her famous family. Her charisma. The way every goddamn head turns when she walks into a room.

The first time I saw her—that first moment—I had to go talk to her.

I never do that.

Especially at a fucking twelve-step meeting in West Hollywood.

Being with her, I felt important—beautiful, for the first time ever.

She introduced me to her friends, family.

People in LA knew our story.

I finally had an identity, and I needed to hold on to that.

So we planned on getting married.

I made payments on a goddamn ring.

We made love all morning—all night—all afternoon.

We never wanted to get out of bed.

She told me her secrets. She gave me her past.

But then, well, then we went down.

Relapsing—shooting heroin, cocaine, crystal—popping pills till we couldn't even feel them anymore—smoking crack. We sold our clothes, books, CDs for drugs. We fought—yelled— screamed at each other. I felt her fingernails dig into my face— tearing. I ran to get away as she bit down hard at the bridge of my nose, pounding her fists into me—accusing me of hiding drugs under the tiles in the bathroom floor.

We stayed locked in our apartment.

I went into convulsions shooting cocaine.

My arm swelled up with an abscess the size of a baseball.

My body stopped producing stool, so I had to reach up inside with a gloved hand and pull out solid pieces of excrement the size and density of goddamn hockey pucks.

We both lost most everything we had—our relationships with our families, the respect of our friends.

And then I tried to steal a computer from my mom's house.

The cops showed up, and I was faced with the choice, you know: detox or jail.

I chose detox.

But my family was determined to get me away from her, so they shipped me out here to Arizona.

She went into UCLA's county program, and then the owner of the old sober living we'd both been at allowed her to come back for free.

That was over a month ago — three days before Thanksgiving, to be exact.

And at first, you know, we talked all the time.

Her detox was even worse than mine, and my detox was the worst hell I hope I'll ever have to know.

But I'm twenty-three — my body's still pretty young.

She's almost forty, and her body just couldn't take it.

First two major seizures landed her back in the hospital, and then they discovered she had gallstones, which had to be removed.

She was sick, fucking sick.

But I talked to her every day, borrowing people's calling cards so I could dial out on the one phone they had set up for us in a little enclosed room off the kitchen.

I'd sit in the wooden office chair that rocked back and forth, listening to the static hum of the space heater and my love's sweet, sweet voice. I'd have to close all the blinds 'cause I'd be crying so much — my body still vibrating with tremors from my own detox — freezing — always freezing, in spite of the space heater and the jackets and sweaters I'd borrowed from my roommate 'cause I had almost no clothes of my own.

She would tell me she loved me. We'd make plans for when I'd be able to get back to LA.

But then one morning before group, I called and things were different.

It was her voice—vacant-sounding, the sweet seductiveness gone.

I told her I loved her.

She said she didn't even know what that meant anymore.

My stomach went all tight suddenly—twisted up—knotted—the pressure building like I'd been swept down, down into the deepest ocean.

I called everyone I knew, asking for money to help me get back to LA to be with her. No one would even speak to me. I guess I'd used up every last favor from every last person in my life.

At one point I even thought about hitchhiking.

But, honestly, I'm still too weak.

And, besides, I know damn well she's not gonna fight for me anymore.

I mean, at one point she would've.

At one point she actually believed in me.

Before we relapsed, I'd been offered a book deal to write a memoir about my life. I'd finished half the manuscript, and I'd received nothing but positive feedback. I'm pretty sure she saw success in my future. Hell, maybe that's why she stayed with me.

But now I've lost all that. The book is on hold. Actually, I may have blown the whole thing completely. I have no money—no place to live—no car—no cell phone—nothing.

My only prospect of getting out of here is to go into sober living and start working some shit-ass minimum-wage job. I'm just not glamorous enough for her anymore. She'll find someone else — someone with money — someone in the entertainment industry who can open doors for her.

I know how she works. I know her so goddamn well.

We explored each other fully.

Physically and otherwise.

There was a time making love, locked in our goddamn apartment, where she lay on her back. Without really thinking about it, I began rotating my body, fucking her from every angle until I was facing completely away from her, and then back around the other side.

Goddamn, I still want her so much.

She can't be the one to leave me.

She just can't.

So I will leave her.

I won't call her — not ever again.

It's over.

I'm gonna start telling people today.

I mean, I'm gonna go do it right now.

So I walk up to the smoke pit.

It's been over a month of this shit already.

It's time to end it.

Ch.2

The Safe Passage Center in Arizona is basically just made up of a bunch of cheaply constructed little boxes on the top of a barren, dry, dust-blown hilltop about an hour and a half away from Phoenix. All the groups and weird, New Age-y therapies are held in these sort of converted trailers at the base of the property. The clients, or patients, or whatever we're called, all stay in a bunch of shoddily built imitation log cabins — usually three people per room. The only privacy comes from a cheap wooden screen set up between the beds. I actually try to spend as little time in my room as possible. It's pretty depressing in there. Plus, whenever either of my roommates comes in, I get stuck talking to him forever. Mostly, I just hang out in the main lodge — playing board games — trying to teach myself guitar on this acoustic six-string someone left behind. One of the rooms has a fireplace and, for some reason, my friend David has taken it on himself to make sure the thing is blazing constantly. Hell, I'm fucking grateful. Being by the fire's about the only way I can get warm 'round here ever. The unrelenting December wind tears through my skin and bleeds out my veins. The parched, frozen earth drains the last embers of heat from inside me.

But the fire heals. And around the fire my new friends and I spend hours laughing and messing around like little kids again—everything pure—unrestrained—stripped wide open. David, the fire builder, does a rockin' Johnny Cash imitation, so I've taught myself to play a few songs—"Boy Named Sue," "Folsom Prison," "Ring of Fire"—and we have us some good old-fashioned sing-alongs. Another friend of mine, Jason, has been teachin' me how to get better at Scrabble. But most of the time, well, we just talk is all. We sit around, tell stories, try 'n' figure out what the hell we're doing in this goddamn place, how we got here. And then, of course, we do spend a good bit of time talkin' shit about other patients and staff members. I mean, we gossip a fair amount—maybe more'n we should. But, fuck, you know, what the hell else is there to do trapped up here on this goddamn compound? Besides, we gotta keep from getting too indoctrinated with all their cult bullshit. Hell, they even have their own way of speaking here—little catchphrases—ways of expressing themselves that everyone ends up adopting before they leave.

Like, check it out, instead of saying "I think," we say "I make up." As in, "I make up that Richard is avoiding talking about the real issue." But, actually, we're only supposed to use "I" statements. So what we really say is, "What I make up is that, for me, I always want to avoid talking about the real issues, so maybe that's what's going on with Richard."

It's all pretty annoying, but somehow we all end up buying into it.

'Cause see, the thing is, the people who come here aren't just addicted to drugs, like in most rehabs. I mean, there're some people who aren't even addicts at all — they just have, like, mental problems — bipolar disorder, depression. When I first got here, there was this one woman who'd been diagnosed with multiple personality disorder. Some of 'em are recovering from serious sexual trauma and molestation. Some of 'em self-harm, or have eating disorders or sex and love addictions. Some of 'em think about killing themselves every single day. This one woman, Carol, is fifty and a virgin except for the three times she's been raped. My friend Marc had been having sex with his older brother starting at, like, ten years old.

Basically, it's a lot of really delicate people. So the rehab has, like, five million rules designed to keep everyone safe. First of all, we're not allowed to touch anyone — not even a handshake. If we wanna give someone a hug 'cause they're leaving or something, we have to get a counselor's assistant to come witness the, uh, transaction. We're not allowed to keep any sharp objects in our rooms. We're not allowed to watch R-rated movies. We're not allowed cookies or ice cream or sugar cereal at all, 'cause of all the people with food issues. Exercise is allowed only with prior counselor approval for basically the same reason.

Everything has to be supervised.

We are like little children.

And if I don't comply, I'll be told I have to stay longer—or, worse, I'll be transferred to some even more militant institution.

Because, like I said, I don't have a penny to my name; I'm completely dependent financially on my family in terms of helping me start some sort of life after treatment. Problem is, my dad buys into this rehab shit so much that he'd do literally anything my counselor tells him. He'd leave me rotting here for the next ten years if she told him to.

So I've gotta be good.

I've gotta comply with all the goddamn rules—or, at least, not get caught breaking 'em.

I've gotta tell 'em exactly what they want to hear so they can report back just how goddamn "well" I've gotten at their bullshit center.

I mean, hell, I've been in and out of rehab so many times, it's practically ingrained in me to lie about having "found my higher power" or about how much I'm getting out of working the twelve steps. They want me to say I've had a spiritual awakening, so I say I've had a spiritual awakening. They want me to say that making a "searching and fearless moral inventory" of myself—as we're directed to do in Step 4—is some life-changing experience for me. So, yeah, I go on and tell 'em all about how powerful the whole thing was for me—even if, in truth, I didn't feel anything at all and I never have. They don't have any other solution they can suggest. If the twelve-step thing doesn't work, well, they just won't accept that.

So I'll tell 'em I've found God.

I'll tell 'em the steps are working for me.

And I'll tell them I've decided to leave Zelda.

They're gonna eat that shit up — the counselors — my friends here — everyone.

Even if, like I said, she's the one who hasn't called me.

I'm gonna make it so they all think it's my decision.

I'm going to show them how much I've changed — how healthy I'm becoming.

So I walk up to the smoke pit — layered with a borrowed sweatshirt and jacket against the bitter desert winds. The only pants I have are my soon-to-be-ex's tight-ass bell-bottoms. It wasn't till I was already in Arizona that I realized my bag was filled with basically nothing but her clothing. I guess that's what I get for letting her pack for me.

Anyway, when I make it to the little smoking hut, Jonathan's the only one who's still there.

I forgot we have our community meeting in, like, two minutes.

Jonathan's become a pretty good friend of mine. He's a musician in his mid-forties with an odd-looking face — mostly because he was in a car accident as a teenager, and his parents forced him to undergo countless reconstruction surgeries, telling him they were necessary when they really just didn't like the way he looked.

Jonathan turned to alcohol and cocaine pretty hard-core once he came of age.

But now he's sober.

Hell, he's crafted himself as the goddamn poster boy for this rehab.

And, for some reason, he seems to have adopted me as his

little pet project—convinced he can save me, whatever that means.

But, anyway, Jonathan is there, in the smoke pit, sitting cross-legged on one of the stained, dirty, what once must've been white plastic chairs.

He smiles real big up at me—his wraparound dark glasses reflecting the faraway sun like spilled ink bleeding out in every direction.

"Hey, little brother," he says, his West Texas accent sounding almost like an imitation of itself. "Yer goin' to group, ain't ya?"

I nod. "For sure."

He hands me a cigarette before I can even ask for one—which I was about to.

My broke-ass status is known to pretty much everyone.

"Thanks, man," I say, lighting the unfiltered Camel that's strong as hell.

I take a couple of drags, looking up at the clear, cold sky.

"Jonathan." I clear some shit outta my throat. "I wanted to tell you that I've been thinking a whole lot about what you've been saying. I mean, about the whole girlfriend situation and all."

He cuts me off before I can finish, holding up a hand like I'm some dog he's commanding to "stay."

"Hey, come on, now," he says, each word painfully drawn out. "That's yer decision to make, and yers alone. I ain't gonna think any less of you either way. That's a promise."

I dig my beat-up old Jack Purcell sneaker into the dry, red earth—kicking up a thick smudge of dust—watching it drift slowly upward—suspended for a moment while the wind lies idle.

My free hand reaches up to scratch at my ear needlessly.

"Well," I say, stuttering some, "I've decided. I mean, I'm going to end it. There's no way we'll ever be able to stay sober together—I see that now. And, besides, I really think I'm starting to understand what our relationship is all about. I mean, you're right, we were totally just using each other. I honestly don't think she's even capable of love. I feel like . . . you know . . . I feel like loving Zelda is like trying to love a black hole. I can't do it anymore. I have to end it."

I breathe out deep and long and slow.

Fuck.

Fucking, fuck.

Jonathan pushes himself up from the chair.

He takes off his sunglasses.

I watch his pupils suck in all at once, retreating from the dull midmorning light.

His head nods up and down—up and down.

"Ain't that somethin'? Well, little brother, I gotta admit, I sure am proud of you."

His blue, bright, almost transparent eyes are fixed on me, so I can't help but turn away.

"Man," he says, "I know how hard it can be to break out of a messed-up relationship like that. Hell, my ex-wife and I are still playin' the same fucked-up games we've been playin' for the last ten years. Yer damn lucky, my friend, to be twenty-three and already starting to face this shit."

Before I even know what's happening, he gives me a hug—ignoring that whole "no touch" policy thing.

I hug him back—overwhelmed by the smell of pomade and whatever else he uses to keep his hair pressed down so goddamn flat.

"This is yer chance, Nic, I hope you know that. I see the way you've been fightin' this place. You've been fightin' everything and everyone. And, hell, I don't blame you at all. I mean, you remind me exactly of myself when I was yer age. I don't know, maybe that's why I wanna look out for you. I'm nearin' on fifty years old. I've spent my whole life running from myself. I've wasted so much time. But I'm tellin' you—right here—in this godforsaken place—where yer standing at twenty-three and I'm standing at forty-nine—this is where the answer is. You start opening up and doing all the shit they tell you, I guarantee, not only are you gonna stay sober, yer gonna come out of here lovin' and respectin' yourself like you never have in yer whole life."

He takes drags at the butt of his cigarette, exhaling loudly and saying, "Goddamn, do I wish I'd had this opportunity at your age." And then, stamping out the cherry and putting his sunglasses back on, "You better not fuckin' blow it, ya hear. I swear I'll hunt your ass down."

He laughs and laughs at that, and I laugh, too, just 'cause it seems polite.

"You can relax, little brother, the sermon's over. Let's get on to group, huh?"

He starts off down the hill, but before he can get too far, I stop him, saying, "Hey, Jonathan."

He turns back, taking off his sunglasses again, I guess to show that he's really listening.

"I, uh... you know... thank you. I wanna change. I really do. And... well, I believe you that this is the place where that can happen."

He nods his head, smiling with his mouth closed.

"It is, little brother. I wouldn't lie to you."

He turns away from me again.

"Come on," he calls back. "I'll even bring out the guitars after dinner if you want. This is a day to celebrate."

I follow on down after him, feeling safe suddenly—like being curled up small—following him down to the group room in one of the converted trailers, and he opens the door and holds it for me to go past.

We're late, of course, but not by that much.

Still, I'm sure I'll get some shit for it from someone, so I don't look around at all till I've already grabbed an open seat near the back.

This guy Richard's on one side of me—a fat creep who always wears one of those ridiculous Greek fisherman's hats.

He leans over and whispers, "You're late," in my ear.

He laughs moronically, putting his elbow into my side.

"Check out the new girl," he says, gesturing with his bulbous head. "I bet she's your type."

I tell him to shut up, but I still look just the same.

A twisted cord lying loose in my stomach is pulled tight all at once.

The girl's around my age, for sure.

Long, straight black hair—eyes almost feline.

Pale, pale skin.

Thick white cutting scars up and down her forearms.

Fuck.

I sit back in my chair.

I know exactly what's gonna happen.

I breathe out.

She introduces herself to the group as Sue Ellen.

Her accent is very Southern.

I study her face—pained, shy, uneasy.

Her dark eyes catch mine.

Fuck.

Ch.3

For some goddamn reason my counselor, Melonie, scheduled to meet me at seven thirty this morning.

I gotta say, I'm pretty well convinced it's 'cause I'm in trouble. I mean, that's usually what my one-on-one counselor meetings are all about. I guess the way Melonie sees it is that I'm not taking this place seriously. So her solution is to sit there in her goddamn expensive-looking office chair — fat spilling out like the Stay Puft Marshmallow Man — smiling — doling out each new punishment with sociopathic calm — always knowing just how to fuck me the very fucking hardest.

For a while I couldn't have any kind of interaction with any kind of female on or off the premises — including phone calls — even with my goddamn mom.

I wasn't allowed to write in my notebook, play the guitar they have in the lodge, or read in my cabin.

Her justification was that I was using all those things as a way of not facing my real issues.

And, of course, she didn't stop there.

Like I said, before I relapsed I'd been writing a memoir for this publishing company in New York, and I'd actually finished about half of it before I started using again—going completely crazy—I mean, out of control. I'd call up my agent and editor totally incoherent, asking for money, rambling on about I-can't-even-remember-what.

Honestly, I thought I'd blown it.

I couldn't imagine them stickin' by me through all this shit.

But they have—I mean, since I first checked into detox—they've been nothing but supportive—calling and e-mailing me—encouraging me to take as much time as I need to get well.

And, fuck, man, thank God.

Writing my book—finishing it—getting it published—that's, like, the one thing I have to hold on to. I mean, really, since I was, like, six years old, my dream has been to get a book published. The fact that I've gotten this far still seems like a total miracle.

But, according to Melonie, as long as I'm thinking about writing my book, I'll never get better. She says it makes me see myself as a character in a story rather than a real person. She says the only reason I even want to write a book in the first place is to impress other people. She also says I'm using this whole book thing as a way of avoiding "what's really going on."

Christ.

I almost cried when she told me.

"Nic," she said, smiling all big but not like she meant it. "Writing a book is a fantasy. You know how many people actually make it as book writers?"

My shoulders rose and then fell. My eyes rolled back.

"No, I don't," I told her. "And I bet you don't, either."

Her pig face went all scrunched up—globular, pale, fleshy cheeks flushed red—the black center of her mud-colored eyes fluttering back and forth.

"N-n-no, I don't. But I can tell you one thing for sure, it's not many. The fact that you insist on maintaining this delusion of success for yourself only further demonstrates to me how narcissistic you really are. You still think you're special—better than the rest of us. You think you're too good for this place— too good for the twelve steps—too good for God. Well, I've been doing this work a long time, and I've met a lot of people, and I can tell you right now, Nic, you're just about as average as they come. So you better stop thinking about what you're gonna do when, or if, you get out of here, and start taking the work we're doing here very, very seriously, or you're not going to have any future to look forward to whatsoever."

She took some deep breaths like she was all winded or something.

I crossed and uncrossed my legs and then crossed them again. My voice came out trembling—my teeth bit down together.

"Yeah, no, I understand what you're saying...and, uh, I agree, I am average. I mean, I'm less than average. I'm a total fucking mess—and, uh, I've always been a failure at everything.

But writing, well, writing's always been the one thing I could actually do, you know? It's really the only chance I've got. Otherwise, I'm, like, totally unemployable and, uh, hopeless. So I've gotta keep trying to write. Even if I don't make it, I mean, it's worth taking a shot—'cause I've really got nothing else."

Melonie laughed.

She laughed right in my face.

"The twelve steps are the only chance you have," she told me, her words coming out eerily calm and even suddenly. "There's nothing else to say and nowhere else to look. You can either accept that and live, or reject it and die. It's up to you. But for now you are absolutely forbidden to do any writing on your book or any writing at all. And you're not allowed to talk about your book to anyone—not me, not the other clients, not people you talk to on the phone—no one. And if I get word back that you have been talking about it or that you've been doing any kind of writing, we will immediately have a meeting with Linda, the director, and we may be forced to transfer you to a higher-care facility with more structure and more intense supervision. Do you understand me?"

I didn't answer right away.

I mean, what the hell was I supposed to say to that? She had me. She'd ground me down to nothing.

That was the last meeting we had together. So you can imagine how goddamn excited I am to be meeting with her today. I mean, I'm sure that someone's snitched on me about something and that's why she's dragged my ass out of bed so damn early.

'Cause, see, the thing is, besides Melonie, there are, like, fifty of these people called counselor's assistants—you know, CAs—who are constantly swarming the grounds like an infestation of head lice.

As far as I can tell, their only real job is to spy on us—or me, in particular—and report back to our counselors whatever it is we've been doing wrong.

And, fuck, man, somehow they're able to catch everything.

I mean, at least with me.

Other people can be walking around holding hands and flirting like crazy, but if I so much as even look at a girl, I'm telling you, Melonie'll get me—every time.

And she knows I can't do shit about it.

Like I said, I've got no money—no one to bail me out. If they kick me outta here, I'm on the streets—the fucking streets of Phoenix, Arizona. If it was San Francisco or LA, at least I'd have a chance. But here? Man, I don't even know where the nearest store is.

Not to mention that the longer she keeps me here, the more money my parents have to pump into this bullshit place.

It's brilliant, really.

I mean, at this point my parents are so desperate they'll do just about anything Melonie tells them. She's replaced a God I'm pretty sure neither of them actually ever had in their lives in the first place.

And if I try to argue, shit, they all just assume I'm resisting 'cause I secretly wanna go get high. If I try to call this place out on its bullshit, the staff just dismisses me, telling me it's my "addict" talking. As if, because I'm a junkie, I've somehow lost all ability to reason—to analyze and critique situations. Maybe when I was high I didn't know the difference between reality and psychosis, but I'm sober now, and I'm telling you, when it comes to this place, the emperor has no clothes—no clothes at all.

But I'm as good a bullshitter as anyone.

I can't wait to see Melonie's chunky, placid, dopey-looking face when I tell her me and my girl are over. That I'm ready, like Jonathan said, to commit fully to the hard work that lies ahead of me here.

Ch.4

So I wake up, right? Even before the bedside alarm clock goes off—just lying there awhile—the thick comforter pulled right up to my neck—staring at the goddamn Lincoln Log ceiling.

Gray light, all dull and muted, floods the room.

I turn onto my side—shut my eyes—open them—just trying to get my head to shut the hell up.

There's this feeling of...I don't know.

Hopelessness, I guess.

Images of suicide are projected against the textured blur of my unfocused eyes.

Blood turns to poison—gasoline—lit fires.

A gun barrel is there, pressed up against my temple—cold, heavy, tangible.

My finger squeezes the trigger tight—my arm jerks back.

A noise so loud my eardrums burst open.

A serrated kitchen knife plunges in behind my ear, slicing through the vital arteries there.

There is a chain wrapped serpentine 'round my throat—a dog's choke chain and leash—secured to a heavy wooden beam beneath the ceiling.

I kick the chair out from underneath me—feel the metal cutting in, the heaviness of my body. My lungs spasm, legs twitching, stomach convulsing. Sexual arousal. Fluids draining out.

But, honestly, if I was gonna do it, I mean, really fucking do it, I'd take the easy way—the only way: a shot of black tar so thick my hand would have to struggle against the plunger.

No pain.

Just bliss.

And one final nod.

I've told Melonie about it.

I mean, it kinda freaks me out—these fantasies of death.

She tells me there's actually a term for it, so I'm obviously not that unique or anything.

Suicidal ideation.

I'm pretty sure that's it.

She also tells me that killing myself would be a permanent solution to a temporary problem.

Thing is, my problems really don't seem all that temporary.

I mean, why do you think I started getting high in the first place?

I was twelve years old.

My friend's brother got us some weed—a dime bag, that's all.

We hiked down to a creek near his parents' house—trees

grown over thick—mud and veins of ivy pulling at our shoes like thousands of clutching fingers.

The smell.

Damp, rot, sweet.

We huddled together, terrified of cops and parents and parents' friends.

The bowl was passed to me.

I took a hit, holding the smoke in my lungs for as long as I could—feeling the drug reach out into the cavities of my brain—spinning webs of pixie dust and cotton candy.

I felt open like a child—full of wonder—innocent, like I could never remember being.

I had permission to do anything—act any way I wanted.

I was high.

That was my purpose.

But most of all, more than anything else, smoking herb gave me freedom.

I didn't care anymore.

I didn't need to hold my family together.

I didn't need to rescue my mom from her abusive husband.

I didn't need to worry that my dad loved his new wife and children more than me.

And nothing, I mean, no one could touch me.

It was instant relief.

At only twenty bucks a gram.

But, unfortunately, I mean, what no one told me, was that my tolerance would build. By the end of high school, I was smoking all day, from the moment I got up to the moment I passed out—but it wasn't really working for me anymore.

I was barely getting high at all.

The relief had been taken away.

And I was stuck with the pain of living as myself again.

I needed something — something to take it all away.

And then I found hard drugs.

After that, man, pot seemed like baby aspirin.

And I went down.

I mean, down, down, down.

Sleeping in the devil's bed.

As Mr. Waits would say.

But, you know, after all these years, even hard drugs aren't really doing it for me anymore.

And maybe that's the scariest thing of all.

'Cause if I can't find something else — some way to live with myself — then, yeah, suicide's gonna be all I've got left.

And, honestly, it doesn't seem all that bad.

Or that far off.

But I figure I can keep holding on for at least one more day.

I mean, that's what they say, right?

One day at a goddamn time.

Hell, one fucking second at a time.

It's Tuesday morning.

Six fifty-five and I-don't-know-how-many seconds.

All I've gotta do is get out of bed.

So I do.

I mean, I sit up, the sheets and blankets falling down around my waist.

My roommate David, who sleeps directly across from me, must've gone to the gym or something, 'cause he's not in his bed. Fucker must've been the one who turned off the heat, 'cause I definitely switched it on in the middle of the night, and now it's freezing.

I mean, goddamn.

I can barely get my clothes on, I'm shivering so bad.

Plus, like I said, basically the only pants I have are a bunch of my soon-to-be ex-girlfriend's tiny fucking bell-bottoms.

Struggling to get into them is a bitch, but since I've dropped, like, fifteen pounds in the last six months, it's not as bad as it could be.

I swear my body's been practically eating away at itself—little by little—day by day.

Back when I was sober, man, I'd basically killed myself with exercise.

I mean, every day.

Training for races and triathlons—obsessively biking, swimming, and running.

I was strong, really strong.

To look at me now, I mean, you'd never even know it.

I can't walk up the hill to the smoke pit without feeling like I'm gonna puke.

I'm pale, white, and sickly.

My arms are scarred to shit.

My skin's all broken out.

My bones are jagged—protruding sharply down my spine and hips and shoulders.

Anyway, at least this way I can fit into these tight fucking jeans.

So that's something.

But besides these bell-bottoms, pretty much all the clothes I have with me are Zelda's—or her famous ex-husband's—or were given to me by her.

The long-sleeve T-shirt I wear.

The fringed tapestry jacket that looks like a converted throw rug, or something Neil Young might've worn on an old album cover.

The Rod Laver Adidas she bought me 'cause she hated my old shoes.

The knit hat she gave me—made by her cousin.

The thick, boxy silver ring from her collection—a symbol of our engagement—worn on my left ring finger, of course.

I put a burned CD into my Discman and secure the headphones.

It's one of hers. The title is spelled out almost illegibly in her scratchy handwriting, the black Sharpie smudged in places. *If I Could Only Remember My Name*. David Crosby.

I press Play—walk out into the still, frozen morning.

My breath catches.

I pull the thin jacket tighter around my broken frame.

Coffee and a cigarette—some toast and jam, maybe.

I'll meet with Melonie—tell her it's over, that I'm ready to move on.

Stupid cow.

She'll be so pleased with herself, taking full credit for my sudden transformation—a result of her profound insight—her expert counseling skills—her intricate knowledge of the human psyche—her brilliance—whatever.

I mean, fuck it.

I don't mind giving her that satisfaction.

'Cause I do need to move on.

It's the only choice I've got.

The song plays loud in my ears.

It's called "Music Is Love."

I walk over to the main lodge.

The fire burns hot—light flickering—shadows playing violently across the chairs and tables.

I keep my head down—pour the weak Folgers coffee into a small porcelain cup—add vanilla creamer—stir.

I grab a pack of cinnamon bread, putting a couple of slices in the pop-up toaster, and then start heading out the side door to go smoke.

Jonathan actually bought me a carton of cigarettes when he went out on pass—a carton of my brand—so that was super amazing of him.

I push open the heavy wooden door.

But then a voice calls out, "Hey."

I turn.

They say self-hatred is a form of narcissism—and obviously Melonie would call me a narcissist—so of course I assume the "hey" is directed at me.

Surprisingly, this time it actually is.

That new girl—Sue Ellen, right?—is sitting up close to the fire, reading the New York Times Arts and Leisure section—obviously.

She's wearing these kinda deco cat-eye glasses and a striped wool hat.

Her hair is dark and tangled-looking. Her neck cranes back, long and elegant.

I point to myself stupidly.

"Me?"

She laughs.

"Yeah, you. Where're you from? You look familiar to me."

I rub some of the sleep out of the corner of my eye.

"I don't know, uh, LA. I grew up in San Francisco. What about you?"

She cocks her head.

"Charleston, South Carolina, but I've been to San Francisco. What's your name?"

I tell her, but she still can't seem to place me.

"Huh, weird, I swear you look familiar."

"Well," I say, "my mom's from the South. But, uh, I've never been down there. I always figured I'd get lynched or something."

She sits up real suddenly.

"You know, not everyone in the South is a conservative bigot. And it seems pretty ironic that most Northern liberals I know are just as closed-minded about the South as they always claim we are toward the rest of the world."

I scratch at the back of my head, kinda just studying her for a minute, watching her heavy eyelids fluttering anxiously, thinking she really is quite beautiful. Her features are delicate—gaunt cheekbones and thick, flushed lips. She hides behind her hair like I do. Her skin is pale, pale white. Her long, slender hands fidget constantly—fingernails bitten down, scabbed and bloody.

My eyes dart up at the bland yellow paint on the walls.

"Okay, okay," I tell her. "Point taken. Anyway, it's too early for this shit. I gotta go smoke."

She jumps up from her seat suddenly, grabbing up her newspaper and things.

"I'll come with you. And by the way, you got cool style. I've been wanting to tell you that."

I push the door open, holding it while she walks past— inhaling the smell of her.

A feeling of sexuality comes over my body.

My eyes close and open.

I laugh out loud suddenly.

I mean, it's all so ridiculous—everything spinning around and around and around again.

She walks with her body pressed close to mine.

She asks me, "What are you laughing at?"

And I say, "Nothing."

Ch.5

When Melonie sees me, she sure as hell ain't smiling.

She stares very deliberately into my eyes, but I look away, saying something stupid like, "Man, I'm so sorry I'm late."

She makes a sort of grunting noise, struggling to lower her massive body onto the cheap swivel office chair.

To say she's morbidly obese is kind of an overstatement, I guess, but she's definitely fat and getting fatter all the time. Plus, she wears these ridiculously tight clothes—baby doll T-shirts—low-waisted pants that must cut off her circulation completely—high-heeled sandals, her foot fat pinched and swelling so the veins bulge out underneath.

But it's not like I'm judging her. I mean, I just get pissed off 'cause she's always harassing me about food and my body size. Last time we met, she accused me of trying to maintain my skinniness 'cause I'm afraid of having a grown-up body and becoming an adult. She even has me showing my plate of food to the CAs at lunch and dinner so they can make sure I've finished everything.

It's bullshit.

I sit down and cross my legs, then uncross them again.

I cross my right arm over so I'm grabbing my left shoulder.

I can feel Melonie staring at me, but I keep avoiding her eyes anyway.

"Look," I try again, "I'm really sorry. That new girl was talking to me up at the smoke pit, and I guess I felt too bad just cutting out on her. I mean, she was starting to go into her story a little, and I didn't wanna make her think I didn't care or anything."

Glancing up, I see that Melonie is definitely not smiling.

She shakes her head slowly back and forth, the pores on her cheeks catching the light, revealing a landscape of soft, downy hairs.

I can't help wondering if she ever shaves them.

"Nic," she says, startling me slightly, "it sounds to me like, once again, you're letting your codependency get in the way of your treatment. Instead of stating your needs, you were content to sacrifice your own mental health—all because you didn't want to offend someone you only met today. A girl someone, no less. Are you noticing a pattern yet?"

I nod my head slowly, basically just 'cause it seems appropriate.

"It sounds to me," she goes on, "that this is exactly what you've been doing your whole life. Just look at your relationship with your biological mother—your relationship with

Zelda. How many times are you going to forfeit your own needs before you have nothing else to give? And that includes your life, Nic, let's not kid ourselves. Because obviously you don't value yourself enough to arrive on time for an appointment with me that very well could be the very thing that finally saves you."

If I could roll my eyes, I would.

She concludes by telling me that I'd never be late for scoring drugs like I would for therapy.

My neck's getting sore from nodding so goddamn much.

"Yeah," I stutter out. "That's crazy. I never thought about it like that before. It's so weird that you can be acting out on all these old behaviors without even realizing you're doing it. I mean, you just keep repeating the same destructive pattern over and over."

She holds her hand out, palm facing forward—gesturing "stop," I figure—so I do.

"What are you trying to say, Nic, that I keep repeating these destructive patterns?"

I'm not sure what she's getting at, and my head kinda cocks to one side like a dog's would.

"Nic, you said, 'You keep repeating them.' But you're not talking about me, are you? You're talking about yourself. That's why we encourage clients to use 'I' statements here. Each one of us needs to own what we're saying about ourselves, understand?"

My head does its whole involuntary nodding thing again.

"Yeah," I tell her. "Sorry, you're right. I'm the one who keeps repeating these behaviors over and over. But I want to change. I really do. And I've been trying. I've been trying to take steps in that direction. And I know the first thing I have to do."

I swallow real loud, choking on some invisible nothing. A kind of heat pushes up against the back of my eyes.

This isn't supposed to happen.

All I'm doin' is playing Melonie so she'll give back some of my privileges.

But when I try to get the rest of the words out, my voice cracks on the first syllable.

The room is unfocused.

Instinctively, I sort of fold in on myself—crossing my arms like an X in front of me—holding on tight to both shoulders—shivering.

"The thing is," I manage to get out, in a voice that seems very far away, "I'm breaking up with Zelda."

The tears come—lower lip trembling—rocking back and forth in my chair—my knees pressed together—one foot stepping on the other.

"I have no choice," I hear myself saying. "There's just no way we're ever gonna make it. I have to let her go. I have to. Y'all've been telling me, but I still couldn't see it. I mean, I wouldn't let myself see it. But now, man, now it's like I can't see anything else. She's poison to me. Man, fuck, I threw away my whole life for her. But it wasn't enough and it'll never be enough and I have to end it now before I get sucked back in again. I fucking have to. There's nothing left for us—not one goddamn thing. She's a vortex, a black hole. I see it, man, I fucking see it. And I know it's over. I know it's the end. But, Christ..."

My voice catches again, and now I'm crying hard, with snot pouring down and my stomach convulsing.

"I'm so scared," I say, feeling it. "I'm so goddamn scared. I mean, I love her. I love her fucking hard. And no matter how much I've tried to quit loving her, I just can't cut her out—man, there's no way. As long as I live, I know I'll never find anyone who can compare to her. And I know I'll never love anyone as intensely as I love her. And I know I'll never stop dreaming about her—every day and night. I have to live with that—with fucking missing her for the rest of my life. I have to. And I'm so fucking scared."

My hands cover my face. The crying hurts—it strangles me. I fight for breath. My eyes are straining closed. I bring my legs up on the chair, knees bent, pressing them tighter and tighter against my body.

"Hey!" Melonie shouts at me. She claps her hands twice. "Hey, Nic, where'd you go?"

I breathe, breathe, breathe, breathe, breathe.

"Nic," she says again, leaning forward, her elbows resting on her gelatinous knees. "Nic, listen to me. I need you to sit up straight, okay. You need to sit up straight right now."

I try 'n' do what she says.

"Okay, good. Now I want you to put both feet on the floor. Good. Press down on the carpet. I want you to ground yourself. When you panic like that, all you're doing is making things worse. Panicking is a way for people to not have to feel their real feelings. By panicking you work yourself up into such a frantic state that it's no longer about what's truly going on, it's about the act of panicking. Understand? As long as you keep running from your feelings, you'll never move past them. Right now you're scared. You're sad, too, but mostly scared. So what I want you to do is check in with your body. Try to find where it is exactly that you feel this fear. Is it in your head? Your stomach? Your legs? Then sit with the fear. Explore it. Try to understand it. Believe me, Nic, the fear of the fear is always much, much worse than the fear itself. Because when you sit with it, embrace it, the fear will begin to lose its power. And eventually it'll be gone completely. And then you'll be free. But as long as you keep running, Nic, you'll never move past it. The fear and trauma will haunt you the rest of your life. Do you understand?"

I tell her I do, wiping my nose on the inside of my sleeve. The crying has stopped by now. My eyes are all swollen, and my throat is sore.

"Good," she says, straightening up so her back goes *pop*. "So look, I have some business stuff I need to go over with you. But first I want to say two things. One is that, trust me, you are absolutely incapable of loving anyone. What you think is love for Zelda is actually something else entirely."

My hands grip the metal arms of the chair, and I clench my teeth.

Still, I don't say anything.

She continues with an even, meaningless smile.

"Zelda used you. She's getting older and I'm sure terrified of what that means for her—since, from what I can tell, she's always been dependent on her looks. You come along—young, attractive, and completely in awe of her — and she takes advantage of you with no thought to your well-being at all. She used you for her emotional and physical validation, then she tricked you into using again with her. You're right, Nic, she is a black hole. So whatever love you think there is between you is not love at all — it's codependency and mutual exploitation."

I breathe in deep through my nose, helpless to do anything but nod my head.

I mean, what choice do I have?

I need her on my side if I'm ever gonna get out of this place.

So I nod and nod like the idiot I am.

And Melonie smiles — so goddamn pleased with herself.

"So the last thing I want to talk to you about is your twelve-step meeting schedule. From what I remember, you told me that you don't believe in the twelve-step program, is that right?"

My teeth clench together again.

"Well, no, not exactly. All I was saying is that I feel sort of let down by it, you know? I mean, every time I've gotten sober I've been, like, so fanatic about the program. I give it everything I have — going to meetings every day, working with a sponsor, studying the twelve steps and all the literature until I can practically recite it all by heart. But the thing is, no matter how much I keep trying to do it right, I keep relapsing, you know? And I guess I just can't figure out if it's because the program doesn't work for me, or because I'm not working the program right."

Now it's Melonie's turn to nod self-consciously.

"And the higher-power thing? How are you feeling about that?"

I crack the knuckles on my left hand.

"I don't know. I mean, I guess it's sort of the same thing. I've tried so hard to believe, right? I've prayed and meditated and studied. But it's never worked for me — I keep relapsing — and, you know, in the center of me, after everything, it just feels like there's nothing there."

Melonie's still kind of bobbing her head for no reason.

"Okay, Nic, that's okay. But the thing is, without twelve-step meetings, without a higher power, you have absolutely zero chance of staying sober. Now, I am impressed with the progress you've made regarding your girlfriend, and I'd like to take you off probation so you can go on outings with the other clients, but I'm afraid I'm not going to be able to do that until you agree to go to twelve-step meetings at least six nights a week. And I need you to get a sponsor and start working the steps as soon as possible, okay? It's the only chance you have, Nic. And, believe me, there's nothing so special about you that makes you any different from the millions of other people whose lives have been saved by the twelve-step program."

"Yeah," I say. "I know. And I really do want to get involved in the program again. I mean, I've seen the way it's helped all my friends back in LA."

She swivels 'round slowly in her chair, grabbing a stack of papers and a clipboard off her desk.

"So you can agree to six meetings a week?" she asks.

I tell her I can, and she checks off a little box on the page in front of her.

"Also I need you to get a sponsor by the end of the week, okay? And find a higher power?"

I actually almost laugh at that.

"Yes," I say. "Absolutely."

She checks another box and then looks up at me, smiling.

"Well, congratulations. You're officially off probation. And, honestly, Nic, I'm very impressed with the change I see in you. Good job."

I smile back.

I mean, what choice do I have?

Ch.6

Because I'm finally off probation, Melonie went ahead and okayed me for the Sunday outing—a hike somewhere—a place called Tent Rocks, I think. The van's not loading up for another ten or fifteen minutes, but I'm already up waiting 'cause I'm pretty anxious to get off this goddamn compound.

Not that it'll be my first time.

I've gone out twice this week to twelve-step meetings—plus on a group trip to Target and Borders. Of course, I still don't have any money, but this stealing thing I've gotten into is a hard habit to break.

When I was with Zelda, we subsisted entirely on stolen food from grocery stores and drugstores and wherever. We'd even drive down to the Grove shopping center with the sole purpose of roaming from shop to shop, stealing books and

CDs, clothing, computer supplies—basically, whatever we could get away with.

And, it's crazy, you know, 'cause I never really thought jacking shit could become some kind of addiction, but still, now that I'm sober, I find myself walking outta places with books in my hands and candy bars in my goddamn pockets—none of which I need or even want particularly.

It's super dumb.

I mean, dumb.

There's actually a part of me that wants to call up Zelda just to ask if she's having the same problem, but I figure that's probably just some excuse, or whatever. I mean, as it is I have to spend, like, every second I'm awake trying not to think about her—keeping myself busy—messing around on the guitar, talking with my friends, playing board games—fucking Scrabble—going to groups. Hell, the other day I ended up spending almost two hours watching this guy Kevin solve the New York Times crossword puzzle.

I think I contributed about three answers.

I mean, even here, waiting for the van, I pace back and forth.

I light a cigarette, listen to my old Discman—playing The Rise and Fall of Ziggy Stardust over and over. David Bowie singing about a Starman waiting in the sky.

If only there really was someone waiting out there—waiting to take me away from all this.

David Bowie singing, "If we can sparkle he may land tonight."

Suddenly something hits my shoulder kinda hard.

I take off one of my headphones and turn to look back behind me.

I guess, not surprisingly, it's that Sue Ellen girl.

She punches me in the shoulder again, this time even harder.

For some reason that makes me really fucking laugh.

I tell her, "Ow, man."

She hits me again.

"What you listenin' to?"

Her voice is jarring — maybe a little too loud.

She takes off the baseball hat she's wearing, shakes out her hair — looking up at me through narrowed eyes — her body thin — delicate-looking — I mean, fragile.

She catches me staring.

"Hey ... Nic ..."

This time I'm able to dodge her punch.

"Damn, girl, all right.... It's David Bowie. I'm listening to *Ziggy Stardust*. You know that album?"

Somehow the green of her eyes seems to clear or brighten or something.

"Are you serious?" she asks me, her mouth remaining slightly open. "That's my favorite album ever."

I laugh.

"Right on. I wouldn't've thought y'all listened to a whole lot of David Bowie in the South."

She smiles, tucking her hair back behind her ears.

"Yeah, well, there's a lot about me you don't know."

I start to say something in response to that, but then a sharp, burning pain shoots through my hand and, instinctively, I drop the smoldering end of my cigarette butt that I'd totally forgotten about, swearing loudly.

Sue Ellen laughs and laughs.

She puts her hat on over her face so I can't see her eyes at all.

"Sorry," she says, her voice kinda muffled. "I don't mean to laugh. I've been up since five thirty writing this stupid good-bye letter, so I guess I'm still a little punchy, you know? Have you had to write one of those?"

I shake my head but then remember pretty quickly she probably can't see me.

"No, uh, no. What do you mean? What kinda good-bye letter?"

She pushes the hat up so her eyes are just barely visible beneath the brim.

"Oh, you know—just some lighthearted Sunday morning fun. My counselor wants me to write a good-bye letter to all my friends and family who didn't stand by me, or even believe me, after it happened. I mean, the way my dad acted, you woulda thought I was the one who did something wrong—it was like he couldn't even look at me. So I'm supposed to write this letter saying good-bye to all these people, including my dad, my boyfriend, and basically all my friends from school, who I'm supposed to be cutting outta my life for good. Do you know Amy, my counselor?"

I half nod.

"Well, she says I have to start the grieving process with everything that happened—otherwise I'll never be able to, you know, like, go on with my life. Even though, honestly, I'm not really sure why having to think about all this shit all the time is supposed to help anything."

"Yeah, I don't know. I mean, they talk about that kinda thing a lot here—all that Elisabeth Kübler-Ross shit—you know, that doctor who talks about the five stages of grief, or whatever. Like, denial, anger, bargaining, depression and, uh, acceptance, I think. Basically, the idea is that in order to get over any trauma that's happened to us in our lives, we have to go through that entire cycle—that's the only way we can move on."

I find myself doing something awkward with my hands— overgesturing, maybe, like a politician at a goddamn press conference.

I can't help it.

"What happens to most of us is that we get, you know, stuck in one part of the cycle. At least, that's what Melonie tells me. She says that addicts usually can't get past denial—which, uh, I think is the first stage. I mean, we don't let ourselves feel any of it 'cause we're just loaded all the time. You know, the whole fuck-the-pain-away thing?"

Sue Ellen sits down on the gravel, her knees sticking out through the frayed tears in her jeans.

"Yeah, yeah," she tells me. "But I'm not an addict, so what's wrong with me?"

She stares off at something in the distance that probably isn't there at all. Her body rocks back and forth, her hands clutching the strings on either end of her knit woolen scarf.

"Wait a second," I say, sitting down just close enough to feel the whispering of her body as it moves past—tick, ticking like a goddamn metronome. "Wait, you're not an addict?"

Her jaw seems to clench tight so the bone is protruding just below her cheek. She stamps her boot on the ground—gravel exhaling dust like glitter in the sun, suspended there, sparkling, until wind I don't even feel comes to scatter it invisible.

Sue Ellen's face is flushed.

"No," she says—her teeth clenched tight. "No, I'm not. I don't know why that's so hard for people to believe. I didn't come here for that. I didn't do this to myself. It's so much more complicated than that. They promised my mom over the phone that they could help me and that I didn't need to be an alcoholic, or whatever, but now it's like they just won't leave me alone. I mean, the way they talk about it, *everybody's* an alcoholic, and everybody's codependent, and everyone's a sex addict with eating-disorder issues. It's fucking bullshit."

Suddenly I find myself talking at the ground so I don't have to see what her eyes are doing. My pulse sounds loud in my ears.

"Hey, it's cool. I mean, I agree, that's the problem with all rehabs. They look at us, you know, the patients, like we're all the same. But we're not. I mean, obviously. We all cope with things differently and all have different things to cope with. But the way they tell it, there's only one solution—which is basically to do exactly what they tell you and never question anything. It's fucking ridiculous. I mean, trust me, this is like the sixth rehab I've been to. The only way to make it through these places is to try 'n' sift through everything they say, you know, and just hold on to the five percent of good mixed in with the ninety-five percent of bullshit. 'Cause, yeah, the majority of what they feed you is worthless. The counselors all have their stupid egos and their stupid power trips, and most of 'em are recovering addicts themselves, so they aren't a whole lot healthier than we are. If they all insist on treating you like an addict, that's 'cause they don't know how to think independently, without relying on their goddamn textbooks and case studies and blah-blah-blah. If they're having trouble figuring you out, then that's a good thing. It means you're more complex than a statistic on a fucking pie chart."

I glance over quickly, but I'm caught right away. I mean, she's looking right at me.

"You know," she tells me, "that's really smart, what you just said. Are you an addict?"

My head nods sort of mechanically.

"Yeah, they got me on that. I more or less fit their little behavioral profiles to a tee. But, uh, what happened to you? Do you mind telling me? I mean, it's cool if you don't want to."

She leans her head back so I can't help but stare at her neck stretching up toward the cold, clear blue sky.

"It's funny," she says, her voice suddenly distant. "I couldn't talk about what happened with anyone. None of my friends would talk to me. My dad wouldn't listen to me. It was like somehow I was the one who'd done something wrong. Everyone just wanted me to shut up about it. So eventually I guess that's what I did. I shut up. I made myself shut up. But now, since coming here, it's like all anyone wants to do is talk about it. Every goddamn counselor and therapist has made me tell it all to them over and fucking over. Honestly, I don't see how dwelling on this shit could possibly help anyone. They should be helping us move on, right? Not making us wallow in self-pity about shit that happened in the past. But, fuck, I mean, if you wanna hear it, fine—I'll tell you. Anyway, it's really not that interesting."

Now, this is a fucked-up thing to admit, but I suddenly realize that, uh, I'm starting to get sort of aroused. I mean, enough so that if I have to stand up right now, it's gonna be pretty embarrassing—even if it does seem to be somewhat of a miracle.

Ever since going into detox, I haven't so much as stirred down there even once. I guess part of me figured that after having been with Zelda, you know, I wasn't ever going to be attracted to anyone else. I mean, Zelda was the exact combination of all things built to satisfy completely every aspect of my sexual template. Just ask goddamn Melonie; she'll tell you. It's got all sorts of shit to do with my mother moving away when I was little—about my need to save her from her fucked-up relationship with my stepdad—you know, all that Freudian shit—for whatever it's worth. The bottom line is, Zelda marked me deep.

But feeling this sudden, visceral attraction to the new girl, well, it's pretty cool. I mean, maybe I actually will be able to move on from Zelda. All I need is a girl like Sue Ellen in my life to help me forget. It's simple, really. I'm not sure why the hell I never thought of this before. Sue Ellen might just be the goddamn miracle I've been looking for.

So I listen to her story.

She talks fast, like she's trying to get it all out before she even has to think about what she's saying.

It's a story I've heard before.

I mean, it's the same story millions of girls could tell.

She was going to school out in California—college, that is—studying art. You know, illustration. It was the middle of her sophomore year. She was sharing a small house off campus with some other girls. Well, basically her friends started partying all the time, and she was surrounded by all these drunk-ass people. It spiraled out of control. She wouldn't tell me what happened, exactly; she just said she felt pissed off and alone. Her friends turned against her.

Sue Ellen had never felt she was popular anyway.

So she was left with absolutely nobody.

She'd had this idea that college was gonna be about learning, and that the other students were going to be all excited about knowledge and ideas. Instead it turned into a free-for-all. She couldn't relate to any of it. And she began to feel more and more like there had to be something wrong with her—like she was the mistake, like she was the fucked-up one. And so she withdrew even further into herself.

She transferred to a local art school in Charleston. She moved in to her own place there. She started smoking pot and drinking more—hanging out with any guy who'd give her even the slightest bit of attention. She spiraled, destructed, dropped out of her classes. And finally, just before Christmas, at home with her family, she decided she couldn't take it anymore. She wanted to disappear. She wanted to make it all disappear.

She lay in her bed.

Quiet.

Waiting.

The struggle of living life just didn't seem like it was worth it anymore.

"I try to look at everything as a cost-benefit ratio," she says, pulling her knees up closer against her chest. "And at that point, the cost was definitely outweighing the benefit."

So she thought about how she could make it go away.

She was ready.

But her mom sensed something—she was worried about her.

"She lives her whole damn life in denial," Sue Ellen tells me. "But at that point, even she couldn't deny what was happening to me."

And so Sue Ellen's mom was able to convince her to see a doctor.

And it was the doctor who suggested long-term treatment.

Both Sue Ellen and her mom fought the idea at first, but things just kept getting worse.

She was out of options and out of ideas.

She was desperate.

She had nothing left.

And so eventually, finally, she agreed.

She said yes to the doctors and yes to her mom and yes to giving it just one more try.

Anyway, she figured, it couldn't possibly make things any worse.

So two weeks later she was boarding the plane to Phoenix.

And now here she is—rocking back and forth on the ground next to me.

A girl from Charleston, South Carolina.

I remember something I once wrote about Zelda—something from a short story I'd never shown to anyone.

I wrote that my ultimate sexual fantasy with Zelda was just to hold her while she cried.

It was a fantasy I would later fulfill with her.

Many fucking times.

But here, now—close enough to Sue Ellen to feel her, without really feeling her—I remember that same desire.

I want to hold her.

I want to be there for her.

But for now all I have are my words.

I mean, they're meaningless, but I speak them anyway.

"I'm sorry," I say. "I mean, fuck—people are such assholes, right? And we're so goddamn sensitive to it—like we just feel everything so much...more than normal people do. You know what I mean?"

She nods, pulling her knees up tight against her chest.

"And, look," I tell her, "you don't have to be ashamed about that shit. I mean, not to freak you out or anything, but when I was younger, I used to be a sex worker...you know? And, man, I couldn't talk about that with anyone. 'Cause the thing is, for me, hustling wasn't even really about money. I mean, sure, I was strung out and living in a goddamn park, so it's not like I had a whole lotta options. But still, you know, more than just the money, it was about trying to feel like I was actually worth something—like, if guys wanted to sleep with me and would even pay me for it, then maybe I'd finally feel beautiful, or confident, or whatever. Of course, that's not how it worked. I mean, I just ended up hating myself even more after that. Plus I got beat up, raped. I woke up in the ER on life support. And I was so scared all the time, you know, just fucking terrified."

My voice catches suddenly.

I swallow loudly.

"Fuck, I'm sorry," I tell her. "I didn't mean to start rambling like that. All I'm trying to say is that, you know, as corny as this sounds, you're not alone. And, I have to say, I really do believe that this place can help. So, anyway, I don't know, I'm really happy you're here. And, uh, I'm really happy to have met you. And I guess I just feel this connection with you. And, uh, I really gotta shut up now. I mean, it's way too early. And I don't even know what I'm talking about, anyway."

Thankfully, Sue Ellen laughs at that.

She snorts a bunch of snot up her nose.

She wipes away still-wet tears with the back of her hand.

"No," she says. "I appreciate it. I really do." She laughs again. "I mean, thank you. And, uh, I'm glad you're here, too. Really."

Now it's my turn to laugh at that.

"All right, well, enough of that," I tell her. "Let's talk about light shit, okay?"

"Yeah," she says. "Light shit."

She pushes herself up off the ground—turns—looks back at me. "You coming?" she asks.

I nod.

Our eyes lock together.

I tell myself this is what I want.

I mean, I know it's the best thing.

We can make it work.

I just know we can.

And everything's gonna be all right.

Ch.7

When I open the door, the cold rushes immediately into the lodge, as though it had been pounding there the whole time, fighting desperately to smash through the windows—to tear the frames from their hinges—to come flooding in—to drown us all in icy seas—snowcapped waves. As though our world inside should never have existed at all.

I slam the door shut—pull my jacket tight around me—leave footprints in the muddy snow as I trek to the smoke pit.

A whole bunch of us are there, for some reason talking about how terrible Christmas is. Smoking cigarettes, huddled in against ourselves, under the protection of the little wooden shelter.

Sue Ellen is sitting with her legs crossed, rocking back and forth, smoking all exaggerated, like a teenage girl.

"I think this last Christmas of mine has to be recorded in

some book as, like, one of the worst Christmases in the history of Christmases," she says, exhaling through a big O she's made with her mouth.

She goes on to tell us, first off, that she's part of a big family, and that her cousin, Lily, who's twenty-five, announced at Christmas Eve dinner that she was six months pregnant. According to Sue Ellen, the pregnancy was the result of her cousin not wanting this deadbeat, unemployed douche bag to break up with her. Said douche bag had agreed to marry her, but they had nowhere to live and no money. Well, if that didn't cause enough of an explosion, Sue Ellen's brother came to the Christmas dinner drunk as shit and then proceeded to get a whole lot drunker. He started yelling at everyone, screaming obscenities, talking about how he knew they all hated him — all this before storming out the door, turning on the car, and driving over the front lawn before screeching out of there. The police called about twenty minutes later — her brother was in custody after having crashed his car into a nearby lake. The punch line of the story was her sister's husband saying, "Man, this sure beats karaoke." Which, I guess, is what they usually would've done.

Anyway, we're all laughing super hard at the way Sue Ellen tells the story. And, of course, I can't help staring at her — her pale skin stinging, red from the cold. I'm staring, staring, and that's how Melonie catches me. I mean, I didn't notice her walking up at all.

She clears her throat, and I glance over in immediate terror to see her bundled-up, wide pig face, bordered by a thick black scarf and a black, furry hat.

"Nic," she says, not smiling at all, her eyes looking at me intensely. "I need to talk to you in my office before group, okay? Can you walk down with me?"

My stomach tightens.

"Is it all right if I finish my cigarette?"

She pauses for a couple seconds.

"No," she says, shaking her head. "No, you'd better come now."

I stamp out the rest of my cigarette and then follow Melonie down the hill.

Honestly, I'm not sure what the hell Melonie expects, exactly, when she sits me down and says, "Nic, I want you to tell me the truth now: Is there something going on between you and Sue Ellen?"

I try to make my face look as disgusted as possible.

"What? You mean romantically?"

She nods.

"No way," I say, kinda loudly. "Not at all. I mean, I think she's fun to talk to and all, but that's it. She's like a little girl, you know? Like my little sister. Besides, I'm not even into girls my age. Believe me, we're just friends, that's all. I could so not be interested in her."

Melonie reclines slightly, and I figure that must be a good sign.

She smiles some.

"Oh, good, Nic, I'm so glad to hear that. But you do understand why I asked, don't you?"

My shoulders rise and fall. I'm trying to look, what? Incredulous? Something like that.

"Honestly," I tell her, "not really. I mean, we have been spending a lot of time hanging out, but I figured anyone who had eyes could see all I want is to help her."

Melonie leans way forward, resting her elbows on her knees. She makes her eyes intense, so it's like she's about to drop one of her profound insights on me.

"It sounds to me," she says, pausing a whole lot like some bad TV actor. "It sounds to me like she reminds you of your mom—or even Zelda. Sue Ellen is just another woman in trouble who you think you can save. I believe you when you say you have no romantic intentions toward Sue Ellen. Still, I can't help but notice that you're repeating a similar pattern. You couldn't rescue your mom, and you couldn't rescue Zelda, so now you've found someone new to reenact your fantasy with—even if it is on a strictly platonic level. Why don't you check in with yourself and see if that resonates at all?"

I nod my head, okay.

I mean, I gotta say, at this point I've definitely been here long enough to know how to handle this. To get all defensive—tell her to fuck off, like I wanna do—is only gonna be taken as an admission of guilt. What I'm supposed to do, if I want it to look like I've made progress in the program, is just to accept the feedback, ask myself whether it feels true, and if it doesn't, just let it go. So, yeah, knowing all that, I just nod my head, saying, "Yeah, okay, I'll think about that. I mean, that could be playing a part in this, for sure. Right now it doesn't feel like any of this is even that important, but I'll take it in, for sure."

Melonie seems very pleased. I stare at her little baby teeth all lined up straight in a row. She's smiling real big.

"Good, Nic, good. You know, you're really making so much progress. I mean, God, when I think about how you were when you first got in here, I can't even believe you're the same person. There was a while there where I didn't think you were gonna be able to make it here. I was honestly thinking about having you committed to lockdown psych ward. But now I just look at you and, I'll tell you what, Nic, you have single-handedly made me the proudest I've ever been in my five years of substance-abuse counseling. I was starting to have doubts about the effectiveness of my work, but you've made me see that what I'm doing really is important. You've helped me to care again. I'm very grateful to have been able to work with you."

She laughs. "You're like a second son to me."

I laugh at that, too—but mostly 'cause something just started eating away at my stomach lining.

"Yeah, right, the son you never wanted."

She shakes her head. "No, I'm serious, Nic."

I look up at her, and she's smiling with her whole body, and I suddenly can't help feeling a heat building in my eyes. I mean, she is just a stupid ol' cow, but still. I feel tears burning down my face. My voice cracks some when I try to speak.

"I'm really grateful for you, too. I mean, you've saved my life. I owe everything to you. And, uh, I just...you know... thank you so much."

Of course, now she's crying, too.

She stands up and I stand up and we hug each other.

For the first time I actually do feel aware of the progress I've made. I mean, even if I keep making mistakes, I've still been clean for almost three months—I've broken it off with Zelda—I've started talking to both my parents again—I've made friends here—I'm enjoying my life—sober.

I cry about it.

I mean, I don't even care how pathetic I must look in front of her.

"Well, good," says Melonie, wiping her face with a tissue. She sits back down. "Enough of that, right?"

"Right," I say, both of us laughing.

She rolls up her sleeves and fans herself with her white, pudgy hand like she's having a hot flash or something.

"So, anyway," she tells me, struggling for breath suddenly. "Like I said, in regard to this whole Sue Ellen thing, I really do believe you. But the thing is, based on what her counselor's told me, I'm not so sure Sue Ellen is looking at your friendship in the same way you are. I realize that you are very open and sensitive and caring, but for someone like Sue Ellen, that can open the door for a romantic attachment. You're a handsome kid, Nic—though I know you don't think so—and you can be very charismatic. So my worry is less for you and more for Sue Ellen. And her counselor agrees that she may be looking for something more than just friendship and that it's keeping her from fully engaging in work here."

I interrupt. "Oh, man, well that's totally the last thing that I want."

She continues. "I know, Nic, I know. So that's why I want you to sign this contract, okay? Saying you and Sue Ellen, at least for the time being, won't talk to each other, interact in any way—passing notes, whatever—or be in the same room alone together."

I tell her I understand. I don't fight at all. I sign the piece of paper and stand up to leave.

"Thank you so much, Melonie. I mean, for everything."

She hugs me again, saying, "Thank you."

I shut the door behind me.

A shiver wraps itself serpentine around my spine.

I walk out into the snow.

* * *

After my conversation with Melonie, I realize I have only a short time before group, so I figure I'd better write some sort of letter to Sue Ellen—just telling her that I'm sorry and that I really do care about her. It seems like the right thing to do.

I hike back up to my cabin, which, thankfully, is empty, so I sprawl out on my plush bed. Honestly, the beds here were, like, the only thing that kept me going the first couple weeks I was here. It was such a relief after coming from detox, where we slept on hospital beds with rubber sheets—freezing always—with only one thin-ass blanket apiece.

But here, yeah, the beds make you never want to get up ever.

I take out one of the composition books I brought with me from LA. The first half is already filled with rambling, repetitive attempts at writing while coked outta my head.

But today I flip straight to a blank page, scribbling Sue Ellen's name at the top.

I write about how I'm starting to fall for her.

I write about how I've made the decision that I want to be with her.

I write about how amazing and strong and beautiful she is. How brilliant. How sensitive.

I even find myself using lines that I clearly remember having written to Zelda when we first started hanging out.

I mean, in a way it feels almost like I am writing all this for Zelda.

Writing to her.

Writing about her.

I substitute the name.

But it's okay.

I know this is the best thing for both of us.

Sue Ellen needs a love like this.

She needs a love like I could've given to Zelda.

I fold the note in on itself several times and then hurry off to the main lodge to find her before group.

"Sue Ellen, hey," I whisper, standing right up close next to her. "Hey, we've been put on contract saying we can't communicate with each other anymore."

She squints up at me. "What?"

I kinda shrug my shoulders.

"I know, right? But it'll be okay. Here, read this when you're alone and then, uh, write me back, okay?"

Still staring up at me, she takes the crumpled piece of paper from my hand. Her face somehow looks even younger than I remembered it.

In my note, I tell her to meet me in the woods below the cabins after curfew if she feels the same way about me as I feel about her.

Time moves slower than it should, but finally ten thirty comes around, and I feel my way through the tangled bramble in the half moonlight. The night is cold, and I've got about five layers of sweaters and shit on. But, I mean, still...it's fucking cold. Brush tears at my legs, and branches sting my face and shoulders. My tennis shoes lose their grip in the fine powdered sediment on the rocky ground. I stumble. Honestly, I'm not even sure why the hell I'm doing this. I'm tired and trembling. The moon disappears behind drifting clouds, and the darkness closes in absolutely. I stumble and slide. Already I know this was a stupid idea. Anyway, she probably won't even come.

But somehow I know that's not true.

I mean, of course she'll come.

There's movement in the bushes directly behind me.

"Hey," I whisper kinda loudly. "Hey, it's me."

The moon breaks through the clouds again. The light is dull and full of shadows. Sue Ellen is there in front of me. She has on a knit hat and a long, thick scarf. Our hands tremble as I hold hers gently in my own.

"Thanks for coming," I say, like an idiot.

She shivers and then presses herself up against me. The warmth and smell of her makes me instantly aroused again.

"I can't believe this is happening," she whispers back to me.

I put my arms around her and bring her in even closer, saying, "Yeah...I know."

Her neck stretches up so her mouth is very close to mine.

"I'm scared," she tells me.

And then we kiss until she pulls away.

I read through the script.

"It's okay. I could never hurt you."

And that's the truth.

Or, at least, I'm gonna make it that way.

Ch.8

A couple of my friends here have already moved on to Day Program, which means they're staying at a kinda corporate-suites hotel in town — only coming to group during the day — sort of an intermediate step between inpatient and the real world.

Almost everyone here transfers to Day Program for at least a week or two before being discharged and, surprisingly, Melonie seems to think I'm almost ready.

I guess the plan she's worked out with my dad is that I'll do the Day Program for about a month and then maybe try 'n' get an apartment with my friends here — eventually finding work, most likely at a coffee shop or something terrible.

Of course, I'll keep going to twelve-step meetings every night, and I'll attend the alumni group here on Wednesdays.

Honestly, I normally wouldn't've agreed to any of this.

I've always said I would never live anywhere in this country besides San Francisco, LA, or New York.

I guess I just need the feeling of being where things are happening.

But for now, well, I've agreed to try Arizona — though only because Sue Ellen is gonna be sticking around for a while, too. Not that we're gonna stay here for more'n a couple weeks. Sue Ellen's agreed to come to San Francisco with me just as soon as she can figure it out. Her mom'll help her get an apartment there, and as soon as I finish the second half of my book, I'll use the advance money to pay her back — because, of course, I'll be living with her.

Considering how things would be without Sue Ellen, I really am super fucking grateful for her. She's given me the hope and promise of a good life. And I'd like to think I've done the same for her.

We pass notes back and forth throughout the day, we meet in the woods every night, and I sing songs to her by the fire — even though we both pretend that we have no contact at all.

There's something really great about all this. I mean, if we weren't on this contract and we didn't have to sneak around, it wouldn't be anywhere near as much fun. We both get to have this exciting little secret — something to hold on to when shit gets too hard. As for the whole duplicitous, lying thing, I really don't feel all that bad about it.

When I first got here and was receiving all this criticism from every damn counselor in the whole place, I used to fight back as hard as I could. Anything I disagreed with I had to argue about — you know, prove my point. But the more I fought, the more they accused me of reacting against my own denial.

"Just take in all the feedback we give you," they'd say. "Sit with it, then ask yourself if it fits. If it doesn't fit, don't worry about it—let it go. But if it makes you feel the need to defend yourself—if it triggers a response of anger or resentment—that probably means it's hit a nerve and needs to be explored further."

Well, their rule here prohibiting us from forming romantic relationships with one another doesn't hit any sort of nerve in me at all. I've sat with the idea and I've decided it doesn't fit. Besides, it's not like this thing with Sue Ellen negates the rest of the work I've been doing here—or the progress I've made. If anything, it's because of the progress I've made here that I'm able to sustain a relationship with someone so, you know, normal.

Anyway, I'm not sure whose idea it was to go horseback riding today, but I'm actually pretty excited. The ranch is in a tiny town about forty miles away. There are mountain trails on all sides leading to condemned silver mines and abandoned Native American cave dwellings.

The only disappointing thing is that Sue Ellen can't come with us—I mean, because of our whole no-communication/ contact thing. But she still lent me the money to go riding, so that was really cool of her.

Besides me and Kevin, there're, I think, seven or eight people going. Both Cat and Tim have rental cars, so we're just gonna be, like, caravanning over there. All of us waiting are excited and loud and talking all at once. Well, all of us except me. I'm smoking one cigarette after another.

It's fucked up. I mean, as much as I wanna get outta this place, in some ways I can't imagine ever leaving. The harshness of winter has melted away with the snow and the icy wind. The sun finally has some warmth, and the sky is clear above us, with thick clouds like caterpillars bordering the mountains and the desert horizon. I used to think of this place as a prison. The sagebrush and reddish dirt were like steel bars closing in, the isolated compound like an island asylum offering no chance of escape. But now, I mean, fuck, it's beginning to seem like being at this place is the only real freedom I've ever known. It's the outside world that's the prison. The outside world of jobs and cars and cell phones and apartments and grocery stores. Appropriate clothing, plans for a Saturday night, loneliness. This here, the Safe Passage Center, this is an oasis — a Shangrila — a sacred temple.

I stamp out another cigarette.

Man, I don't ever want to leave.

I stare off — my eyes burning slightly.

I stare off until something suddenly whacks me upside my head.

"Hey, Nic, come on."

It's Megan's voice.

I mean, it's Megan.

She laughs. "Get it together, space boy. Shit. Are you ready, or what?"

"Uh, yeah," I say. "I'm ready."

She grabs my arm, pulling me toward the driveway. "Well, they're here."

I look over.

Of course, she's right.

We divide up, get into the two rent-a-cars, and take off fast.

Since Tim insisted on me taking shotgun, I'm sitting up front with him, resting my feet on the black imitation-leather dashboard of the Chrysler Sebring—lighting another cigarette, even though there's a big NO SMOKING sticker on the passenger-side window.

I gotta say, man, driving in an actual car is surreal as hell.

And maybe even a little scary.

It just feels like, I don't know, like the outside world—like freedom. It's a reminder of what waits for me. A reminder of decisions, responsibilities, negotiating the fucking craziness.

"A plague seems quite feasible now."

David Bowie was right.

So I stare out the car window.

I tell Tim, "This is so weird."

I can't see his reaction.

"No shit," he says. "When I first got the car, it was like I'd totally forgotten how to drive. And sleeping by myself in the hotel room? Shit, man, I never thought I'd say this, but I missed being up at SPC. It just wasn't the same as listening to Brian snore at three o'clock in the morning, then going to the lodge to make hot chocolate and reading till Marion caught me."

That gets a smile outta me. "Come on, you can't miss Marion. She's a troll—biding her time till she can eat us up—grind our bones to make her bread—that sorta thing."

Tim laughs. "Yeah, whoa, I never thought of that. A troll...
totally. Or maybe a witch—with that wart on her face, and
the way she walks all hunched over."

Marion's one of the counselor's assistants. She's known for
being a real hard-ass, though she's always been pretty nice to
me, despite her resemblance to a troll—or, uh, a witch, right?

Mostly I'd say the reason she likes me is 'cause I keep trying
to speak to her in German, her native language.

The only two phrases I know are "Do you like my ass?" and
"You are a monkey face."

For some reason she thinks that's just the funniest thing ever.

Plus, we play gin rummy together.

"I don't know," says Kevin, startling me from the backseat.
"It's the accent that really gets me. She's like straight outta some
German fairy tale."

She's Austrian, actually, but whatever.

"*Tim, go to yar room. Da funniness is ovah. I'm da party poohpa.*" Kevin's imitation is more Arnold Schwarzenegger than Marion,
but it gets the car laughing.

"Yeah, well," says Tim. "Maybe I don't miss Marion, but I
do miss being up there. All you guys gotta really make the
most of it, 'cause when it's over, it's over. You know?"

"Sure," I say, studying him. "But, uh, *you'll be bahk.*"

Tim laughs at my bad imitation, though his eyes don't
change much—remaining dull, almost vacant-looking.

"Yeah," he says. "I know. But it's just not the same."

I watch him watching the road in front of him.

I think for about the thousandth time just what a handsome
kid he is.

I mean, handsome.

"Hey," he calls out kinda suddenly—to me more than anyone else. "I forgot to tell you, I went and bought all these CDs.
This Al Green one was only five bucks. Can you believe that?"

I smile. "Well, I'm not sure how popular Al Green is nowa-
days, but, yeah, that's a good deal. What album is it?"

He hands me the all-white cover of *I'm Still in Love with You*,
with Al Green's dark skin as the only contrast. It's actually one
of my favorite records ever.

"Right on," I say.

Tim pushes the CD into the player, clicking the button to
advance two or three tracks. Al Green's voice sounds clean and
beautiful coming through the car speakers.

A love song.

Of course.

I wanna say that these kinda songs make me think about
Sue Ellen—make me long for her. But honestly, I don't think
about Sue Ellen at all. I mean, I can't even make myself do it.
Listening to music like this, I see Zelda in front of me. She's
there at the back of my eyelids. She's standing against the sky,
the glaring sunlight, the flat, bare desert. She's standing against
mountains jagged on the horizon, jagged like her shoulder
blades, her spine, the bones jutting from her hips.

Tears come hot in my eyes—blurring everything—the
sweet, salty liquid running down my jawline.

Megan notices from the back.

She puts a hand on my shoulder.

She leans forward, her mouth parted slightly, not even an
inch from my ear.

"Hey, sweetie, it's gonna be okay. You'll move on. I promise. It's a big world out there. And there's a whole lot more to life than you even know."

Somehow Kevin must've heard, 'cause he yells out, "And we're going horseback riding. Who woulda thought?"

Tim shakes his head. "I know, right? I mean, hell, I haven't seen a horse in, man, I don't even know. This is a far cry from shooting heroin in a hundred-dollar-a-week hotel room."

I breathe in, then exhale long and slow. "Thanks, you guys. You're right. I mean, we really have come a long way, haven't we?"

Megan's hand on my shoulder squeezes tight. "Fuck, yeah, we have."

Kevin stutters his words out, all excited. "And now we have each other, right? We're friends. I've never even really had friends before."

"Me either," I say. "This is all pretty new to me."

The CD switches over to the next track.

I go on and look out the window again.

We've gotten off the highway and are driving through a sorta creepy little town that looks almost abandoned. There's a bar with boarded-up windows—a closed-down five-and-dime—trailer-style houses with dirt yards and corrugated siding and dogs chained out front. Chickens wander the empty dirt roads. We drive over a small wooden bridge, and I can't help but hold my breath. The road leads up toward the dusty mountains—barren, dotted with low-lying bramble and tumbleweeds. Tim pulls over into a makeshift parking lot, and I realize we're here. In fact, Cat and her group are already out of the car, standing around waiting for us. She yells out at Tim, "What took you so long?"

He flips her off, the two of them laughing real hard.

And then we all laugh along with them—you know, just laughing together.

"Man, we sure are a motley crew, aren't we?" says this middle-aged guy Johnny, who's in my home group, and we all laugh even more at that.

I mean, it's the truth.

There's no way under normal circumstances we would ever be hanging out together.

But, well, here we are.

We get on our horses and follow along the narrow trail.

Our guide tells us to kick into a gallop.

We do.

And we take off.

Ch.9

Melonie really is just fucking glowing.

I mean, glowing the way pregnant women must look when people say they're glowing.

She really is glowing like that.

And she's glowing like that 'cause of me.

Or at least I hope that's it.

The last thing we need is a little Melonie offspring added to our already grossly overpopulated world.

So, for the sake of the nation, I'm assuming her glow is all about me.

"How does it feel?" she asks me. "You're finally ready to take the next step in getting your life together. I can't tell you how proud I am."

She doesn't need to tell me. I'd say I've pretty well got it.

And in terms of her question, well, my answer is that it's

strange to have even the smallest bit of hope again. I was close to giving up. I was closer than I've ever been.

"I look at you, Nic," she continues, "as one of my greatest successes. I will always hold your transformation as perhaps the best work I've ever done."

She beams, all cherubic-looking. Glowing. Obviously having no problem letting herself take all the goddamn credit.

"I brought your case up at the staff meeting, and we voted unanimously that you are ready to go into Day Program at the end of the week. We also voted for you to be taken off all your contracts. So you don't have to worry about not communicating with Sue Ellen anymore. Though, of course, I trust you will continue to uphold healthy boundaries with her...and everyone else, for that matter."

I nod.

The sunlight is streaming through the slats in the plastic blinds drawn over the window. There's no air-conditioning and the door is closed and I think I drank too much coffee, 'cause I'm starting to sweat all over the place. Whatever the hell's left in my stomach is stuck fast to the quickly turning walls—the bottom dropping out like those centrifugal-force rides they have at state fairs. My tongue is swelled up so I'm choking.

It's what I get for tryin' to live on cigarettes and coffee.

But, of course, I can't excuse myself, not even for a glass of water.

The moment's way too goddamn touching.

"You know," says Melonie, her eyes clearly tearing up, "I want to tell you that, after you leave here, you are welcome to call me anytime you need to talk. In fact, I want you to call me—even if just to check in now and then. I sincerely hope we can continue to build our relationship. As I said before, I really do think of you as a son. And you've inspired me to rededicate myself to this field."

I look down in a display of humility.

"Thank you," I say, even though the twisted-up feeling in me is just getting worse.

I wonder if maybe it isn't the coffee.

I mean, I've been in and outta therapy since I was seven years old. And after all that time, I'd say I'm pretty hip to the, uh, protocol, or whatever. At least, I know a couple of things. The doctors are supposed to stay neutral—professional— detached. They're not supposed to get personally involved. Not ever.

"Is something wrong?" she asks, her expression going all concerned again.

I smile it away. "No," I say. "No, not at all."

She smiles along with me. "Well, good."

We sit there like that.

Smiling back and forth.

When the fifty minutes are up, I immediately go to find Sue Ellen—walking some of the sickness outta my body—stopping only to watch a raven land clumsily on a gnarled tree branch. It cocks its head back twice before flying off again and joining the other birds gathered at the edge of the rooftop.

Sue Ellen is sitting, like always, up at the smoke pit. With long legs crossed, one hand compulsively ashing a cigarette, the other pulling at her flat-ironed black hair. Her oversize sunglasses teeter precariously on the end of her aquiline nose. Her jaw click-clicks like maybe she's grinding her teeth or something. There's a thick wool knit scarf wrapped around her neck, despite the sun, and she's wearing two sweaters—a cardigan and something tight and low-cut that I don't know the name for. Her blue jean bell-bottoms are cut short at the ankles.

"Hey, Sue Ellen," I say—louder than I need to. "What's up, girl?"

Everyone turns to look at me with these sort of horrified expressions on their faces, like I just climbed out on the ledge of a tall building and am threatening to jump.

Ray hunches over, putting a finger to his lips—eyes darting—whispering, "Nic, shh, what are you doing?"

I walk over next to Sue Ellen. "No, it's okay. I've come to announce that, as of about three minutes ago, Sue Ellen and I are officially off our no-communication contract."

She stands up. "Is that true?"

"Yeah, totally. We can talk as much as we want."

"Or as little."

She laughs at her own joke, and then everyone takes turns congratulating us. I mean, honestly, I think they all approve of me 'n' Sue Ellen as a couple. At least, they all act super supportive. They can tell the difference, you know? This isn't just some desperate, quick-fix substitute for getting high.

We really care about each other.

This is love.

Believe me, if it was anything else, I would never be capable of doing something like this. I mean, I've been on the other side.

When I first got here, there was this kid Matt, from Maine, who immediately took it upon himself to really try 'n' mentor me. He was a tough kid—tatted up—with long, wiry hair and a thick, thick accent. He'd really fought the place when he got here, just like me, so I guess that's why he took an interest. He'd sit up smoking with me, even when my body was still seizing from the detox, telling me about the way he'd been when he first got to treatment—how he'd packed his bags five different times with the intention of ditching this place. He'd been running the streets his whole life. The hell if he was gonna let these touchy-feely, soy-fed, patchouli-smelling, incense-lighting, mama's little pansies order him around. All he had to do was clench his fists and the whole lotta them would flinch back.

But by the time I met him, Matt was like a totally different person. He'd become gentle and caring. He reached out to me when no one else did.

"I know this place seems like it's all full of shit," he told me, his bug eyes popping out beneath his thick brow ridge. "But just try doing, like, one or two things they tell you to. That's what it took for me, man. One day I just decided, you know, 'Matt, you're gonna fuckin' try this thing.' I got a little boy in foster care 'cause his mom 'n' me are both dope fiends and can't take care of him. I know for damn sure his mom ain't gettin' clean ever, so that means I'm the only chance he's got. 'Cause the hell I'm gonna let my boy be raised by some god-damn strangers. So I told myself to give this place a shot, you know, and I started participating in group and then, man, here I am. Gonna be outta here in a couple weeks, and they already got me parental visitation rights. I know it ain't too much, but it's a start for now."

But then, a few days later, after a group trip to the aquarium in Albuquerque, we were all gathering down in the community room for our nightly meeting. Both Matt and this girl Rachel were absent, which was weird 'cause I'd been with them all day on the outing.

When the meeting was over, I ran up to the main lodge and saw Matt in there, with Rachel, closed off in the counselor's assistant's office, surrounded by, like, every staff member in the entire place.

An hour later two taxis showed up, one for Matt and one for Rachel. I watched them load up their different bags 'n' things. Matt's head was hung real low. He couldn't make eye contact with any of us. He couldn't even come say good-bye.

Of course, it didn't take long for the details of what had happened to get passed down to us. It was basically what I'd expected — one of the counselor's assistants, this club-footed woman named Sonia, was going from cabin to cabin reminding everyone about the community meeting. When she got to Rachel's, however, she heard some sort of noise and stuck her head in the door. According to the rumors, Sonia hadn't actually caught them in the middle of the act itself, but they were lying naked in bed together. Within less than two hours, they'd been removed from the premises. No trial. No jury. Just execution.

And as much as I felt sick about it, I had to admit that I understood why they'd been kicked out. I mean, it's like that

Peaches song that used to be so popular. "Fuck the pain away."

They used to play it at, like, every goddamn club in New York when I lived there.

I guess that's no wonder.

"Fuck the pain away."

I mean, fuck it, drink it, shoot it, smoke it, snort it, cut it, binge it, purge it all the fuck away.

Get high. Relapse. That's what we do.

And that's what Matt and Rachel did.

So, yeah, no big surprise they were thrown outta here.

Even if that kid of Matt's ends up having to stay in foster care.

Even if one of them gets loaded and ODs, or both of 'em do.

I cried, actually, as their taxis drove off, the smear of red taillights disappearing behind the first bend in the gravel driveway. There was a feeling like ... like the time in San Francisco when this guy on the street sold me forty dollars' worth of H that ended up being just a chunk of black-colored soap. I felt embarrassed — sickened — like I never wanted to tell anyone how easily I'd been suckered. And, man, this rage was surging through me — pounding — like blood filling my head so my ears exploded wide open — leaving me blind and dizzy and fantasizing about tracking down the motherfucker and bashing in his skull. With Matt getting kicked out, there was a rage like that. I'd trusted him. I'd genuinely believed all that bullshit he'd been telling me. I'd looked up to him. I thought he'd really changed. But it was all a con, man, a fucking con. He'd ripped me off, just like that guy in San Francisco. So, uh, yeah, there was a whole lotta rage inside me. And there was a whole lot of sadness and embarrassment, too.

But, then again, I was also worried about him, you know? I was worried about what would happen to him now that they'd kicked him straight the fuck out on his ass. I mean, people die from this shit all the time. Last year alone I lost two people—one to an OD and the other to a motorcycle accident. It never gets any easier. And there's no telling which one of our dumb asses is gonna be next. Hell, Matt could get himself dead, and I'd probably never even know. It's not like I have his goddamn phone number or anything.

But this thing with Sue Ellen, well, it's totally different. We're not fucking any pain away. We care about each other. I mean, we've fallen in love. And that hasn't gotten in the way of the work we're doing here—not at all. If anything, we're just pushing each other to go deeper with all this shit. It's cool, you know, 'cause we get to really support each other—lift each other up when we're feeling weak, or scared, or just overwhelmed with hopelessness. She validates me and, well, I validate her, too. I make her feel beautiful, valuable, worthy of love. Honestly, there's no way she would've been able to open up as much as she has without me there telling her over and over that I want her and need her. That's not me bragging or anything; it's just the truth. She relies on me and I rely on her. We write each other letters. We look out for each other. There's not one goddamn person who could find fault with that.

And no one does.

I mean, I'm pretty sure they all just think we're sort of, uh, cute, or whatever.

And now that I've announced we're off our contract, everyone seems genuinely excited — acting all supportive and everything. We stand around laughing and talking like that till it's time to go to group. I can't help but notice that the ravens have gathered in the branches all around us — waiting impatiently to pick through whatever trash we've left behind.

Ch.10

Sue Ellen agrees to meet me in the woods near the boundary of the property — mostly 'cause I just want to talk to her in private, that's all.

The sun is setting quickly against the distant, silhouetted mountains — a child's faded chalk drawing in orange and red and pink and purple.

We find a somewhat hidden shelter between the thorns and the parched, tangled branches — about three hundred yards behind our section of cabins and fifteen feet up from the encircling barbed-wire fence. That always seemed like a nice touch, you know, the barbed wire. Just in case we ever thought about escape.

Sue Ellen looks up at me — eyes searching, lips parted. She puts her small hands in my jacket pockets, pressing up against me.

I kiss her and she kisses me.

We kiss desperately—like we really need it—like we've been wandering lost for days in the woods—starving—weak and dying from dehydration.

I suck on her tongue, and then she pulls away.

"I'm sorry," she says, whispering so we won't get caught. "It's just...I don't know. I'm really scared, Nic. We're so close to leaving, and I can't help feeling like we're never gonna see each other again."

My gloved hands take hold of both her shoulders.

I crouch down so I'm right at eye level.

"Listen: I am not going to leave you, okay? I'm going to do whatever it takes to be with you. I mean, I love you. I'm in love with you. That's the only thing that matters. Besides, we're going to move to San Francisco together. We'll build a life, you know? You and me."

Her face goes flushed. There are tears forming. "But I don't know if I can do that to my mom. She doesn't understand. She won't listen to me. She won't even listen to my counselor. We had a conference call, and I tried to tell her how codependent she is on me and how I need to go away on my own, but she just started sobbing and asking me what she'd done wrong and everything. She wants me to come home."

My jaw clenches, and then there's that dropping-out feeling in my stomach again. "You can't go home," I tell her. "That'd be like death for you. The only way you're gonna move past everything that's happened is to get away from all those old places and people. Your mom'll understand that. I mean, tell her it has nothing to do with her. Tell her it's just about you making a fresh start. Tell her she can come visit whenever she wants, but you need to have some space from everything that's happened. Besides, you're gonna have a really awesome support system out in San Francisco. Tell her a whole bunch of us are moving out there. I'm sure it'll be okay. If she wants what's best for you, then she'll let you go."

Sue Ellen presses her body up against mine, and I kiss her forehead.

"It's gonna be okay," I say. "I just love you so much. And I swear I won't let anything happen to you. Tell your mom she can talk to me if she wants. I'm sure I can convince her everything'll be all right. I mean, better than that."

She laughs a little.

"Yeah, right. I can just imagine it: 'Hey, Mom, this is my drug addict friend. He wants you to let me go live with him in a random city on the other side of the whole country. But he promises everything'll be okay, so it's all good.' Ha. I'm sure she'd love that."

"Well," I say, laughing along with her, "you could downplay the whole drug addict thing. Come on."

I stretch my body out on the sharp, rocky ground — pulling at Sue Ellen's sweater — trying to get her to lie alongside me.

She drops to her knees but won't go any further.

"The thing is," she whispers, "I'm having a hard time playing it down myself. I mean, how do I know you're not going to relapse? How do I know I can trust you not to bring that shit around me?"

My jaw click-clicks back and forth.

I stare straight up at the sky being drained of its last bits of color.

When I speak, my voice cracks, and I have to clear my throat before answering her. "Sorry, yeah, no, I understand. I'm not trustworthy. I've proved that enough times. Everyone who's tried to help me has ended up getting burned. In fact, about the only thing I've ever been trustworthy of is being fucking untrustworthy. And I'm not saying that to be all 'poor me,' or whatever. I've been a shit bastard my whole life. There's no excuse, you know?"

Sue Ellen's lying next to me on the dirt and rock.

I turn toward her.

Our eyes struggle to maintain direct contact. Her pupils are all dilated against the coming darkness.

I go on talking, mostly just 'cause of all the silence around us. "The only thing I can tell you, girl, is that, honestly, things really are different this time. I mean, I know that's like the biggest cliché in the world, right? But what can I say? It's the truth. I've finally learned to start loving myself here. And I can see now that loving myself is loving you. 'Cause you're a part of me. You always will be. I think I was born to love you. I think we were created to meet here and love each other and hold each other as we go out into this fucked-up world together. And I'm not saying I believe in fate or God or whatever, 'cause I'm not sure I do. But if there is a God—some sort of spiritual force guiding us, like they tell us here—then it's pretty obvious to me that us finding each other is all a part of some greater plan. I mean, it's a gift—a fucking miracle. I'm not gonna turn away from that. I will not shrink back."

A shiver crawls its way through me, and I squeeze her hand maybe a little too tight, 'cause she pulls back suddenly.

"You can be sure of me," I tell her, not letting go. "And there's not one person in this whole place who can deny what we have. I mean, hell, it's what they try to teach us every day—to let go—to trust in spiritual guidance and intuition—to give ourselves over completely—to listen to that 'still, small voice inside,' as they say. Well, that voice in me has made me love you, and I'm pretty sure that voice in you has done the same, so there's nothing we can do but follow that. 'Cause as long as we do, we will be taken care of—we will—and everything'll be all right."

"Sure," she says, eyes going bloodshot, glossy—tears forming at each corner but refusing to fall. "But what'll we do? How are we going to live?"

Her lips part as I lean forward, and we hold each other, kissing softly, pausing. I whisper, "Don't worry, okay? Your mom will help us get started, but then we can both get jobs. And as soon as I can finish the second part of my book, I'll be able to pay her back. Seriously. You can tell her that's a promise. And otherwise, I mean, we'll explore the city, go to shows and movies and galleries—get involved with twelve-step stuff out there—you know, live—together—in love."

As we kiss again I can feel her tears hot against my face.

"But you don't even believe in twelve-step stuff," she says, half choking on her words.

We both laugh at that.

"Well, I believe in the community of it—even if I don't really dig on the program. I mean, that's what's so awesome: We can go practically anywhere in the whole country and get totally hooked up with cool people who are working on the same shit we are—or at least've been forced to be a little more introspective than a lot of folks out there. Anyway, trust me, Sue Ellen, you are gonna absolutely love it there. It's the most beautiful city, and there's just this feeling, like, I don't know . . . like you can finally breathe there or something. You'll see. It'll be amazing—living there together, you and me."

I kiss her again—rolling onto my back—her straddling me, letting her weight rest against my body.

We kiss and kiss and touch and whisper that we love each other.

The night closes in—gray turning black.

I know they're probably serving dinner up at the lodge, but we decide to stay just a little while longer. Kissing till my body is consumed with fever—a vague oblivion in my bloodstream, like getting high, maybe, but not at all the same or even comparable. But something, you know, at least more than nothing.

"We should go," Sue Ellen whispers in my ear.

My head nods in agreement as she pushes herself up to standing.

The harsh beam of a flashlight hits my eyes right then, but, I mean, who knows how goddamn long she's been standing there. Her voice calls out to me specifically, saying my name with that thick accent. Marion—the goddamn troll.

"Neek, oh boy, vahss is going on here?"

The light gets out of my eyes, and I can see her bulbous head shake back and forth, back and forth.

I try slowing down my breath, even though my heart is beating so hard I feel like I might be sick. "It's exactly what it looks like," I say, hoping to God my voice isn't wavering like I'm scared, which, of course, I am.

Marion's head keeps shaking as she makes a "tsk-tsk-tsk" sound, literally. "Vell den, I am truly sorry to be de vone. I valk de perimeter each night at dis time."

I force myself to laugh. "Yeah, uh, obviously I didn't know that. Are we totally fucked, then?"

She nods slowly. "Ah, Neeky, you are so stupid. I mean, vhy do you do dis? Vhy?"

I finally stand up all the way. "We're in love," I tell her.

She laughs and laughs. "Vell, who knows, maybe you vill be very happy. It could be good for you both. But it could be very bad. Da, da, you are, as you said, fucked. Neek, you go to the office now. Sue Ellen, you come vis me."

I reach over to squeeze Sue Ellen's hand, but she quickly pulls away — hunched over — a mess of tears. She walks toward Marion in a sort of trance. And I watch them both walk off together.

Sue Ellen's shadowed frame is bent and defeated.

A new sickness cuts its way through my stomach, like swallowing crushed glass and antifreeze.

For the first time I finally admit to myself that maybe I've made a big-ass mistake by getting involved with Sue Ellen. I keep asking myself, over and over, if I've actually hurt her more than helped her — if I've robbed her of her chance to really heal at the fucking Safe Passage Center. If nothing else, I know all our plans are ruined now. We had our chance, but we screwed it all up.

And the other thing I know is that now, after all this, I have no choice but to stick by her, no matter what happens. I mean, this is my fault.

So I start up the trail, my hands shaking bad.

I may have done some fucked-up things in my life.

But I'm gonna make this one better.

I have to.

I mean, I have no choice.

Ch.11

So, of course, Melonie is here.

Along with Marion and this wormy counselor Mathew.

Plus Shoshana, another counselor, who basically looks exactly like Melonie but with a different face.

They call this meeting with me a "round table"—and I can tell how serious it is, 'cause they've brought the head of the entire program in to watch me squirm. But it's still Melonie who's doing all the talking.

"The point is," she says, her face flushed almost purple, "you've violated the trust of the entire community. And by your actions, whether you know it or not, you've essentially spit in the face of everyone who's tried to help you. To say I'm disappointed would be such a gross understatement. I feel personally violated, Nic, I really do. It's obvious you have absolutely no respect for me whatsoever. I see issues of borderline personality all over this—borderline, with sociopathic tendencies. You're in a lot of trouble, buddy. If you don't get help soon, I imagine you'll be dead within three months."

I watch the seconds tick by on the circular wall clock above me.

"Okay, hey, Nic!" Melonie practically shouts at me, snapping her fingers in front of my face, making me want to break them off. I mean, goddamn, even if I had zoned out for a minute, you still don't do shit like that.

"What?" I say back, holding my jaw locked and my fists all clenched up. "What? What? What?"

She leans back and smiles.

I mean, fuck. I swear to fucking God.

"There's no need to get defensive, Nic. We're trying to help you. The staff here has been working hard to find a program for you to transition into. As it is, I think we've found the perfect option. And just so you know, I contacted the director and explained your situation to him in detail. He agreed that you are a perfect candidate for what they have to offer. And, luckily, they have one open bed left, so you'll be able to leave first thing tomorrow. I spoke with your father, and he's completely on board with all of this. In fact, he's not willing to speak to you until you've checked in to the program."

My breath gets caught in my throat suddenly. I feel my heart pounding through my head—blown-out speakers buzzing, loud and distorted.

"Wh-what program?" I stutter.

"Well, it's an all-male sober living house, which I'd say is absolutely essential for you. They offer group during the day, but after thirty days you'll be required to get a job in the local community—a city called Gallup, New Mexico, about an hour outside of Albuquerque—in the middle of nowhere, so you'll be completely safe and isolated. Of course, they require you to attend twelve-step meetings and get a sponsor to help walk you through the steps. You'll have extensive chores and restrictions on your writing and drawing and playing guitar—also essential to your recovery. But, as I said, the most important thing is that you will only be with other men, so you'll have no opportunities to engage in your sex and love addiction. And, because the program requires a one-year commitment, you'll be able to get a substantial period of abstinence under your belt."

She pauses—I can only imagine for dramatic effect and for giving me time to squirm.

"Of course," she continues, looking around at her fellow counselors as though trying to impress them with her bitchiness—I mean, her expert handling of this unspeakably evil act I've committed. "Of course, you do have a choice in all this. But if you decide not to attend, I'm afraid you're going to be asked to leave the premises within the next hour. Otherwise you'll be able to spend one last night here, say your good-byes, then leave for the airport tomorrow morning. Those are your only two options—and I need your answer right now so we can protect the community."

I tell myself not to cry. Seeing me cry will only satisfy her all the more.

But I go ahead and cry anyway.

I can't help it.

I mean, a year? In the middle of nowhere in New Mexico? Surrounded by nothing but fucking men?

There's no way I can do it.

I actually lived in an all-male sober living once. It was my nightmare of what a goddamn frat house would be like. I lasted there a week. That's all I could take. I mean, it was so goddamn depressing.

And that's the thing I don't get—how are people supposed to stay sober when they hate their lives? Fuck, man, my will to live isn't all that strong in the first place. Facing a year at a place like that, I just know I'm gonna relapse—or take my own life. It's not worth living sober and being miserable. It's not. I keep thinking that if I ran my own sober living, it would be all about trying to help the residents feel excited about life. At least, I know that's the only way I'll ever stay clean. So this Gallup place . . . hell, Melonie says I'll be dead in three months if I don't go. Well, I guarantee you I'll be dead in three months if I do. There's not even a fucking question.

Of course, I have no money.

That's literally zero dollars and zero cents.

Thank God my mom sent me a carton of cigarettes, so at least that's something, but it doesn't exactly help with the whole food, shelter, and transportation thing.

It's a big fucking risk.

But Sue Ellen will help me. I know she will. Besides, I got her into this mess—telling her I loved her—that we were going to be together—that we were built for each other. How much of an asshole would I be if, after having gotten caught, I just pussed out and abandoned her completely?

So, yeah, they're all just gonna have to back the fuck up, 'cause I'm done with this shit.

I wipe my stupid tears outta my eyes. I stand up. "All right, then," I say, my voice definitely shaking all over the place. "I'm gonna go pack. And, don't worry, I'll be gone within the hour."

Melonie immediately jumps up in front of me.

"Don't do it, Nic. It'll be the worst mistake you've ever made in your life. You have to listen to me."

There's actually panic and a kind of fear in her voice that just makes me all the more determined.

"Look, I'm sorry," I tell her—as detached as possible.

I walk toward the door.

I'm really done with all this.

I step around Melonie and just keep walking.

"Do you think you're in love with her?" she asks the back of my head. "Is that it? 'Cause, oh boy, you've got another thing coming. I feel sorry for you, Nic. I really do. But I can't stop you from self-destructing—and obviously you can't, either. So, fine, go pack your things. I'll have your discharge packet ready at the CA's office when you're done."

I walk out into the quickly fading sun, up the trail— hopefully for the last time.

My hands are trembling.

What am I gonna do now?

Ch.12

It's actually this lawyer kid, Jason, who's saving my ass—at
least for tonight. He's already on Day Program and has a room
at the Residence Inn, so he kinda reluctantly agrees to let me
stay with him—though he wants me out by tomorrow. Honestly, I feel like he's being kinda fucked up about the whole
thing. I mean, he totally knew what was up with me and Sue
Ellen. We all used to hang out together. I really thought he was
my friend—in fact, one of my better friends in this place. We
would talk and joke around and confide in each other and play
Scrabble. But now, since I got caught, he's suddenly acting like
I'm this dangerous predator. Hell, he was totally into that Jessie girl who'd been a call girl, and he was constantly trying to
get together with her. And he would've, too, if she hadn't kept
blowing him off. So his puritanical, I'm-Mr.-Poster-Child-of-

Recovery thing is pissing me off. Though it's not like I can do anything about it. I mean, I need his room.

Besides, I was able to talk to Sue Ellen, and she told me real quick that her mom had gotten her a room at that same Residence Inn for a couple nights—just till she could get a flight back to South Carolina. I don't think either one of us would be comfortable spending the night together. I mean, it's just too much pressure. But we are anxious to hang out and talk and all, so staying with Jason is perfect.

He drives me to the hotel in his stupid rental car, and I bring my bag up to his room. All I've got is one bag, plus an over-the-shoulder backpack thing and that guitar from the Safe Passage Center, which I figure they owe me.

Immediately Jason is sort of pacing back and forth across the tacky, worn-thin, patterned wall-to-wall carpeting—a grayish-black color, probably to help hide all the stains. But actually it's a totally fine room, with a separate sitting area and a couch and a mini-kitchen with mini-appliances. There's some abstract, corporate framed art on the walls that look like bad Miró imitations.

"All right, Nic, all right," says Jason, definitely not sounding like my friend anymore at all. "I'm trying to be cool about this, but I need to know, what's your plan? I can't have you staying here after tonight, okay? You need to get your shit together, man."

I think I maybe roll my eyes a little. "Of course," I tell him, looking down at the cheap, dark-colored fake tile on the kitchen floor. There's a swarm of ants moving steadily along the grout beneath the sink—keeping perfect pace with one another—falling in line—instinctively, unthinkingly working,

working, working—serving the queen—each individual ant indistinguishable from the rest.

"Well?" Jason demands, pretty goddamn forcibly. "So what is your plan, then?"

My attention stays fixed on the blind obedience of the ant colony.

"Honestly," I say—distant—escaping the terror and humiliation of being in my body. Watching myself watching the ants from a corner of the textured, off-white ceiling. "Honestly, I don't totally know. I wanna be with Sue Ellen. If I have to, I'll go back to South Carolina with her. I mean, I love her, man, I really do. And I'm gonna take care of her. But, look, you know, I really appreciate you letting me stay here tonight. I swear I'll get out of your way tomorrow. It's just for a night. You've been so good to me, man. I mean, I'm really honored to have you as a friend."

Which is true—except he's being such an asshole.

And he's still pacing, running his right hand over and over through his greased-back hair. It's weird, you know, 'cause I swear people really do mold themselves to look exactly like they're supposed to look. I mean, like, take Jason. He's a young lawyer from Manhattan, and he looks exactly like a fucking young lawyer from Manhattan—sharp, handsome, clean-cut, with expensive clothing and greasy hair and just kind of a greasy slimeball look in general. That is, a very traditionally handsome greasy slimeball look. Not too far off from *American Psycho*'s Patrick Bateman, you know?

Something like that.

"Jesus, Nic," he says, louder than he should. "Do you really expect me to believe that? Well, I don't. And I'm not gonna sit back and cosign your bullshit while you throw your life away— especially since you're trying to take Sue Ellen down with you. My counselor pulled me aside after group today. She explained everything to me. You're toxic, man, and as long as you remain in the community, we're all gonna be unsafe. Besides, you and I both know you're not capable of loving anybody. I mean, whatever happened to learning how to love yourself first? Whatever happened to taking things slow?"

My body shifts around uncomfortably.

"Nothing," I tell him, exhaling loudly at the same time. "Hell, I know I still have a ton of work to do on myself. And I know Sue Ellen does, too. But there's no reason we have to stop doing that work just 'cause we're not in the program anymore. I mean, even the counselors keep telling us this is a lifelong practice. It's not like the only way we can make it is to stay at Safe Passage Center the rest of our lives. Believe me, the last thing I want to do is endanger you, or anyone else. But I don't see how my decisions can possibly do that. I mean, y'all can think for yourselves, right?"

Jason's pace speeds up even more. "Nic, listen to me, you're making a mistake. And the thing that pisses me off more'n any-thing is that you're gonna take Sue Ellen down with you. You're a user, Nic. I know. How many times have you had to borrow money from me since being here—a fucking lot, right?"

He pauses as though actually expecting an answer, so I sort of half whisper, "I don't know. You always made it seem like you wanted to help. I don't have any money, and that sucks.

But I can pay you all back for everything. Once I finish the second half of my book, I'll get more of my advance. That's another reason why I wanna get out of here — to start working again and be able to finally support myself."

He laughs, but not like he thinks it's funny at all. "Your book, huh? Yeah, right. You might be able to fool little Sue Ellen with that shit, but not me. You're a con man, Nic — a leech. Hell, I used to be the same way. That's why I can see it in you. We're the same, man. And what is it they say, 'You can't kid a kidder'? Well, that's how it is. Now, look, my counselor specifically told me I was not to have any contact with you once you left the program, but I'm gonna give you this one night. She also told me that if, for some reason, I do have to talk to you, the only thing I'm supposed to say is that I want you to go to the program they suggested in New Mexico. So I'm saying that, Nic. Honestly, I think that's the one chance you've got."

"Yeah, well," I say, or, well, yell real loud. "You know what Jimmy Cliff says, right? 'I'd rather be a free man in my grave than living as a puppet or a slave.'"

Jason stares me down like he doesn't even see me anymore.

"Man, your addict's in full force. I don't know what's the point of even talking to you right now. You're delusional. I mean, it's sad to see."

I turn toward the door, pulling on the big Army jacket my old roommate gave me.

"Whatever," I tell him, kinda quietly. "I'm gonna smoke. Just remember that whole time you were so hung up on Jessie

I never judged you—not once. I supported you. I supported you 'cause I used to fucking respect you."

He doesn't have time to respond before I get the door open and step out into the cold, cold night, slamming the fucking thing behind me.

Ch.13

The wind tears through the sterile, corporate-looking suites—everything radiating harsh yellow from the rows of staked lights in the sparse planter boxes surrounding the imitation cobblestone courtyard.

The wind stings my face as I walk down the short flight of stairs, fumbling to get a cigarette outta my pack.

There're some plastic chairs set up in the courtyard, so I take a seat—turning my head, kinda startled, when I hear the door to the suite below Jason's click open.

At first I just figure I'm gonna have to apologize for smoking in front of the person's door, but then suddenly the face comes into focus and I actually jump.

"Oh, shit, Sue Ellen. Is that your room?"

She seems pretty startled, too.

She clenches her hands, and her eyes go wide, and she sort of takes a step back.

There's something in her voice, like she's trying to keep me at a safe distance—like she's telling me not to come too close, without really telling me anything at all.

"Nic, oh, yeah. Uh, wow, I didn't expect you to get here so fast."

"Me neither. They, uh, they were able to get my meds from the doctor sooner than they thought. You want a cigarette?"

I hold out my pack to her.

Her small, pale hand reaches over to take one.

She sits down on one of the cheap lounge chairs, but not right next to me.

I light her goddamn cigarette and then, just to do it—I kiss her on the forehead, whispering, "It's okay. Everything's gonna be all right. Don't worry. We'll take it all slow."

Then I bend down and kiss her mouth.

She pulls away after just a few seconds. "I'm sorry," she says, her voice coming out curt—her body tensed and withdrawn—angry, almost. "Look, I...I'm not sure I can do this. I mean, everyone's acting like you're gonna die or something if you don't go to that program in New Mexico. I can't deal with this. All my friends are turning on me. I feel like some sort of disease. This isn't right, Nic. This can't be right."

I turn and kick the closest plastic chair with just about everything I've got—watching sort of mechanically as it smashes against one of the planter boxes, knocking dirt and cheap, fake-looking carnation petals out onto the concrete.

A crash echoes down the corridor—amplified—reverberating—loud enough that I'm even a little bit startled.

I make a noise like "ugh," stomping my half-numb, half-pained foot on the ground. "That's fucking bullshit. I mean, I'm sorry, but I've been goin' in and out of these rehab places since I was eighteen, and I'm just so sick of their manipulative crap. The truth is, they don't have a clue what they're talking about. They act like they have this goddamn divine authority—like whatever they say is straight from God's mouth. But it just doesn't work like that. And, besides, all it really comes down to is business, anyway. These rehabs make a shitload of money, and the only way they can do that is to present themselves as infallible institutions that know, absolutely, the difference between right and wrong. That's why if you ever question their system, they have to turn everyone against you—otherwise they'll lose their illusion of absolute power."

I flick my still-burning cigarette against the off-white stucco wall. Sparks pop in the air like red and orange flares. I crush the smoldering end down to burned ash with the toe of my sneaker. My eyes stay fixed on the edge of the wall there, where it meets the bland, nothing stone.

Inhale.

Hold the breath in.

Exhale.

Long...calm and slow.

"The point is," I say, steadying myself, "they rely on fear to control us. And they control us to take our money and boost their own egos. But people like you 'n' me, Sue Ellen, we threaten their system. If they don't make an example outta us, all this false sense of power they've created will be totally gone—and then ain't no one gonna pay them shit. You understand? They're just trying to scare us. But the truth is, I fucking love you. So how could that possibly be wrong? I mean, I know for damn sure the only way I'm gonna stay sober is if I'm able to build a life that I want to hold on to—that I want to fight for. We can build a life that's worth living. And not one of 'em can even touch us."

My knees crack as I crouch down next to her, looking up at her face all flushed with crying. "Hey," I tell her. "It's okay. I mean, fuck 'em, right?"

She sniffs some snot up into her nose—smiling even—hiccuping.

"I'm sorry," she whispers. "I know you're right. I really do love you, Nic. You've made me excited about life again. I honestly didn't think that was even possible. Having to be away from you, well, I can't imagine it. You make me feel good. I don't know what could possibly be wrong with that."

She stands awkwardly, pulling at my arm as she starts toward the door—her hands pale and delicate—an almost weightless pressure.

"Come on, Nic, hurry. If Sam or David sees me, I'm so goddamn dead. They just spent the last hour lecturing me about how I should refuse to even speak to you."

"Yeah," I tell her. "I got a little of that myself from Jason."

She puts her key card in the electric lock, pulling it out quickly so the light flashes green, and she turns the handle and the door swings open and we step inside—safe and hidden from the world.

The room is laid out exactly the same as Jason's, right above it—with the same furniture and dark, tacky, worn-out carpet. But unlike Jason's immaculate, perfectly ordered bedroom and attached mini-kitchen, Sue Ellen's room is already a mess of clothing and books and magazines and CDs everywhere. Honestly, I'm not sure how it was even possible for her to have trashed the place so goddamn quickly—though she obviously managed it all right. I mean, not that it bothers me any. I'm sure if it were my room, it'd end up looking the same way—except that I don't own half as much shit as she does.

As it is, I end up having to throw a bunch of her clothes on the bed just so I can sit on the small foldout couch—stitched in a coarse fabric like the kind used for seat covers on a goddamn airplane.

I pull Sue Ellen down next to me.

This time, we kiss for real.

I put my hand against the warmth of her neck—feeling the arteries there tap-tapping hard against the skin's surface.

Faster and faster.

All the blood in me flows down between my legs as the pressure builds with its own pulse, fucking sore and growing painful.

I almost decide to go masturbate in the bathroom real quick so I can just think straight. Besides, I absolutely do not want to have sex with her tonight. It's too soon—too weighted with crass, embarrassingly pathetic need—as though all this has just been about satisfying a need to fuck and gratify our own stupid egos. Having sex tonight would be like admitting defeat to the counselors and everyone else who're all so condescending and dismissive. This is not about sex. This is not about fucking the pain away. This is about two people following their hearts, even when the whole goddamn world is working against them. This is supposed to be like storybook love, right? I mean, this is supposed to be one of those loves worth risking everything for. And, yeah, having sex on our first night together would definitely cheapen all that.

And, besides, that's totally not what this shit with Sue Ellen's all about.

I mean, it's so much more than just sex and physical desire and whatever.

We kiss each other.

Her pale, pale skin is flushed all over.

Her green-blue eyes are blurred with tears.

"What are we gonna do?" she whispers. "What the hell are we gonna do?"

She cries against my shoulder, and I can feel the wet soaking through my T-shirt.

"Hey," I say. "Hey, it's okay. I love you. That's all that matters. We're gonna be together. I'll come to Charleston. I don't even care. I'll stay with you. I'll get a job. I'll finish my book. I don't need anything else. I mean, all I need is you."

She cries even harder at that—her nose snotty, her eyes, cheeks, and mouth all swollen.

I rub her back like you would a small child's—tracing and retracing the contours of her spine.

"But you won't be able to," she whimpers. "You don't have any money."

My hands grip her tighter. "What about your mom? You think she might be willing to help me get a ticket if I promise to pay her back?"

She shakes her head. "No. There's no way. I can't ask her that."

We stay silent for a minute before I can think of anything.

"Well, what if she rented you a car? We could drive to Charleston and drop it off there. That'd be awesome. I've never seen any of that country down there."

Sue Ellen sits up all at once, tucking her hair back behind her ears. "Hey, that's a really good idea. I bet that won't be any more expensive than a plane ticket."

"Totally," I say. "But, even if not, I'm sure I can borrow the money from someone to get a flight from here. You don't have to worry. I mean, it'll be fine."

She lets herself fall down on top of me again, nuzzling her head into the curve of my neck like a cat would. "And you'll be all right just living with me in the South. It's gonna be a whole different world than you're used to. And, I hate to tell you this, but you're gonna stick out like a sore thumb down there." She laughs like crazy. "I hope you're okay with that."

I go on and laugh along with her. "Yeah, I gotta admit, I never in my life ever thought I'd end up living in South Carolina. But, honestly, as long as I'm with you, I don't care where I live. We could move into a goddamn cardboard box, for all I care. It's you, Sue Ellen. I mean, you've given me a reason. You understand?"

She burrows in closer to me. She tells me she loves me.

I run my hands through her hair. "It's gonna be okay," I say—over and over—as an electrical pulse surges through the wiring of my veins. I feel nausea all in my throat—everything burning—dizzy—teetering.

"It's gonna be okay."

I swallow it all down. I mean, what else can I do?

This is my life.

Fuck if I know how I got myself here.

But here I am.

When I was a kid, the grown-ups told me I could accomplish anything if I just set my mind to it.

So what have I accomplished?

Survival.

And the only thing I can hope for now is just to make shit not suck so goddamn hard.

So I might as well try 'n' believe this is what I really want.

Because it is, you know?

It really is.

I mean, it's gonna be okay.

It's gonna be okay.

It's gonna be okay.

I'm going to worship Sue Ellen like I did Zelda.

I'm going to make her matter just as much to me.

So I guide Sue Ellen over to the bed and lie her down on her stomach—legs pressed together so I can straddle her from behind. I gather her long hair up in my hand, draping it off to the side so her long, pale neck is exposed. Her body tenses up beneath me—both in fear and anticipation.

I kiss gently behind her ear.

I kiss down her whole body.

I kiss her all over.

As hours pass.

And then we do make love—even though I hadn't wanted to.

And we make love again.

And we talk and talk.

And we kiss each other.

And we make love again.

And we don't sleep.

Until it's morning.

And finally we pass out.

But then there is a pounding at the door—loud and hard and relentless. I ignore it for as long as I can, but the knocking just won't stop. Standing up fast, I feel the blood rush out of my head so I almost go unconscious. I feel sick and shaky. The world's turning a whole lot faster than it should be.

A ball of white, glaring light makes me flinch as I open the door. I've got a sheet wrapped around my waist, but that's all.

"What?" I ask, stupidly—still half-blind.

It's Jason, of course.

Seven thirty in the morning, and he's already screaming at me.

"This is it, Nic. I'm through with you. Here's your shit. Now, I don't want to talk to you again until you've gotten back into treatment somewhere, is that clear?"

He's sort of piled my guitar and suitcase next to the door, so I start dragging the shit in, saying, "Believe me, man, that's not gonna be a problem."

Jason's jerking all around almost like a goddamn tweak head.

"Yeah, well, you're setting yourself up for a big fall, man. And the most unforgivable thing is that you've decided to take Sue Ellen with you."

I can't help but freeze up for a second at that.

"Look, Jason," I say, turning to face him. "I know where you're coming from. I mean, this is your first time in treatment, so I get why you've bought into it so goddamn blindly. But one day, man, I swear, you're gonna look back on all this and be embarrassed as hell. You'll go back out there in the real world and you'll get some perspective and you'll realize what a total jackass you've been. You might even remember how to think for yourself again."

I blink, blink the world in and out of focus—trying to remember just where the hell I was going with all this.

"Anyway," I stammer. "It's gotta feel pretty good knowing how goddamn right you are."

Jason runs his fingers through his overly gelled, greasy-looking hair. "I don't have to listen to this shit," he tells me.

For once I actually agree with him.

"All right, then, thanks for everything," I answer. "Why don't you go process this shit in group, or whatever? I'm sure they'll tell you just exactly what you want to hear."

I slam the door in his face—my whole body trembling. My heart all sped up. My breathing strained. A pain in my stomach makes me double over as if a knife's been buried in there. I crawl back into bed under the rough cotton sheets.

Sue Ellen must've slept through the whole goddamn thing.

I press up against the warmth of her bare skin, feeling the steady rhythm of her lungs contracting.

Expanding.

Contracting.

I close my eyes.

Her body twitches and stretches and turns and turns again.

I pray for sleep.

It still won't come.

Ch.14

The plane lurches to one side, and I hear someone a couple of seats ahead gasp real loudly, shrieking, "Oh my God!"

Looking through the thick, scratched plastic window, I see nothing but perfect square parcels of desert flatland. The window across the aisle shows only cloudless sky.

The plane bucks—convulsing—racked with bursts of seizure.

Different passengers start yelling and pleading and whimpering.

I hear their desperate breathing all around me.

The plane shakes and drops a bunch of altitude all at once.

Honestly, I'm just praying the fucking thing will go down.

I mean, how amazing would that be? To have the decision made for me by some act of fate. No more struggling. No more trying to decide whether life is actually worth living anymore. No more holding on to that stupid, completely unrealistic, tiny parasite of hope that won't stop spawning in my blood— driving me forward when I should've ended it all a long-ass time ago.

The plane stutters, lurches, kicks, and stalls.

I'm waiting for the fall, praying. A chance at a good death.

No ODs, sexual violence, suicide, or disease.

Me and all the other passengers, the same—innocent.

But, of course, we're not the same at all.

I hear them panicking—praying for life—both aloud and silent.

"Oh God. Oh God. Oh God."

The two people sitting next to me are grabbing their armrests, faces gone colorless, sweating, heads bent back toward the sky—eyes closed—the veins and tendons in their necks all bulging out.

Someone yells, "Fuck," a couple of rows up as the plane hits a mass of tremors—the overhead compartments bursting open all at once, so our luggage and coats and things are dumped out into the aisles.

There are tears and sobbing all around me.

I hear it. I hear them screaming. And it's no good.

I don't want to die like this—with all these frightened people clinging to their lives like they really do have something to live for.

And who am I to say otherwise?

Most people want to live and, honestly, I've really never

been able to figure that one out. I mean, most people are lonely and lost and broke and frightened. Most people are deep in debt, with shit jobs or no jobs and no health care and no shot at the future. But yet they still wanna live. I don't get it. I don't. Somehow they've found a reason. Somehow I've never found mine.

Maybe I never will.

I stare out the scratched window—trying hard not to look at anyone—imagining how my family will take the news of my death. Hell, they'll probably be relieved. I mean, no more worrying. No more disappointments. No more borrowing money to pay for my rehab. No more dealing with my bullshit.

The plane drops a couple hundred feet, and a bunch of overhead compartments open all at once.

I'm ready—fucking ready.

But then, suddenly, inexplicably, the shaking stops. We've leveled out. We're flying straight. The sobbing and praying came through for them. We're going to live. Or, at least, the airplane's not gonna kill us. The captain makes an announcement over the loudspeaker apologizing and reassuring us—trying to keep us calm with some dumb pilot-talking-over-the-loudspeaker humor. The passengers laugh hesitantly. They sigh and wipe their faces and start nervously half whispering to one another. Hell, I guess I'm happy for them. I mean, I'm probably even happy for myself—in spite of everything. 'Cause, yeah, that stupid hope is inside of me, too. I'm just like everybody else. Everything has fallen apart, but I still don't have the common sense to just give up already. Instead, I boarded the plane—not to Charleston, South Carolina, but to Albuquerque, New Mexico. The goddamn head of the Gallup House is gonna meet me at the airport. I fucking gave in.

Honestly, though, I was outta options. Aside from trying to hitchhike clear across the goddamn country, Gallup House was the only shelter I was gonna get.

Sue Ellen's mom wouldn't go for the whole rental-car idea, and she wasn't gonna pay for my flight, either.

I asked to borrow money from some old friends in LA—and, of course, from my mom and dad—but I knew I wasn't gonna get a fucking penny.

The days of people bailing me out are gone forever. Everyone's tired of my shit. And they've all but given up on the possibility that I might actually change. To them, man, I'm done. Lost and not coming back.

But there is one person who still believes in me—probably just 'cause I haven't had the chance to hurt her yet.

Sue Ellen wants to help me. Too bad she's got no money of her own.

Still, she did manage to convince her mom to pay for a room at a Super 8 motel near the airport, so at least we didn't have to separate immediately. We holed up there for about three days—doing pretty much nothing but making love and talking and watching movies on Sue Ellen's computer.

The room was tiny and stank of sweat and stale smoke and fresh smoke. The walls were painted a pale yellow and covered with brown splotches like grease stains. The sheets were coarse and all twisted up around us—the tattered wool blankets heaped on the floor—smoke from our burning cigarettes filling the air, thick and suffocating. Our clothes were strewn everywhere. We'd stay locked in there for maybe fifteen or sixteen hours at a time. We talked and talked and talked and talked. And if I'd ever doubted it, I mean, after all that, I know I really could grow to love her.

But I guess all that's gonna have to wait.

I mean, we can still make plans to be together, even if I'm pretty sure we both know it'll never happen. I'm lookin' at a year in New Mexico with nothing but a bunch of recovering alcoholic men. Hell, and who am I kidding? It'll be a year if I'm lucky. It's not like I'm gonna make enough money there to strike out on my own. Nah, I'm at the mercy of my fucking father. And he'll just do whatever the counselor people tell him. So I could keep getting bounced around from one center to the next for the rest of my goddamn life. I'm sure my dad thinks that's exactly what I need. At least he'll sleep better that way — and be able to devote all his attention to his real kids.

But for now, yeah, I'm gonna try with Sue Ellen. She bought me a calling card before I left, and I promised to phone her every day — which I will, I mean, I want to.

At the airport, man, she cried so hard. She held on to me and cried and cried, and I wanted to cry, too, but for some reason I just couldn't. I forced myself to walk away, down the corridor to my gate, and I swore I wouldn't look back, but then I did and I felt my stomach squeezed so tight the crying finally came. She was still watching me go, and I wanted to tear off my skin and cut myself deep, up and down both arms, and rip my eyes out. I mean, Jesus Christ, it's just not fair. We actually had a shot together—a shot at a life we both maybe wanted to live. But now...fuck, now we've got nothing.

Nothing.

And there's just no way out.

My plane doesn't crash.

It touches down in Albuquerque.

Ch.15

In twelve-step meetings and rehabs, they always say this thing about how the definition of insanity is doing the same thing over and over but expecting different results. Of course, they mean it in the sense that as addicts, we keep trying to use again even though we suffer such devastating consequences every time. But, I'll tell you what, walking off the plane to go meet up with the director of this fucking program feels pretty goddamn familiar. The only difference is that this time I'm not expecting different results. I know how insane it is for me to be here. So I guess that makes the rest of the people in my life the fucking crazy ones. And, me, well, I guess I'm finally fucking sane.

Not that it matters.

I still have no choice but to play along.

So I walk down to the baggage claim.

The director of the program has no trouble identifying me

from the description Melonie must've given him. I mean, I definitely don't look a thing like the other passengers standing around. Especially 'cause I'm wearing this stupid, fringed tapestry jacket that was Zelda's ex-husband's and these bell-bottoms that were actually Zelda's.

"You must be Nic," he says, sounding very masculine and chummy, like we just met at a goddamn football-watching party or something. He shakes my hand, doing his best to show me just how confident he is. A confidence, I'm sure, that can be achieved only after spending a year or more at his very own recovery frat house high up in the New Mexico desert. He smiles at me like, "Trust me, little queer boy. Give me just one year and I'll make a man out of you yet." Seriously, I mean, these all-male treatment programs really are cults—run by smooth-talking con men with their smug "I'm enlightened" Tom Cruise smiles. And this douche bag here's not a fucking bit different. He shakes my hand hard, like a man should.

"Chip Barnes," he says, proudly. "Glad to meet you."

He's short and squat with a thick, '70s porn star mustache.

He's wearing a shiny suit and a pair of snakeskin cowboy boots.

Christ.

I get my bag, and we walk out to the parking lot together.

His car, of course, is this monster sport-utility vehicle. It's got a built-in camera on the back bumper so you don't have to turn around when you're backing up. The leather interior smells kind of lemon-scented. I ask if I can smoke, but I'm just being an asshole.

He tells me I'll have plenty of time to smoke when we get to Gallup.

He laughs deeply, like he just said something really funny.

Fucking Chip Barnes—the man who's finally going to set me straight. The man who's gonna teach me whatever it is I'm gonna need to know to become a confident, successful, influential male.

Driving his luxury SUV.

Air-conditioning on full blast.

Hair slicked back.

Smiling that fucking smile.

Not shutting up once the whole goddamn ride.

"Nic, I can already tell, this is gonna be exactly what you need. Alcoholics Anonymous was founded on the principle of men working with other men."

He laughs at the joke he's about to make. "And that was back when being a man actually meant something, you know what I mean? Not like today, where we're supposed to be ashamed to even own a pair." He laughs some more, smirking and laughing and smirking again. "Am I right?"

He takes one hand off the wheel and punches my shoulder with it.

"Yeah...ha-ha," I say.

The bland desert stretches out on either side—dull shades of brown, all burned and peeling. The brush is tangled, brittle. The cacti rot beneath the dust and sand—the car exhaust— the hazy, cancerous sky.

And Chip Barnes, well, he keeps driving. He keeps driving and talking and talking and driving. As we pass strip mall after strip mall. As we pass a rash of housing communities—with one oversize home after another, pressed up practically touching one another. Indoor living. Giant air-conditioned cages with no yards or individuality. Stalinist Russia on steroids. The American dream.

Is this what I'm getting sober for? Is this the society I'm trying to become a productive member of?

I listen to Chip as he goes on blathering. I listen to Chip and I nod my head. I listen to Chip outlining the next year of my goddamn life.

"Based on what we know about you," he says, still smirking his smirk, "the team and I have decided that it'd be best to keep you on phase one for at least a couple months. All that means is that you'll be going to group on-site during the day and then out to meetings at night with the guys. As long as you're on phase one, you won't be allowed off the grounds unless accompanied by one of the senior residents—that's phase four or higher. They'll be responsible for signing you out, so if anything happens, it's on their head. That's one of the ways we try to create accountability around here. Anyway, as part of phase one, you're not allowed to use the phone or computers unless, of course, there's some sort of emergency you make us aware of. As well, because we want to keep you focused on your recovery, we don't allow any non-twelve-step-related reading material, and you won't be able to play that guitar you brought with you—so we'll go ahead and keep that locked in the office. That way you'll be free to really spend some time getting to know the other guys—and really getting to know yourself."

My eyes close as I breathe in through my nose, long and

slow. There's a cramp in my stomach and a cold, glossy sweat broken out all down my back.

My voice comes out stuttering and shaky. I can't help it. "Okay," I say. "Yeah, all that sounds, uh, good, I guess. The one thing is, though, before I relapsed, I was able to get a book deal, which was, like, such a total miracle. I mean, I never really went to college or anything, so I kinda feel like this is my one shot, you know? Anyway, I was able to finish about half of it before I got involved in this relationship and started using again. But I guess everyone was really encouraging about the pages I've already written, so, uh, now that I'm sober, I'm really looking forward to writing again. And I'm pretty sure I could finish the rough draft within a month or two, which would be so awesome — but I'd definitely need to use a computer. You think we could work something out so I could spend some time writing every day — if I promise not to go on the Internet, or whatever?"

Obviously Chip must've been listening, 'cause he responds to what I've said, but without even thinking about it for two seconds. He laughs, almost as if he'd been expecting this question the whole time — which he probably was.

"No, Nic, sorry, I don't think writing a book is something you should be focusing on. You need a real job, where you can just be one of the guys. One of our boys just made manager at the local Albertson's grocery store. So he's worked out a deal with them to start hiring the new guys we got coming in. That's the kind of job I want for you."

My teeth grind together so it's actually painful. My jaw pops back and forth.

"But," I say, still stuttering my goddamn ass off, "I mean, why couldn't I do both? I've worked jobs like that before. Hell, I worked at a grocery store in LA for almost six months. I've got no problem with that. But can't you guys give me some time to write as well? Honestly, man, that's like the one thing I have to hold on to."

My voice cracks, and I hope to God I don't start fucking crying.

"If I didn't have this book," I try again, "I don't think I would've even made it through detox. It's, like, the only chance I've got."

Chip's expression doesn't change. He's just silently laughing—grinning like a bastard. "See, that's my point, Nic. Seems to me like your priorities are all screwed up. Writing a book isn't gonna get you anywhere. What you need to do is focus on working the twelve steps and on building your relationships with other men. Nothing else should matter to you right now. You don't need to be writing. You don't need to be hanging out with girls. You don't need anything that your brotherhood can't give you. All that other crap is just a distraction—a waste of time."

"Yeah," I say, inhaling through my nose all at once. "Sounds to me like the twelve steps and your stupid male bonding are the real wastes of time. If who you are is any indication of what that'll do for me. I'm not sure managing a sober frat house in the middle of nowhere exactly qualifies you to make any sort of judgments about anyone else's life."

I mean, I figure why not fight back? Obviously I'm fucked either way.

But, still, his goddamn expression doesn't change. "I'll tell you what qualifies me to pass judgment on how you're living your life. I have over fifteen years of living clean and sober. Seems to me you're having trouble even getting a couple days without being locked up in some institution."

He snorts at his little comeback.

Man, it really is all I can do not to punch him in the face.

I'm shaking all over.

I want to cry and scream.

"Believe me," I tell him, "if just staying sober's what it's all about, I woulda had this shit beat when I was eighteen. Anyone can stay sober. It's actually having a life that's worth staying sober for that's the hard part. Honestly, I rather be strung out, or dead, than a self-righteous 'sober man' on a goddamn power trip. No, I'm not interested in sobriety like that. So, yeah, go ahead, put me on phase one. I don't fucking care. Fuck." I pound my fist into my leg. "I can't believe this shit."

For the first time since we started driving, I realize he's gone silent for a second. I mean, he isn't even smiling. Veins protrude like parasitic growths along his neck and forehead. His tan face is turning almost purple.

I guess I got what I wanted.

Though now, well, I'm not so sure I want it anymore.

All his smug, serene whatever has turned into rapid, screaming craziness.

He lets me fucking have it.

"If you're trying to tell me you don't want to be here, then fine. I don't care. You can take the coward's way out—since that's obviously what you are. Anyway, you wouldn't be the first. I've seen it a hundred times before. In fact, I've seen *you* a hundred times before. You think you're unique? Ha, you're not unique. Nic Sheff after Nic Sheff after Nic Sheff have come through here. Usually they end up walking down the street to the Greyhound station and catching a bus outta here. Then a week or two later they come crawling back, licking their wounds and begging me for another chance—not so high and mighty anymore. The ones who don't come back, well, usually I get a phone call from their parents saying that their son is dead or in jail. That's what happens to people who don't give themselves over to this program. And you think I'm gonna give a rat's ass when I get that call about you? No way, not me. I'll be sleeping soundly, knowing that I offered you everything you could have possibly needed to get better, and you still wouldn't take it. I'll tell you what—the twelve steps work— my program works—they work for everyone and anyone. The only people who fail are the ones who don't do exactly what I say. People like you, who are too arrogant and, frankly, too much of a damn pussy to do what it takes to really commit to this thing. So you want me to drop you at the bus station? That's fine. We'll go there right now. But I got a feeling ain't no one gonna be helping you get that ticket. And by tomorrow night you're gonna be selling your ass just to have a place to sleep. 'Cause, I'll tell you, these high desert nights are cold as sin. But I'll drive you to the station. That's fine by me. In fact, you better decide right now, 'cause if you wanna be admitted to my facility, you're gonna have to shut your mouth and do exactly, I mean *exactly*, what I say. 'Cause as far as I'm concerned, we're done already. So if I hear you're giving anyone any problems — talking to the guys about how this is some cult or anything like that — well, I'll lock the door on you and throw away the key, and you'll never set foot on my property again. You understand me?"

I stare at the creased black-leather dashboard — my eyes stinging — still fighting back the tears that're trying to get through.

I breathe.

I breathe some more.

Should I try this thing?

Should I pray that Sue Ellen will have mercy on me? After all, a Greyhound ticket's gotta be cheaper than a flight. I can't believe I didn't think of taking a bus before. But what if I can't stay with her? What if I'm throwing away my last chance? What if I really do need this program?

"Look," I say, surprisingly calm. "I'm sorry. It's been a fucked-up, you know, emotional couple days. The truth is, all I really want is to get well. But I'm just so frustrated. I mean, I've tried this shit so many times, but I still keep fucking up. I don't know. I feel like there's gotta be another way, 'cause nothing I've been doing has been working. And I'm so sick of hearing that my only chance is the twelve steps. Honestly, I'm scared that, for some reason, they just won't work for me. I'm scared I'm a lost cause. So I'm sorry I took it out on you. I mean, I'm sorry I was being an asshole."

At this point I'm really not interested in what he's doing with his face, so I keep my focus kinda blurred out the window.

"Hey, it's okay," he says, already sounding a whole lot more cheerful. "That's my job, all right? And I can assure you that you're not a lost cause. The twelve steps are the answer for everyone—I mean, every last one of us. I can promise you that. So if I were you, Nic, I'd stop worrying about what might be wrong with the program, and I'd start trying to figure out what's keeping you from fully committing to it. In fact, since tomorrow's Sunday and you don't have group, I want you to write me a thorough list of everything that is blocking you from working the steps."

He pauses a second.

"And, as well, I want you to write a list of all the things that have kept you from developing meaningful relationships with other men and how that is fueling the fears you have about being here. Does that all sound good?"

I realize, suddenly, that we must have turned off the highway at some point, 'cause Chip's stopped his car in front of a single-story, sort of '70s, Brady Bunch–looking ranch-style house. There's no sign out front, but this is obviously the place.

My stomach goes all knotted again, but I try not to let on. I mean, I'm even able to put on a goddamn smile.

"Sure," I say. "That seems like it'll be really helpful."

I finally let myself look over at him, and I can see he's just beaming at having turned me around so fast.

"Well, good. I'm gonna drop you here, but I need you to go check in at the office right away. I'll make a time to sit down with you first thing Monday. And, seriously, Nic, if you start feeling squirrelly, you have one of the guys give me a call. The Greyhound stop's just down the block that way, so I don't wanna come back on Monday to find you skipped out on me."

He's nice enough to point toward the bus station for me before continuing on.

"Remember, God created this program for you as well as me and the rest of us alcoholics. All ya gotta do is start giving yourself over to our care, and the healing can begin. You got that?"

I nod.

"Yeah," I say. "Thank you."

He helps me get my stuff out of the trunk, and then we shake hands.

He tells me, "Good luck," getting back into his prized car and driving off.

I don't go right in like he told me.

I sit on the curb and smoke a cigarette.

The neighborhood suburban and crumbling all around me.

I sing that Talking Heads song quietly to myself.

I repeat it over and over.

This is not my beautiful life.

This is not my beautiful life.

I shut my eyes. I hold them closed. But it's no good.

I mean, I'm still here.

And this is the only goddamn life I'm ever gonna have.

Ch.16

So I made it through the first night.

Even if I did wake myself up screaming, not knowing where the hell I was.

But then I turned to see my new roommate sitting up on the narrow built-in twin bed, looking like I'd just freaked him the fuck out.

I told him I was sorry.

He grunted, lying back down so he faced the textured, off-white painted wall. He pulled the blanket up, hiding most of his head. It was the weekend, so I guess everyone was allowed to sleep in, but it was no use to me. The images from my dream played over and over against the blurred nothing of my unfocused eyes. It was a dream about Zelda. Of course. She'd been given some sort of poison and was dying on the floor of my dad's house in Point Reyes. My fingers couldn't dial the right numbers on my phone to get her help. I couldn't find a hospital. Everything was closed. No one would answer my questions. Until, finally, someone told me I should forget about trying to save her. She was gone already. The person said all I could do was bury her. Screaming, I held her.

I mean, fuck. After everything that's happened, I still dream about her almost every night. I keep waiting to dream about Sue Ellen, but it hasn't happened yet.

Anyway, I gave up on trying to go back to sleep. It wasn't gonna happen. Besides, I figured I should get outta there so I didn't keep my roommate up any more than I already had — even if he did seem kinda like a dick. I mean, I guess that's not true. He was totally indistinguishable from most of the other guys there. The night before, I'd sat around talking with a bunch of the kids in the little courtyard. They all looked the same — tan, muscular, close-cropped hair stuck up with gel in the front. They smoked Marlboros, and quizzed me about using and girls, and kept one-upping all my stories. There were a few, like, hipster kids there — with shaggy hair and bangs swooped to one side — Converse sneakers — tight-ass jeans. But, really, they were the same as the others. All they talked about was drugs and wanting to fuck — taking a definite pleasure in bragging about how much more they'd used than everyone else. Even some of the older guys came over, and they were talking about drugs and fucking and all the shit they were gonna do when they got the hell out of this place. No one offered any hope. No one seemed to want anything except escape.

So I smoked one cigarette after another.

And I began to fantasize about ways of ending my life.

Because having to live like this, man, I'll tell you, it's not worth it.

But today is a new day. The sun is growing warm — the winter giving way to spring. Of course, I'm tired as shit, but I've agreed to go with a couple of guys to a twelve-step meeting, just to check it out, you know? The two guys are in their forties, I'd guess, and neither one of 'em was around talking shit last night, so maybe that's something.

But, anyway, the meeting's only a couple of blocks away, so we all walk together. Thank God my mom sent me those cartons of cigarettes when I was back at Safe Passage, 'cause otherwise I think I really would snap completely. But she came through with that, so I've been chain-smoking all morning.

From what I've seen of the town, it seems pretty desolate — torn apart by chain stores and fast-food restaurants. The houses are all duplicates of one another, pressed tight together with competing green lawns that are ridiculously out of place in this dry desert wasteland. We pass a gas station with a big mini-mart, and this guy from the house, Peter, mentions to me that it's the recommended place for everyone to buy candy and drinks and cigarettes.

I thank him.

Across from the meeting there's a concrete park with teenagers skateboarding all over the place. I have to sort of laugh at how angst-ridden and full of rage they seem to be — pierced and tattooed, with dyed hair and chains on their wallets — yelling at each other and spitting and saying "dude, dude" all the time. Still, some of them are crazy good, and I use watching them as an excuse not to have to talk to all the people gathered out in front of the meeting. Those moments at the beginning and end of the meeting are always awkward as hell. Fuck, in LA, man, they even had ten-minute coffee breaks around the hour mark of the meeting. Most everyone would kind of mill around talking all jovially and everything—laughing and slapping one another on the back. But, honestly, unless I'd come with a couple of friends, all I'd do at these breaks was check old voice mail messages or randomly decide to text someone just so I'd at least look like I was doing something important.

Because I'm new, though, a bunch of different men introduce themselves and tell me, "Welcome." I don't know what to do but thank them and pretend I have to go do something else. Basically, I just end up walking back and forth to the coffee urn about ten times—never actually getting any coffee.

Finally, though, the meeting is called to a start, and I take my seat. I guess 'cause we're using the basketball court of the local school, the overhead lights are bright-ass fucking bright.

So, yeah, like I said, they start the meeting, and it's basically the same as every other meeting I've ever been to. Man, I remember how amazing it was the first time I went to one of these things. I'd been checked in to my first rehab a couple days earlier, and they finally felt I was ready to go off the grounds with the rest of the patients. We had to take a city bus down to the Marina, so I was quizzing everyone the whole time about what to expect, since I had absolutely no idea. But none of their explanations really made it any clearer.

The first part of the meeting, when they read the preamble and all this different stuff, made no sense at all to me, but then this elderly British woman went up to the front and started telling us her story. It was so crazy. I mean, despite the fact that she was from a totally different generation and the details of her life were totally different from mine, all the feelings she described about why she started drinking and what drinking gave to her and how her life had begun spiraling out of control—all of it was so dead-on to everything I had experienced. It was the first time I realized that I really was an alcoholic. And, in terms of the meeting and this program she was talking about, I knew right then it was exactly where I belonged. It's a feeling that's lasted since I was eighteen right up to now— despite my relapses and sometime doubts. I know this is where I belong—where I have to belong.

But today, man, fuck.

This guy is telling his story up at the front, telling the same story I've heard a thousand times before. Everyone's sort of laughing in unison at his jokes—nodding their heads in agreement with almost everything—becoming emotional—then laughing again.

But me? Me, I don't feel a goddamn thing. The man talks about the solution—finding God—being saved by the different people in the rooms—his sponsor—his sober brothers. He talks about taking commitments at meetings—greeting people at the door or cleaning up the cigarette butts or whatever— different things that helped him become more connected with the program. And he's right, you know; it all brought me closer to the program and my friends and my sponsor. But suddenly I realize I have no connection to any of that shit anymore. The sense of hope I always had—the complete faith in everything they preached — it's all gone. Sweat breaks out all along my neck and back and chest. My balance goes. The sickness keeps burrowing in.

So I stand.

The meeting's not over, but I go on and push my way through the crowded aisles — almost everyone turning to stare and silently criticize me in their heads for not being, you know, serious enough. At least, that's what I imagine. Their collective eye definitely follows me out the heavy fire doors of the gym. Doors that slam conspicuously hard behind me. I mean, fuck.

The pavement is already hot from the blur of sun, which is somehow bigger than I've ever seen it — filling half the goddamn sky. My sweat soaks through my shirt as I strip off my jacket and lie faceup on the burning concrete. I light a cigarette and try to smoke on my back without choking. Man, I wish I could just stay right here forever — being swallowed by the sun — my head all filled with strobe lights and static. I could just drift off and never wake up. I mean, halle-fucking-lujah. The smoke fills my lungs, and I curl onto my side, one arm buried between my legs as I tuck my knees up to my chest, fetus-like. The heat is scalding. I decide just to sleep here for the rest of my life on this goddamn glittering sidewalk. My eyes stay closed. My mind goes blank.

Of course, it can't last. Pretty soon that Peter guy from Gallup House is shaking me and loudly whispering, "Hey, get up, you're embarrassing us."

I do get up, jaw clenched, my eyes fixed on his. I don't say a word.

"You're also not allowed to leave a meeting before it's over," he tells me. "That's a rule we all have to follow."

I laugh just to piss him off, lighting another cigarette and saying, "Man, come on, I'm just goin' through some shit. Anyway, why the hell do you care? It's not like it affects you at all."

His nose lifts, all indignant. "I'm taking you to the office and reporting this to Adam." He tugs at me kinda roughly. "Right now!" he almost shrieks, acting like I'm fighting him, even though I'm totally not.

"Fuck, all right, fine, whatever," I say. "At this point, honestly, man, I don't even care."

I realize that's the truth right after I say it. But, I mean, I still make him get his fucking hands off me.

His eyes go kinda wild as he yells, "Well, we'll just see about that now, won't we?"

He stomps off toward the office and I follow, dragging my feet on the ground behind him.

Not surprisingly, I guess, Adam seems to take my transgression just as seriously as everyone else. His face goes very kinda angry, or whatever — jaw set, eyebrows all furrowed and shit. He tells me to take a seat and I do, on one of those low-to-the-ground office chairs with the little wheels. It makes a metallic, sort-of-groaning noise as I lean back.

"So, Nic," he says, his voice deep and affected. "I'm Adam, the weekend manager. We haven't had a chance to meet yet."

I don't say what I wanna say, which is, "No shit."

I really don't say anything at all.

"Well, look," he continues, crossing his thick, tanned arms, all covered in coarse-looking white-blond hairs. "When I talked to Chip this morning, he told me you two made some kind of a deal that you were going to change your attitude and not make any trouble. He also told me that if you went back on this deal in any way, I was to ask you to leave immediately. Now, do you remember having that conversation with Chip yesterday?"

What I really want to do is roll my eyes, but I'm able to stop myself. "I remember," I say, sucking in a lot of breath—holding it—exhaling. "But I wasn't causing any trouble. It's just...for some reason when I was listening to that speaker, all this shit started coming up for me. I don't know, it's like, I used to get so much out of those meetings, but today I couldn't connect at all. I mean, it just seemed like such bullshit. And that was really scary to me, man. I'm serious. I know how much I need those meetings, so feeling like that, fuck, it freaks me out. I'm not sure I'm ever going to be able to buy into that shit again. And, believe me, I want to super fucking bad."

My body's rocking back and forth involuntarily. I look around the cramped, institutional white-painted office. There are no photos on the wall, no inspirational posters, no art prints, nothing—nothing to focus on but the shelf holding the client folders. Actually, I'm pretty sure mine hasn't even been started yet. I mean, I definitely can't see it up there.

"Hey," says Adam, I guess noticing that I've spaced out for a second. "Is this boring you? 'Cause there's nothing keeping you here if you wanna go. Hell, I'll even help you pack. Because I can tell you right now, this is not how I want to be spending my Sunday, either. So if you wanna leave, leave. Otherwise, I'd stop giving excuses and start improving your attitude. 'Cause all I hear you saying right now is that your addict has total control over you. So if you want to give in to that, fine. Otherwise I don't wanna hear one more complaint about you criticizing the program, or anything else, 'cause we got no tolerance for that here."

I really do wonder for a second if this guy might just be fucking with me or something. Maybe this is like some initiation, some hazing thing for the new people.

"Wait, are you serious?" I ask, allowing myself a kind of forced laugh. "I can't talk about having doubts or anything? I mean, I'm telling you, I'm genuinely freaked about this whole thing. Should I just, like, pretend I'm not feeling this stuff?"

Man, his expression goes even angrier than before. "I'm not gonna debate with you, okay? We don't debate here. You listen. So if you think you can start doing that, then you're welcome to stay. If not, just come into the office and we'll get your discharge paperwork all ready."

He turns back toward the small computer monitor in the corner and immediately starts typing something.

Me? I walk over to the house pay phone.

The pay phone that'll be off limits to me for however long they feel like making it.

I have no change, but I have that phone card Sue Ellen bought me, so I go on and give her a call. There are a few guys outside smoking pretty close to me, so I turn my back and hope to God they're not rats, like everyone else in this goddamn place.

Sue Ellen answers after the third ring, the connection all

crackling like a beat-up old record spinning around. Still, her voice comes through soft and sweet and beautiful and like the best sound I've ever heard in my goddamn life. It takes about two minutes to convince her to get me the bus ticket. I mean, I can hear her anxiety, and I'm scared, too, but she tells me to go to the station—my ticket from Gallup, New Mexico, to Charleston, South Carolina, will be waiting for me. Besides all the fear and everything, I can tell we're both excited. Before we hang up, we both say, "I love you." It feels very real.

So immediately I go back to my dingy-ass room and pack my things quickly—filling my duffel bag with the few clothes I have left and then putting into my backpack some stuff I figure I'll need on the bus: a notebook, some pens, a Michael Chabon novel I borrowed from Jason before things got bad, a couple of packs of cigarettes, some energy bars left over from my mom's care package, and a bottle of water. Now, I guess, all that's left is to get my guitar back from Adam and, I hope, convince him to give up all my meds. I tell myself for, like, the thousandth time that it's all gonna be okay. I tell that to myself over and over, even though I know damn well just how many things could go wrong. I mean, what if Sue Ellen asks me to leave after a couple weeks? What if somehow my dad figures out how to get in touch with her parents, convincing them not to let me in their house at all? Actually, I'm sure that's the first thing he's gonna do, 'cause I know he's gonna flip his shit when he finds out I split outta here. And, uh, that's putting it mildly. I figure I'll give him a call from the road just to let him know I'm all right. Even though that's gonna be a fucking shit show, for sure. But, the thing is, this really is the right thing for me.

And even though he won't be able to see that now, I know someday he will. As it is, I'd say the best thing for both of us is just not to communicate at all for a good while. I'll tell him that when I call. I mean, it's gonna be all right.

I sling my bag over my shoulder and walk toward the office. When the other guys see me all packed and everything, they don't say a word, but they stare longingly — there's no mistaking it. Our eyes meet, and they are all so goddamn defeated.

I look away.

It's over now.

I'm walking free.

Ch.17

The bus shudders to a stop and the doors open, letting in the night air all hot and thick—almost tropical—sticky—wet.

I've been riding for two days now, and I'd say I have about two days left.

I stumble to my feet, legs cramped and aching, barely able to walk down the aisle and the three steps to the pavement outside. My vision is still blurred from having been asleep just minutes before, but I can make out another passenger smoking a little way off. Bugs are chirping and crackling loudly all around us. There is little light. The damp and heat is like another world.

"Hey, man," I call out, the sound of my voice so foreign suddenly. "Where are we, do you know?"

He coughs some before responding. "Louisiana," he says. "What'd you think?"

I light my own cigarette—dizzy, teetering. "Honestly, man, I have no idea."

Part 2

Ch.18

It's night as the bus pulls into the Charleston Greyhound station.

Or, uh, morning, I guess. Around two a.m. eastern fucking standard time.

I haven't slept or eaten for about a day and a half.

I mean, those energy bars my mom had sent ran out after the first two days, and I've been traveling at least forty-eight hours since then.

Plus, my phone card ran out somewhere in the middle of Texas, so I haven't talked to Sue Ellen at all. If she doesn't come to get me at the station, well, I'm not sure what the fuck I'm gonna do. At least it's warm down here—a whole lot better than the freezing-ass nights in Arizona and New Mexico. Still, sleeping outside pretty much sucks, no matter what, and I've been dreaming of food and a real bed for the last eight hundred miles or so. I've even caught myself praying that she'll be there. Praying like—what's the expression? An atheist in a foxhole?

Exactly.

Praying 'cause this could be my last chance.

Praying 'cause this is all I have left.

Praying 'cause I ain't got shit else to do.

But, still, I mean, even if Sue Ellen does show up, well, I figure she's probably gonna be pretty freaked out about me actually being here. I'm sure she's gonna feel a ton of pressure and, as much as I want to be cool about it, this whole thing is a big-ass leap in terms of our relationship. The last thing I want to do is make it all the way here just to have her kick me out 'cause she thinks I'm moving everything too fast. Hell, as it is, I'm showing up with no money and my life in a goddamn duffel bag. If I push even a little bit, she could panic. If she panics, then I'm on the street. So it's all very, you know, delicate. I'm just gonna play it like I'm her friend. I'm not gonna try and kiss her, and we're not gonna have sex, and I'm gonna let her go about her day like she normally would. That's the only way this is gonna work. And even then, well, fuck...

The bus shuts down and the lights come on, and my heart is going like I just slammed enough coke to drop me to the floor with convulsions.

I get my breathing together—or try to, anyway. Sweat soaks through my jeans and T-shirt—my whole body is shivering, despite the outside heat. The driver takes out my bag and guitar from the storage compartment underneath. There're actually about ten other people getting off at this stop. They all seem to know just exactly where they're going, climbing into waiting cars, walking off in different directions, leaving me alone in the deserted parking lot — trash strewn from one end to the other, the lights in the waiting area suddenly turned off by some unseen person.

Fuck.

Through the thick, strangling air and the dim overhead streetlights, I can make out what look like projects on all sides of me — two-story, institutional-looking brick buildings divided into run-down apartments with boards on some of the windows and graffiti all over. There are clotheslines strung up in rows — sheets, dress shirts, pants, dresses, socks, and whatever hang drying in the warmth of the night. A barely noticeable wind rocks the lines back and forth. A man's voice echoes through the street — screaming something I can't make out. I hoist my bag up on my shoulder. There's nothing to do now but walk. That's what you do when you've got nowhere to go — you walk and walk and walk and walk.

So I start walking.

And then a car pulls up next to me.

"Nic, hey, where're you going?"

I turn, half wondering if I'm hallucinating or something.

But, no, she's there.

Holy shit.

She's there. I mean, here. Now. In front of me.

Looking the same as before — green eyes glowing in the dark, like a cat's would.

"Sue Ellen, oh my God, I can't believe you came."

She smiles, and all the breath goes outta me.

"Yeah, well," she says, her voice soft, like a goddamn lullaby.

"I was worried when I didn't hear from you, but I figured I'd go ahead and try."

I tell her about the phone card as I throw my stuff in the back of her new-looking silver Volvo station wagon.

I sit down next to her on the tan leather passenger seat— trembling suddenly—staring.

"This is fucking surreal," I say, stupidly.

She stares right back at me and she is beautiful and I've come all this way and I really do love her—I do—more than I ever could Zelda. That has to be the truth. I mean, I keep telling myself that.

Her pale, small hand reaches up, her fingers lightly running down the curve of my cheekbone.

"It's so good to see you," I tell her, unable to stop myself, the words practically forcing themselves outta my mouth.

She moves her hand up higher, pushing back my long, greasy hair.

"It's good to see you, too," she says sweetly.

A car drives past—the light catching her eyes—her tears like shadows.

"I don't know how I can ever repay you for this, Sue Ellen. You've saved my life. I'm so fucking grateful for you."

She leans forward and kisses me. Her full lips pressing against mine—opening slightly.

I want to take things slow.

I don't want to pressure her.

But she's kissing me, so I kiss her back.

We kiss like we mean it.

I suck on her tongue.

I hold the warmth of her body.

She tucks her head up under my jawline, resting there—taking shelter in the curve of my neck—her arms encircling my frail waist.

"Jesus Christ," she whispers, wiping away her tears with my frayed-to-almost-nothing T-shirt. "You're so skinny. Are you all right?"

"Well," I say, laughing a little, "I haven't eaten in about two days. And, uh, even then it was just a fucking PowerBar."

She pushes herself back. "What? Are you serious?"

"Yeah, I mean, I'm broke. I really don't have a penny."

"But you're gonna be getting money from your publisher when you finish your book, right? So why wouldn't anyone lend you the money?"

Leaning forward, I reach out to kiss her forehead, inadvertently picking up the putrid, rotting smell of my clothes and body crevices.

"Man, I stink bad," I say. "I'm sorry. First thing I'll do is take a shower. But, uh, yeah, you're right, I will be getting that money. It doesn't matter, though. There's not a single person in my life who still trusts me. I mean, you might wanna take that as a warning, you know?"

She laughs, turning the key in the ignition. A James Brown song screams loud from the car speakers, startling both of us—Sue Ellen's hands moving frantically, scrambling to get the volume down.

"S-sorry," she kinda stutters, not looking in my direction. Embarrassed, maybe.

I tell her she should never apologize for the Godfather of Soul.

That gets her laughing again. "Amen to that. But, uh, anyway, Nic, don't worry. I trust you. I trust you more than I have almost anyone, I'd say. Besides, your dad already tried that one on me."

She puts the car in drive, and then we take off down the street a short way before half skidding out in a U-turn.

"What do you mean? He called you?" I ask stupidly.

"Yup. Tried to convince me I should put you right back on the bus as soon as you got here. Said all kinds of bad shit about you...and about me for helping you, actually. I guess he got my number from your mom or something. 'Cause you called her from my cell phone when we were in Arizona, right?"

My whole body stretches out in the seat, and I crack my neck from side to side. The window's halfway down, and I can smell this foreign sweetness in the wet air. I light a cigarette.

"Yeah," I almost whisper. "Fuck, I'm sorry. I called my dad from Texas somewhere. It's gonna be a long-ass time before we talk to each other again—I mean, if we ever do. He's pissed as hell."

"At you and me both," she says. "Do you think he could be right? Do you think this could be the wrong thing for you?"

My hand finds hers—our skin touching—my fingers tracing the lines of her knuckles—drawing shapeless patterns up her wrists and forearms.

"No, Sue Ellen, no way. You're the...the best thing to happen to me in as long as I can remember. That's the truth, you know? There's no other truth but that."

I watch her silhouette nodding.

The streetlights glow a dull orange—bleeding out like watercolors on the coarse black paper of the night. We've made a few turns here and there, and I suddenly realize the street we're driving on is made of uneven brick. On either side are wide sidewalks with rows and rows of old, what I can only describe as New Orleans–style mansions—many with gas lanterns burning on their porches, and intricate carvings along the stairs and columns and railings that I can't fully make out in the dark. In front of us is a little square with green grass and hedges and some sort of large horseman sculpture in the middle. Giant oaks line the streets and crowd the square. Long, tangled moss hangs down from the tree branches. Sue Ellen turns at the square, and we take a sort of roundabout so we can keep going straight, if that makes any sense.

The next street is the same, shrouded with oaks, the tendrils of moss reaching down. The warped, decrepit, haunted-looking mansions lead into a central square—everything deserted.

But as we drive even farther, across a set of seemingly abandoned railroad tracks, the mansions suddenly give way to withered little shacks with cluttered porches and broken windows. Dogs sleep chained to the front stairways. Men and women are out here, talking in groups on the sidewalk, holding beer bottles in their hands, smoking cigarettes. Sue Ellen pulls into a large, sprawling, mostly empty grocery store parking lot—the rectangular fortress with its sliding glass doors is blindingly bright in the surrounding still and darkness. Until that point, it had been almost as if we were traveling through some other world—ancient and full of secrets—everything heavy with black magic and mystery. Already I can say that

Charleston is unlike anything I've ever seen. There is a feeling here like...like the dead really could crawl out of their graves—a feeling like it might all be an illusion, a town from some ghost story that will amazingly have disappeared by morning. But, well, then we get to the supermarket—some place called Kroger. It is giant and uniform. I know where I am now. I'm in America. And so we get out of the car and start walking in. I grab hold of Sue Ellen's waist and pull her to me.

"This is all pretty crazy," I tell her.

She kisses my cheek quickly, like a little kid would. "Yeah, Charleston's pretty cool. Anyway, I don't have any food, really, at my new place, so you should pick out some stuff you like."

I stop her. "New place? What do you mean?"

"Oh," she says, actually giggling some. "I forgot to tell you. I agreed to finish school here in Charleston, so in return my mom rented me my own apartment and she agreed to let you stay with me there. You'll just have to start paying half of the rent once you get a job."

My eyes go wide. "No shit! Really? That's amazing."

"Uh-huh." She's smiling all over. "I took care of everything, didn't I? Now, uh, come on, let's go get you some food."

But I don't let her go in quite yet. I hold her right up to me, and we kiss for a good long time. I think maybe this has all been worth it, after all.

Charleston, South Carolina. Man, I never would've guessed it.

And Sue Ellen? She's just fucking perfect.

I mean, perfect.

Goddamn.

Ch.19

Honestly, I'm not someone who really needs a lot of structure in my life.

I'm not like most people, who seem to go kinda crazy if they've got too much free time on their hands. I don't know — I really can't relate. Between writing and reading and drawing and playing music and taking walks and watching movies, I never have enough time for everything anyway. So in terms of having to work a regular job, well, I can't say I was too excited about the idea.

But obviously I had to work, right? I mean, Christ, Sue Ellen had already started her spring quarter at school, and she was working part-time at this clothing boutique downtown, so I felt like a total asshole sitting around the house all day. Of course, I was writing, but when I talked to my editor in New York, she made it pretty clear that I wasn't gonna see any more money from them till I got a really solid, complete first draft in—and that might take a while. So, yeah, finding a real, you know, job-type job was very necessary.

It actually didn't take long. Sue Ellen and I went to this kinda funky, pseudo-hippy, knockoff San Francisco coffee shop up the street from us. We ordered drinks and sandwiches, and it was all pretty good and the people seemed cool, so I asked if they were hiring. The manager was immediately called from around back to interview me on the spot. She was a middle-aged woman with long, ratty hair that might as well've had flowers all woven into it. She wore a shapeless sack dress with some sort of African-looking print. She wore Birkenstocks. When I told her I was born in Berkeley and raised in San Francisco and that I'd worked at a Peet's Coffee there, well, the interview was over. At that point all she wanted to know was when I could start. And it's a good thing, too, 'cause if she had called my references, I would've been fucked as hell. But, uh, then again, at least that would've held off this inevitable day a little bit longer. 'Cause, as it stands, I've gotta be there in about five minutes for training.

Fuck.

I mean, I feel so stupidly sick and anxious—lying here on Sue Ellen's bed—my bed—the overhead fan spinning and rocking loose overhead—the early summer heat oppressive—suffocating.

But, here, under the fan, I am safe. And the central air-conditioning whirs night and day to try 'n' at least keep the rest of the apartment somewhat livable, even if Sue Ellen does a whole lot of complaining about the power bill. But the house is small—one-bedroom in the back and a combination kitchen/

living room facing the lane...or, well, the alley. In Charleston they call them lanes, but they're really just alleys — alleys where everyone dumps their trash both in and around the designated bins. Honestly, I've never in my life seen as much trash everywhere as I have here. The other day I was walking down to meet Sue Ellen at work, and I saw a passing driver throw her McDonald's trash and empty drink cup out the window and into the middle of the street. Garbage clogs the gutters, breeds giant roaches in the dark places, lies rotting in the sun. Garbage piles high in the abandoned houses and empty lots. The smell of garbage is carried with the wind. The town stinks of it — mixing with our sweat and the shit-smelling fumes from the paper factory down the river. And our little alley, our little lane, is the apex of it all — the accumulation of crawling insects and shit and garbage and black asphalt hot as torched metal. Only here, inside, am I safe — with the air-conditioning and the fan and my books and writing and sex and the VCR. I want to stay hidden in this apartment forever. I want to be kept like a house cat. I don't want to have to face the world. I don't want to have to work, to meet new people, to put myself at risk. Here, protected, I know I can make it. Out there, well, I'm not so sure.

But I've got no choice, right? I mean, I'm not some invalid. I've got to participate in life, just like everybody else does. There's nothing so special 'bout me that should make me exempt. I need to be able to handle this kinda shit. And I will. I'm going to.

I force myself up, put on some pants, and I'm sweating already. Sue Ellen's got her laptop set up to a set of speakers, so

I go put on one of the electric Miles Davis albums I downloaded off her iTunes without actually asking.

The music starts out fast and frantic. In some ways, listening to this shit helps remind me of who I am, you know? I mean, the music I love has always been such a huge part of me. I need to hold on to that.

So I turn the volume louder and go get dressed the rest of the way. Sue Ellen's designated me some space in the closet and one dresser drawer. Like I said, I don't have too much stuff, anyway. All the photos and posters on the wall are hers. The couch and plush chairs and desk and office furniture are all from her family. The rest of the stuff she bought herself, but with her mom's money, of course.

But now that I'm working, well, at least I'll be able to pay for some of our shit, even though the minimum wage here is ridiculously low—like, six dollars an hour. Still, my getting a job is more a symbolic gesture than anything else. It shows I'm not some fucking freeloader. It shows I'm not just hustling Sue Ellen.

And so I pull on my shoes and light a cigarette and walk out into the wet, sticky heat—my sunglasses fogging up so bad I can't even see. The trash is stinking in the alley. Skinny, feral bobtail cats lie sleeping in the shade of parked cars. A young man with short dreads and a muscular body bends over the open hood of his car, messing with I-don't-know-what. The guy I call the "bastard man" is walking down the narrow street in my direction. He makes his rounds of the neighborhood every day about this time—sweating, fat. His khaki shorts hiked up so they cling tight between his butt cheeks. His too-small Hawaiian shirt practically bursting open around his belly. His white socks pulled up to his fleshy calves. Waddling along in his bright white, sensible orthopedic sneakers. His straw porkpie hat pulled down over his eyes. I call him the bastard man 'cause, somehow, his particular mental illness causes him to walk around the neighborhood for hours, stopping every ten paces or so, screaming out "You are the bastard!" at no one at all—or, I guess, at everyone, maybe. The first time he came by, I tried to say hey to him, but he just turned on me and yelled, "The trash goes in the motherfucking trash can!"

Of course, I get how fucked up it is that this guy isn't getting treatment for his illness—most likely 'cause he can't afford the psych evaluation and medication. Another example of how corrupt our health-care system is in this country. On the other hand, there's something oddly comforting about the bastard man roaming free and unharassed around the neighborhood. I mean, he's just accepted as an eccentric part of the community—one of a whole bunch of crazies wandering the streets, like the man who dresses in three-piece suits every day and screams "Jesus" at the top of his lungs, holding some sign about Satan over his head, walking from one end of town to the other, no matter how hot it is outside. They are as much a part of the landscape here as the live oaks, the ancient cemeteries, the Spanish moss, the squares and parks, the projects, the old Southern mansions. And I guess there's something about that acceptance that I really do respect. Or maybe it's 'cause, being totally fucking crazy myself, I've finally found a place where I might just fit in.

So I walk off down the street—quick-like, 'cause I'm about to be late.

The bastard man screams, "You are the bastard!"

And I make sure to throw my cigarette butt in the mother-fucking trash can.

Back when I was in high school, dealing with all the bullshit pressures of getting into college, trying to figure out who the hell I was, battling my parents, challenging every goddamn thing, feeling hopeless, like nothing could ever fill me up completely, I remember thinking what a relief it would have been just to turn that corner, you know? Lose hold of reality. Drift off to some delusional place. Living with eyes closed. Easy. Able to walk around Charleston screaming, "You are the bastard!" Never having to work or love or make anything of yourself. Never having to let anybody down. It would be such a relief. An escape I would never be blamed for. A little lovely dream. A fantasy. Romanticized in movies, books, and songs. *The King of Hearts. One Flew Over the Cuckoo's Nest.* David Bowie singing, "I'd rather stay here with all the madmen than perish with the sad men roaming free."

But as I've gotten older, well, I've come to learn the truth of it. There is no freedom in insanity. There is nothing romantic about wandering the streets disoriented and crazy, mixed up, tangled, bound by obsession. Sometimes I just want to curl up small in an abandoned corner and lie still till the world goes away completely. Sometimes I want to run screaming and screaming. But either way, crossing the street to the coffee shop, I'm suddenly aware that I have a whole lot more in common with the bastard man than I could ever have with these ultrahip-looking art school kids I'm about to be working with.

I can see them through the large front plate-glass window, standing behind the counter, talking and laughing.

When I walk in to introduce myself, neither one of them seems particularly impressed. The boy is super tall and skinny, with these tiny cutoff jean shorts revealing his long, sinewy, shaved legs. He's wearing some kind of off-orange-colored boat shoes with no socks, and his tight, tight self-consciously vintage T-shirt has a picture of a sailboat silk-screened on the front. His head is shaved, and his neck and arms are covered in intricate, expensive tattoos. He has a pair of square, nerdy-chic glasses on that I'd be willing to bet aren't really prescription. His name is Rafi.

The girl is a lot more plain-looking, with short black hair and a narrow face. She's wearing sensible clothes—jeans, a V-neck shirt, and hiking boots. Her name is Elaina. I guess she's the one who's gonna be training me.

"Look," I tell her, as she starts taking me on a little tour around the workings of the shop. "I've definitely been in your position before, you know, having to break in the new guy, so I just wanted to say that you really don't have to worry about me. I'll figure it out as we go along, so you don't need to stress at all."

She turns back, but without really looking at me. She's got her eyes on the ground and her neck bent forward, so it's like she's talking out of her forehead.

"Oh, sure, yeah right, you'll figure it out on your own. I bet you took this job thinking it was gonna be real easy, didn't you? Well, I'll tell you right now, it ain't. We work nonstop for eight hours a day or longer. We're on our feet, moving all the time. If you're looking for a job where you can just slack off, you've come to the wrong place, man. We work hard here. Most new people don't even make it through the first week. I mean, have you ever even worked at a coffee shop like this before?"

She stares me down with her forehead, jamming her hands into her pockets and hunching over a little more. I can't quite make out her accent—Southern, for sure, but a whole lot different from Sue Ellen's. It's almost as if this Elaina girl has some sort of combination between a Southern drawl and a Midwestern twang. At least, her forehead does.

"Sorry, no, I didn't mean it like that at all." I stutter like an idiot, trying my best to keep smiling. Hell, I mean, I should know by now that any powerless person who's finally been given a temporary position of authority is gonna take herself way too seriously. The only thing I can do is try 'n' make her feel important—you know, necessary—like I fear and respect her. Of course, I know I can do it. I've been telling people what they wanna hear since I was four years old. It's as instinctive and automatic as breathing. I can eat shit and suck cock like the best of them.

"Yeah, well," her forehead demands. "What did you mean, then?"

I follow her lead, burying my hands in my own pockets.

"All I was trying to say," I tell her, "is that I wanna make this as easy for you as possible. I've worked at a couple coffee shops before, and I just remember how annoying it is to have a new person tagging along behind you. So just let me know if I get in your way. But for now, I mean, you tell me what to do and I'll do it, no problem."

Her face lifts up into the light slightly, and for the first time I can see that her eyes are green and striking against her tan skin and cropped dark hair.

"Okay, good," she says, her hand reaching up to play absently with the inch-long bar piercing the upper cartilage of her left ear. "Then enough of this touring crap. We gotta get sandwiches prepped for the lunch rush. Let's go."

I follow her behind the counter into the cramped, sweating, noxious kitchen area. She pulls out twenty-five baguettes from the industrial-sized, two-door stainless steel refrigerator. I'm told to split each baguette lengthwise. We go on from there.

The hours pass so goddamn slow.

Rafi and Elaina won't let me make the coffee drinks or do the final preparations on any of the food items, so I'm stuck cleaning every last inch of the kitchen—something that looks like it hasn't been done in, like, five years. Already I've come across more dead roaches and rat shit than I've ever seen in my life. I mean, I actually catch myself gagging—and this from a kid who's eaten out of trash cans to survive.

The rest of the place is pretty nice, though—open and light, with tall ceilings and concrete floors. It looks like it might've been converted from an old barn or something. There's bad but pleasant student artwork hung on the walls, and a stage is set up in the corner for open-mike nights and live music on the weekends. The shop advertises fair-trade coffee and organic produce. It even has vegan pastries and desserts.

The customers are mostly college kids—hipsters with tapered jeans and their track bikes all locked up outside. There's also a middle-age contingency—women with long graying hair and dumpy, sack clothing, men with ponytails and Birkenstocks who look like they might've landed in Charleston by mistake on their way to Berkeley or San Francisco—like Columbus finding the Bahamas instead of a route to Asia.

Of course, every now and then a real-life Southerner walks in, uncomfortably staring at the menu. There was even one paunchy, clean-cut, doughy-looking man with a wealthy, refined Southern accent who slapped the hell out of his little boy 'cause the kid was messing around in line. When I asked Elaina if we could refuse to serve the man, she just made some sort of distorted face and pointed me back toward the kitchen to keep scrubbing behind the oversize refrigerator.

But eventually eight o'clock finally comes. Elaina goes over some of the closing procedures with me, then has me go around collecting all the trash to take out to the Dumpster. I strain against the stinking black plastic bags, heavy with wet coffee grounds and whatever else, practically having to drag them behind me as I push open the back fire-exit doors. The sun is nearly down, but it's still hot as a motherfucker, the sweat pooling on my body, spilling out on the baking asphalt. I remember suddenly that Sue Ellen has class tonight till ten thirty, so even when I finish here, I'm going to have to be alone. The trash clatters and crashes into the Dumpster loudly, and I jump, even though I shoulda been expecting the noise. My breath comes all sharp and metallic. If I could get away with screaming right now, I would scream. As it is, I just whisper hoarsely to myself, "Fuck, Nic, fuck. This is your life. This is your fucking life."

Ch.20

Everything is work.

Either I'm working or I'm exhausted from working or I'm dreading going back to work.

Today will be my sixth opening shift this week, even though I don't get paid overtime. Actually, it's my own damn fault. My boss cornered me about coming in today, and of course I agreed 'cause I don't know how to say no.

Especially when I'm sober.

So the alarm clock beep-beeps at me, and I quickly shut it off to let Sue Ellen sleep in at least a little bit longer. We've been living together only about a month now, but between my work and her work and her going to school, we barely see each other at all anymore. Plus, even when she is home, the TV's always on, so she practically exists more in the world of the *Today* show, *America's Next Top Model, The Hills, E! Entertainment News, Celebrity*

Rehab, and *Gossip Girl* than she does here with me. I swear, it's like those television people are more real than reality could ever be. And if she's not watching the lives of others on TV, she's reading about them on Internet tabloids—Gawker, TMZ, Perez Hilton—clicking from one site to the next. Sometimes she even has both going on at once, the Internet world and the TV world, eyes shifting back and forth. Honestly, at this point, it's more like we're living as roommates than anything else.

But, really, I can't blame her for wanting to escape. Our existence is suffocating. It grabs hold of my throat with both hands—pressing down slowly—crushing the bones and veins and tendons there. I wish TV could take me away like it does for so many people. I wish I could immerse myself in its simple story lines and unambiguous morality. I wish I could find friendship in these onscreen personalities and indulge my consumer fantasies in the luxury-car ads and blowout electronics sales. I wish so badly I could get lost in it like most people do. I wish that's all it would take.

But for me the TV is just bleak and depressing. If anything, having it on all the time makes me even more aware of how hopeless and empty my existence really is. When I was using, I didn't need to watch TV; I was the star of my own fucking reality show. Every day was like an epic—like a goddamn David Lean movie. *Lawrence of Arabia*, *Doctor Zhivago*, or at least the twenty-first-century, fucked-up version of it. Running the streets, breaking into buildings, meeting up with crazy drug dealers, having crazy sex, stealing, running scams for money, living so close to death and life and insanity and greatness. I didn't have time to watch TV then. But now I'm rotting away in front of it—paralyzed—too scared to live my own damn life. 'Cause, really, what life is there to live? Working this dead-end job? Eating takeout with Sue Ellen? Too tired to write. Having to be too goddamn careful of my sobriety to go out and do anything. I mean, shit, man, what the hell kind of life is this? How could this possibly be worth it?

I always said that I'd rather live a shorter life blissed out on drugs than a long, normal life sober and miserable. I guess at Safe Passage Center I'd started to believe that I could actually live sober and fulfilled, but now I know that's just more rehab bullshit. Sure, in the safety and little utopian world they create within the treatment center, everything can be all positive and supportive and exciting. But not out here in the real fucking world, where we have to work eight-hour shifts and we can't relate to anyone—where people my age go out drinking every night and I have to stay in watching *Flavor of Love* season two.

It's just not worth it, man.

It's not fucking worth it all.

It's not worth it as I make coffee in the kitchen, watching tiny brown roaches scurry off to their cracks and crevices as I turn on the light.

That's three trips the goddamn exterminator has made here, and we still can't get rid of these miracles of evolution.

I mean, it's not fucking worth it.

Not any of it.

At all.

I pull on clothes, light a cigarette inside, even though Sue Ellen would flip out at me.

I drink coffee and put on music, real quiet.

There's maybe time for me to listen to one song, I'd say. It's just about the only connection I have to anything beautiful anymore. It's the only connection I have with anything that means anything.

And, of course, at work I can't ever put on any of my CDs 'cause the two managers somehow established a monopoly on the stereo system, so we end up listening to these soulless, hipster emo bands all day long.

So I play Marc Bolan, like I said, quiet—the song's "Life's a Gas."

The alarm next to the bed goes off a second time, and I run in there to shut it off.

Sue Ellen doesn't wake up at all.

I guess 'cause she's been taking Tylenol PM every night to go to sleep.

I bend over and kiss her damp, sweating forehead.

"I'll call you later," I whisper.

She doesn't respond.

I go walk off to work.

The girl opening with me today is someone I haven't seen around before, I guess maybe 'cause I don't usually work this shift. She introduces herself as Carmine, and I introduce myself as me—obviously—trying to suss her out as best I can. From what I can tell, I'd say she's probably a little younger than I am, with a certain quietness about her. A quietness that seems to come from some inner wisdom. And she is beautiful in her quietness. As we set about making the coffee and putting out the baked goods and all that shit, I can't help but keep studying her, not being too goddamn obvious about it, I hope. I mean, I'm pretty sure she doesn't notice.

Her body is extremely thin and sort of pulled and twisted-looking—like maybe she has a kind of scoliosis or something. Her spine is curved like a half moon at the base of her neck, pushing her right shoulder up, creating a fairly large hump there. But her body's deformity isn't freakish-looking at all. If anything, it just adds to how fragile and lovely she is, her limbs like spiders' legs, her eyes large and dark and bored and distrustful, her lips full, pursed, her black hair hanging down long and straight, a lot like Sue Ellen's.

When she speaks, her voice comes out all hoarse and raspy, like maybe her throat is being constricted by her condition, even though I guess that's not how it works, huh? In general she seems reticent to talk to me at first, but I do manage to get a little bit out of her.

"Yeah," she says. "I'm from Broomall, Pennsylvania, but, uh, I've been down here for, like, five years now. I mean, I just graduated from school last spring. I'd like to get out of here, for sure—maybe move to LA or New York or someplace where stuff's actually going on. I'm just trying to save up enough money, that's all. You know, working here and, uh, making some other money on the side."

I decide not to ask her about that second part. Instead, I go on and tell her that I just moved here from LA, and I could definitely see her really loving it out there. While she washes some dishes, I prep the sandwiches, just so I can hang out in the kitchen with her.

"LA's actually a pretty cool place," I say. "I mean, I know everyone disses on it all the time, but, really, compared with other cities, I'd say it's way less pretentious there. Like, well, I'm from San Francisco, and I lived in New York for a while, but both of those places are so full of phonies trying to claim those cities as their own, you know? Someone could've moved to New York, like, a year before, but suddenly they're calling themselves New Yorkers, sneering at you for not being a local. San Francisco's the same way. But no one wants to claim LA."

The long, serrated bread knife I'm working with slips and slices a big ol' chunk off the side of my finger.

"Ah, motherfucker," I say through my teeth all clenched tight together.

Deep, purple-red blood drip-drips onto the vegan sandwiches I've been making.

Carmine laughs at me, throwing over a clean dishrag.

"Here, wrap your hand in that. You're getting blood everywhere."

"Sorry," I tell her, doing what she said with the cloth. "It's gross. I'm sorry."

She laughs again, saying all sarcastic-like, "What? You gotta problem with blood? You a little squeamish are you? Christ, men are so lame. You should try being a woman. We gotta deal with a lot more blood than that every single month."

Narrowing my eyes at her, I speak before I really have time to think better of it. I mean, it just sorta comes out. "Yeah, well, I was an IV crystal meth and heroin addict for about five years, so I'd say I've had my share of getting familiar with my own blood."

She kinda freezes up at that, and I guess I do, too.

"Fuck," I stammer, all quick and awkward. "I'm sorry. I shouldn't've just said that. I'm an idiot. Don't pay any attention to me."

She stares me down a second longer but then cracks up laughing.

"Nah," she says. "I'm just messing with you. I don't think any less of you, and I definitely won't tell anyone. Actually, I think it's kinda cool, really."

I tell her it isn't, but I can tell she's got this new, misguided respect for me suddenly.

"Hey, since you told me that," she whispers, pressing up all close to me, "I'll tell you a little secret about myself. You know how I said I was saving up money to get out of here? Well, I deal pot and pills, so if you ever need anything, you just ask me."

What I'm supposed to say is no. What I'm supposed to tell her is that I'm sober. But what comes out of my mouth is, "Right on, thank you. And, uh, yeah, I won't tell anyone, either. Don't worry."

And so we go on talking like that for the next couple of hours, until we both get off, doing a pretty good job of ignoring most of the customers. It's actually Carmine who suggests that I come over. She asks if I wanna go "smoke a bowl." The way she says it sounds so casual and harmless. A fucking bowl. How dangerous could it possibly be?

My brain processes the long string of thoughts in a virtual nanosecond. I mean, I think about Safe Passage Center and all the other goddamn rehabs I've ever been to. They were all a joke—a waste of time. They were wrong about everything. So when they said I shouldn't smoke pot, even though my problem had always been with hard drugs, they must've been wrong about that, too. I'm not addicted to pot. I'm not even addicted to alcohol. Just 'cause I was addicted to meth and heroin, why the hell would that mean I'm also addicted to pot? It makes no sense. Of course I should be able to smoke pot. Christ, if I'd listened to them, I'd still be at that boot camp place in New Mexico. They obviously have no idea what's best for me.

So what I do is, I light a cigarette and nod my head.

I follow her through the dirty, sweltering streets—oil, thick and glossy, coats the buildings and parked cars and makeshift basketball hoops made of hollowed-out milk crates nailed to trees on opposite sides of the street. A group of scrawny boys pass the ball back and forth, yelling at the drivers who try to interrupt their game.

"Man," I say, laughing at the kids getting all angry and everything. "It really is like another world down here."

Carmine seems oblivious to anything goin' on around us, but she tells me she "knows," probably just to be polite.

She leads me down a couple more blocks, and I talk pretty incessantly the whole time, even though my mind is somewhere else entirely. I mean, basically I'm just going over why this is all okay—over and fucking over again.

'Cause, see, the thing is, the reason I got addicted in the first place was because the drugs took my terror and depression away. But now I've finally learned how to love and value myself. I've grown and changed. So there's no reason why drinking or smoking pot should be a problem. And I'm sure

Sue Ellen will agree. I mean, she's never been an addict, so she doesn't understand this shit anyway. If I tell her it's all right, she'll believe me. She needs me too much to, like, kick me out or anything. I'm not trying to be a dick about it, but that's the truth. Besides, it'll be good for her. It'll be good for us both. We'll finally be able to chill the fuck out a little, you know? Not be so uptight all the time.

So I follow Carmine into her dark, dank, tiny backroom apartment with these kind of creepy but awesome puppets she designed hanging from the walls and the mantel of the boarded-up fireplace. The dolls are kind of a rip-off of Japanimation monster drawings—with tentacles and too many eyes and long, accentuated bodies that I guess remind me of Carmine's. I mean, I'm sure that's the point.

Anyway, she puts on a Tom Waits record and packs her glass pipe with some of the shittiest weed I've ever seen in my life— brown, with tons of stems and whatever. I've always been curious what shwag like this would be like, considering that in San Francisco it was, as far as I knew, literally impossible to find pot that wasn't of the highest dense, white crystallized quality. So, cool, another reason why smoking herb here shouldn't be a problem: The stuff they've got sucks.

But it does get me high.

I take a hit and hold the dirty-tasting smoke in my lungs and exhale, and immediately my brain is coated with a gentle, caressing haze.

"Wow," I say, my voice sounding very out of body or something. "Thank you so much. I really needed that. Do, uh, do you have enough to sell me an eighth?"

She smiles. "Of course, my dear."

Something moves on the bed, a dark shape displacing the light.

Carmine reaches over to grab it, placing it wriggling on her bony, protruding shoulder.

It's a rat.

"This is Franky," she tells me, getting out her scale and doing the whole eighth-weighing thing.

I pet the rat's ragged, coarse hair. It moves suddenly and I flinch. Carmine totally laughs at me.

"So, hey," I say. "Um, I'm gonna try 'n' go write a little now, but, uh, let's hang out later this week, huh? Maybe we can watch a movie or something. I just bought *Barbarella* yesterday for two bucks at Home Run Video."

She doesn't really look like she knows what I'm talking about, but she nods just the same and passes over the ugly sack.

I give her forty bucks. That's half my first paycheck and half of all the money I have in this world.

But fuck it, right?

Walking home, I see the city is transformed, vibrant— everything heightened and rhythmic and alive. Even the heat doesn't seem so bad.

And when I get back to our apartment, I blast music as loud as it'll go and smoke cigarettes and set down to writing again. It's weird, man, but for the first time in almost a year, I actually feel excited about working on my book. The pages come easily, and I'm focused and motivated, and I'm actually not tired for once. It seems like a miracle. I mean, I'm so grateful.

This is what I've been missing, you know?

It's like medicine to me and, well, what the hell is wrong with that, anyway?

A lot of people take medicine.

Mine just happens to be illegal.

And it probably won't be for long.

So I sit writing.

For hours.

Content.

Finally.

Ch.21

I can't remember where I heard it. Some joke about a man jumping off a tall building, repeating to himself as he falls, "So far, so good. So far, so good. So far, so good."

Well, here I am.

Falling.

And so far, so good.

I guess.

It's been about a week now that I've been using — or, well, smoking pot and drinking a little. At first, I mean, yeah, Sue Ellen was definitely freaking out. When I told her I'd bought that eighth, she pretty well lost it. Screaming at me, saying all these fucked-up things about what a weak, nothing person I am. Screaming at me till I'm balled up in a corner somewhere, catatonic, my mind playin' over and over about how the world would be better off without me. 'Cause that's the truth, you know? I mean, everything she says to me, every name she calls me, is completely right on. I'm selfish and lazy and emotional and scared and genuinely unfit for survival. If natural selection could've had its way, I would've been dead a long time ago. Hell, I'm completely dependent on Sue Ellen. She's the only person left who'll still have anything to do with me. So, uh, yeah, I don't blame her for resenting the hell out of me.

Of course, me curling up there on the ground, that just makes it all even worse. She calls me pathetic and a coward and does everything she can to provoke me into fighting her. And, man, I'll tell you, a lot of times I want to, but it's almost like I'm physically incapable of standing my ground. Once she starts yelling, I can't help but totally shut down. I'm like a little kid again, hiding in a cramped corner with the palms of my hands pressed against my ears while my parents, or my mom and stepdad, scream back and forth, throwing things, pushing each other out of the way—my stepfather's glasses flying off—my mom backing up the car as he tries to throw himself behind it to stop her. And now, having just turned twenty-four years old, I'm that same little kid, crawling into the narrow crack between the bed and the wall, my breath shallow and panicked. But, fuck, man, does that enrage Sue Ellen. She ends up beating her fists against me, screaming at me to get the hell up.

But I can't get the hell up.

My body is weighted down heavy, so I can't lift it.

I close my eyes tight and let my breathing calm slowly until I finally just fall asleep hidden in my little corner there.

But when the morning comes, well, somehow everything is okay again. Sue Ellen doesn't apologize, exactly, but she carries on softly with me—kissing my forehead and pressing her body against mine.

That particular morning we actually smoked a joint and made love. After that it was like none of it had ever happened.

"Honestly, Nic, I guess I thought you were gonna maybe turn into a werewolf or something if you smoked pot or drank again," she told me, laughing sweetly. "I mean, can you blame me? That's what all the counselors made it seem like. But you're not a werewolf, are you?"

I assure her I'm not, even if I don't believe it completely.

She tells me she loves me.

And so, just like that, it's all resolved. She gives me some money to go to the grocery store, and when she gets home from class that night, I've made a nice dinner for us both and we split a bottle of red wine. I make sure not to have more than a glass and a half. I remember someone telling me once that you can always recognize an alcoholic 'cause the person can't ever leave any liquor in the glass. So I definitely leave my last glass about a quarter full. And, yeah, it is somewhat of a conscious effort, but not too bad. I mean, I'd say I feel almost like a normal person. At least, that's what I'm trying for.

The only time it's been a real problem so far is at work. I'm just so goddamn miserable there, you know? It's like I can't get through even a couple of hours without going outside to take a quick hit or drink down a shot of cheap vodka I've got stashed in my bag. I mean, that's the only way it's even remotely tolerable. 'Cause, I don't know, way more than the work itself, it's having to be around the other employees that fills me with so much anxiety. Every day before work I feel, like, physically sick—my stomach all cramped up and nauseous, like it used to get in the mornings before school. There's just this pressure I feel to be, well, "on," you know? Like it's just so much effort. And then when I am there and "on," I have this sick compulsion to play this stupid game humans always play when they're hanging out together—this game where one person tells a story about how great he is, and then the next person somehow finds a connected story that tells how equally great, or greater, she is. The game goes on and on like that the full eight-hour workday. And as much as I try to just be like everyone else, I always end up leaving feeling hollowed out, fucking gutted—like I need a drink—like I must be some entirely different species from the rest of humanity. I swear, sometimes I really do wonder if I'd be better suited as a hermit living off in a cabin somewhere—away from all people and pressures and judgments and responsibilities. Hell, it sounds pretty nice. But then again, I'd be stuck with myself—the last person I wanna have to spend a lot of time with.

Anyway, the truth is, I am fucking trying. I mean, I haven't quit work yet, and I've been making some kinda effort to make friends and whatever. Tonight I'm actually going with Sue Ellen to a work party at her boss's house. And, man, I couldn't even begin to tell you the last time I went to any kinda party anywhere—especially a party where I could just drink like a normal person. That definitely makes everything a whole lot easier. Plus, I feel energized like I never do when I'm sober. I guess it's kinda abnormal that both drinking and smoking pot speed me up like a mild amphetamine. Most people say that shit makes them lethargic, but for me it's the total opposite. And it's such a relief 'cause, I swear, being sober—it's like I'm just constantly tired. If I let myself, I could sleep all day and night, always. I'm never not tired. It's such a pain in the ass—and I feel like a pussy admitting it. But, yeah, alcohol and pot are my total saviors in that respect. They're my cure—my medicine. I've said it a hundred times before, but for some reason I have to keep repeating it to myself. I don't know—maybe it just reminds me that it's all okay. I wouldn't deny a schizophrenic psychiatric meds, so why should I deny myself mine? That's logic, pure and simple.

I repeat it over and over.

I tell myself:

So far, so good.

So far, so good.

So far, so good.

Sue Ellen will be home soon. We'll go to the party. There's nothing to worry about.

I take a shower, washing off the thick coating of sweat and coffee grinds and chemical cleaning products and food smells from my day at work. I scrub my body till the skin is red and swollen. I'm using one of those loofah-mitt things—a habit I picked up from Zelda. Whenever we took showers together, she would meticulously scour every inch of my body with a coarse, bristled glove—scrubbing till my dead skin cells had all been washed away completely. Then she would start in on herself. For me, having her take possession of my body like that was the most I could possibly ask for.

But I am alone here in the shower, scrubbing my own body, having to exist for myself and no one else. 'Cause as much as I might try to re-create things with Sue Ellen, I don't know, it's just never gonna be the same. I'm on my own now. I've gotta find some reason to serve myself. But, the difference is, Zelda deserved my love and devotion. Me? Well, I'm grateful I'm drinking again to get me through all this. So you're damn right I make myself a martini to drink while I'm getting dressed — even if it's kinda funky mixed with the toothpaste taste that's left over in my mouth. I mean, I drink it.

When Sue Ellen gets home, she immediately comes to give me a kiss, inhaling loudly through her nose as she swoops in, no doubt trying to smell hints of alcohol on my breath. Obviously she does.

"Have you started drinking already?" she asks, sounding not pleased at all. "What the hell's wrong with you?"

I laugh kinda defensively. I mean, those are basically the first words she's said to me all day.

"Hey, chill, girl, it's okay. I made a drink just now when I got outta the shower. It's not a big deal. I was anxious is all ... about having to be around a bunch of people I don't know. Anyway, I missed you so bad all day. Don't be mad at me. I'm happy to see you."

She glares at me defiantly for a good minute.

"Come on," I try again. "I love you. We're gonna have fun tonight, right?"

I start messing around, poking her and stuff, saying, "Right? Right? Right?"

She finally laughs, and then I know we're okay.

"I love you," I tell her. "Okay?"

Her mouth gives in to a smile, and she says she loves me, too.

"All right, then, don't worry. Why don't you go get dressed? Come on, I'll roll a joint for us."

That was the wrong thing to say.

Her face goes all flushed and angry-looking.

"No, Nic, no. I don't wanna smoke, and I don't want you smoking, either."

I hold both hands up like I'm being threatened with a gun, or something. "Okay, okay. I thought you wanted to, that's all. I don't care one way or the other."

I'm not sure whether she believes that, but it's obviously not the truth.

"Seriously, Nic," she says. "You're kinda freaking me out. I mean, you sound all, I don't know, obsessed."

I laugh that off. "Shit, Sue Ellen, stop worrying so much. You're really making something outta nothing, you know?"

She turns abruptly and walks off to the bedroom. "Yeah, well, I hope so," she says, more to herself than to me.

I tell her I'm going outside for a cigarette.

Obviously I bring the bowl with me in my pocket and steal a few hits off it so she won't know. Then I really do go on and smoke a cigarette to help cover up the smell.

When I get back inside, she seems chilled out some and lets me kiss her.

I put my arm around her waist and hold her to me while we walk the few blocks to the party—the sun mostly set over the trees and houses—the night air cooler than it's been in a long-ass time.

At first, you know, I mostly just kept to myself at the party/ cookout thing. Sue Ellen introduced me to her boss, a girl around my age named Kelly, and a bunch of the other kids she works with. They were mostly all fucking hipsters, like everyone else from the goddamn art school. But still, I mean, they seemed nice enough. I just didn't know what to talk to anybody about, so I sat outside in a folding chair, sort of half listening to people's conversations. Actually, I woulda probably gone ahead and walked back home if Kelly's boyfriend, Russell, hadn't come over right then and sat down next to me, reaching one hand out to shake mine while balancing a heaping plate of food in the other.

"Hey, man," he says, his voice real baritone and, uh, Southern. "You're Nic, right? It's nice to meet you."

I shake his hand. "Yeah, you too. Thanks for having us over and cooking and everything."

He laughs deep at that. "No problem, man. I got that big-mama grill from my folks last year, so any excuse to fire 'er up is good by me. Besides, this is a good group of kids. And I like most everyone Kelly works with. I'll tell you the truth, though, I've always had a special soft spot for Sue Ellen, so I'm real glad she's got a good guy in her life."

I grind the toe of my sneaker into the dirt, saying, "I think 'good guy' is arguable."

He laughs again. "Nah, I can tell. And I really do mean that. Sue Ellen seems real happy, Nic, and I know she's proud of you. She told me about the book you're writing, and I gotta say, I'm genuinely humbled to meet you. I mean, it takes a whole lotta balls to do what you're doing, and I'm just damn impressed."

I feel his thick, fleshy hand squeeze my shoulder tight, and then I can't help it—there're tears flooding my eyes. "Russell, man, that's like the nicest thing anyone's said to me in a long-ass time."

I have to cover my face.

"I'm sorry," I say, trying to pull my shit together. "It's been a hard road, man, and, uh, that just means a lot to me."

"Ah, don't worry about it," he tells me. "Anyway, we're gonna be friends, right?"

I wipe my face, looking up at him from my hunched-over position.

Here I was ready to dismiss him as, like, a good ol' boy, ex-marine, or something—a little overweight but strong and masculine in a way that's always kinda intimidated me. But if anything, he's really the total opposite of that. His face isn't hard or threatening. His smile is open and sincere. His brownish-green eyes, obscured behind wire-rimmed glasses, are deep set with knowing and kindness. I'm actually pretty embarrassed, 'cause the more I truly study his features, the more I realize my initial assessment of him was totally off base. I mean, he's like a big stuffed teddy bear. But, of course, me being from liberal San Francisco, my assumption is that all guys from the South who have crew cuts and wear college football T-shirts and like to grill outdoors and drink Budweiser are all gonna be these redneck, gun-toting, gay-bashing, closed-minded evangelical assholes.

Shit, man, it's pretty pathetic. I mean, here I am accusing other people of being closed-minded when, really, I'm the one who was being a total judgmental asshole. I feel ashamed suddenly, and I want to apologize to Russell, even though that wouldn't make any sense to him.

I mean, what could I say?

So, instead, I try to reach out to him in basically the only way I know how.

"Hey," I say, kinda quietly. "You wanna go smoke a bowl, maybe, when you're done eatin'?"

He leans back in the straining canvas chair. "You know it, brother. Thank you. I appreciate that."

We sort of "cheers" our bottles of Budweiser together, and then Russell starts in on a massive chicken leg. I'd say he's able to get about three or four bites down before, really out of nowhere, this giant cat with scruffy, matted fur and a missing chunk out of its left ear pounces onto Russell's ample belly.

"Hi, there, Jezzy," says Russell sweetly, rubbing its good ear with the palm of his hand. The cat's not impressed. It fixes its scowl on Russell's face and starts meowing and growling and hissing dramatically.

"This here's Jezebel," Russell tells me, laughing a little to himself. "We might think we run things 'round here, but ol' Jezzy, she knows better."

He rips off a pretty sizable piece of chicken from his plate and dangles it up over the cat, who chomps the big piece of meat down faster'n I can fucking blink. The cat then goes on to demand a piece of steak, then a piece of potato. It's not till she's sampled each and every food item on Russell's plate that she finally seems contented, curling up right there on his lap and falling asleep hard—her tongue slightly lolling and some drool hanging down.

"Women!" says Russell.

We both laugh at that.

After eating, Russell takes me inside to go smoke a bowl in the backroom. He's got his own pipe and his own stash, too, so we just match each other back and forth, making small talk and whatever. The room must be used as some sort of study or something, 'cause besides a funky, torn couch and some straight-back wooden chairs, the rest of the space is completely stacked to the top with books—I mean, everything from spy novels to historical textbooks to, like, Bret Easton Ellis and Chuck Palahniuk. He even has a book of military writing by Mao Tse-tung. Fucking awesome.

"Man," I say, probably sounding too excited. "This place is super great. How long have you and Kelly been living here?"

Just about two years, he tells me. They moved up from Savannah, where he used to work leading carriage tours around the city.

"I'll tell you, man, you wanna hear some interesting stories, just talk to a carriage driver. Those guys I worked with were like history geniuses. Did you know the pirate Blackbeard held the city of Charleston for ransom? I mean, that motherfucker stuck up the whole goddamn place. He used to light fuses in his beard when he was charging into battle so there'd be all this smoke comin' off him—scare the shit outta everybody. Blackbeard was a heavy dude. All those pirates were."

"Pirates, huh?"

He goes on to tell me about how almost all the pirate captains were ex-Navy-trained soldiers who had been either disenchanted or disengaged with the service. He talks to me about their ships and military strategies—both of us still passing the bowl.

"Down here," he says, "we all come from a culture of fighters. Sure, there was the Civil War and all, but it's more'n that. The way I was brought up, back in Mobile, my daddy instilled in me that it was my duty to serve my country. Joinin' the service wasn't a question; it was something I had to do."

He tells me about going to school at the Citadel and how, after graduating, he joined the Rangers and was deployed to a bunch of different unstable Latin American countries.

"Basically," he says, as though talking in a dream—his eyes are good and glazed over at this point—"our orders were just to march through the jungle until we met resistance. When we met resistance, well, it was either they killed you or you killed them. I had no idea what the hell I was doing there. All I knew was that these people were trying to kill me. So, yeah, I come back to the States and start doin' a little reading and educating myself—a little growing up—then I find out what we were *really* doin' in those countries. Hell, it makes me sick."

Stuttering out "Jesus Christ" is the best I can do.

"Well, whatever, I was so goddamn young—a little kid. I don't regret it. I mean, how could I? It's made me who I am. I had to go through it. And I got this awesome life now—good friends, good food, good drink, all good things, right?"

I scratch absently at the back of my neck. "Yeah, man, I know what you mean. You really can't regret that shit. I mean, it takes what it takes for each of us to learn and, yeah, like you said, grow up."

His head nods. "Yup, I've lived life just about as hard as I could and, man, I wouldn't take it back, not any of it. Hell, maybe I'll get the courage to write a book someday, too. That's always been a dream of mine."

"Hell yeah," I tell him. "You should."

We go on talkin' like that for a good long while—him mostly telling stories and me mostly listening. I mean, fuck, man, I could go on listening to his stories all night. I just want to absorb everything—hold on to it forever—and I'm pretty damn sure that's not just 'cause of all the chemicals I got pumping through my bloodstream.

But, anyway, yeah, we keep on talking until Russell's girlfriend, Kelly, opens the door and jokingly scolds him for being rude to the other guests, so we both get up and head back out to the party.

"Hey," says Russell, as we half stagger down the hall, "you got work tomorrow?"

I tell him I don't.

"All right, then," he slurs, whacking me on the back in an awkward display of male affection. "Then I'm gonna take you crabbing, okay?"

I nod. "Yeah, sure, what's that?"

He ignores my question. "Good, good. You don't have a phone, right? So I'll pick you up at noon. You got that?"

I nod again, figuring he probably won't remember any of this tomorrow, anyway.

When Sue Ellen sees me, she seems pretty happy Russell and I have hit it off so well. Somehow it seems to mean a lot to her. She kisses me publicly, which is rare for her, but I figure she's a little lit herself.

"I love you," she says.

And I tell it back to her, fumbling to get a cigarette out with my useless hands.

It's then that we hear the cat shriek loud, and I glance over to see it bolting from the grill like a blur of gray shadow, scaling a tree and continuing to meow pathetically.

"Russ," says Kelly, all panicky, "she must've jumped on the grill. We gotta do something."

Russell scratches at his cheek thoughtfully for a few seconds before answering in an even more exaggerated drawl. "Ain't nothin' we can do, honey. I mean, yeah, it's gonna hurt her like hell for a while, but I guarantee you one thing: She ain't never gonna do that again."

Everyone kinda laughs, and the cat lets out one last pissed-off-sounding meow from the top of the tree.

I reach into the cooler to get another beer.

Thinking, man, even that cat's got enough sense not to jump on a hot grill twice, no matter how good whatever's left cooking on there might look to her.

But me? Well, I figure I can outsmart that fucking grill this time.

I put my hand over the coals glowing orange, smoldering.

I lower it.

Closer and closer.

So far, so good.

So far, so good.

So far . . .

So good.

Ch.22

It's barely even light out yet when I convulse awake from a vivid, anxious sleep. Sweat that has soaked into the sheets makes me shiver uncontrollably, and my heart beats fast and panicked. The gray morning fills the room, shining through the slatted blinds, bleeding all color out pale and muted. My eyes are pinned back wide open. My fingers clutch at nothing. My stomach crawls up through my throat and out my mouth as I bolt for the bathroom.

I vomit red, yellow liquid projectile into the porcelain toilet. My brain swells. My skull cracks from the pressure. The vomit comes again—gagging—my face a mess of snot and tears, with veins standing out all over.

The smell's enough to make me pass out right there. I hit the cool white-tiled floor, my burning-up cheek pressing helplessly against it. There's nothing to do but lie here shivering, my knees pulled up tight against my chest.

I try to slow my breathing down.

I try to hold it together.

I try to blink the world back into focus.

As the gray light filters in.

And a fat spider with long, coarse-looking hairs crawls cautiously up the side of the toilet toward the stench there. It disappears behind the dirty rim, and I quickly reach up to flush it away, along with all the vomit—or, well, some of it, anyway.

I pull myself along the floor out into the kitchen, managing to stand, but still really shaky.

What I need is a drink.

I mean, I swear, it's not that I want to or anything, but I've got no choice. It's the only way I can possibly get through this day. And, besides, I have to go crabbing with Russell. So I need this drink.

First, though, I gotta make sure Sue Ellen's really asleep, 'cause she'll freak the fuck out if she sees me drinking at, like, seven in the morning. Already she's been gettin' on my back a whole lot about how much I'm drinking. And she's only aware of maybe half of what I'm actually consuming. So I go sneak back into the bedroom and see that she's definitely still passed out, with the blanket pulled up so that only a mass of tangled black hair is visible against her pillow. Despite getting so sick, whenever I get drunk at night, I'm always jolted awake at six or seven. It's been that way as long as I can remember, even back in high school at parties and things. My friends would sleep all morning, but I'd be up at dawn, thoughts racing, consumed by anxiety, unable to sit still—ending up having to take a walk or something while I waited for everyone else. But what I know now that I didn't know back then is that there is a cure. All I've got to do is take a couple shots and I calm down immediately.

So, uh, yeah, that's the way I play it this morning. I finish off the rest of the vodka in the freezer, and immediately warmth and tranquility fill my mind and body, like I've swallowed the sun down inside me.

It's a miracle, really.

And so what if it's all dependent on a substance? At least with drinking, my life won't fall apart—not like it did with hard drugs. It's just a, uh, minor vice. That's all.

But, anyway, after finishing the bottle, I go clean up the bathroom so Sue Ellen won't suspect anything—trying to cover up the smell with a can of hair spray. I'm not really sure how well it works. Still, I figure by the time she gets up, it should've all aired out a good bit. I leave it be at that and go make coffee and some toast with strawberry jam and butter. The sun is low and bright, its rays like the coils of an electric oven, the temperature gauge rising to the point of self-combustion.

I mess with the air conditioner a little, but even on its highest setting, the apartment is still strangling hot as the paned glass windows compound the sunlight—trapping the layers of humid, palpable, dirty atmosphere in our own private ecosystem. With no chance of escape. I mean, no way out. All I can do is sit naked on the living-room couch—wrapped in a thin sheet—drinking down glass after glass of cold water— trying to quench my unquenchable thirst.

The heat and alcohol leave me sort of blurred out—half awake, half asleep. I put on this zombie movie we got from Netflix, though I can barely focus on it at all. I mean, I guess I must pass out again, 'cause I wake up to the DVD menu repeating over and over. There's a note from Sue Ellen on the coffee table next to me. She says she went to work and didn't want to wake me. She says she loves me.

I get up to go see what time it is, stopping at the refrigerator for a beer—panicking some when I see there are only two left. I'll have to run to the liquor store really quickly with what little money I have left. I chug the first beer all the way down and then immediately pop the cap off the other, trying to, you know, sip at it more casually.

The digital oven clock says it's just before noon.

I take a shower and run up the block to the dingy liquor store, where all the bottles are kept behind bulletproof glass. Actually, the whole counter and the cash register and the little old woman who works there are all kept safe behind the glass as well, so our transaction takes place through a metal drawer that slides back and forth from one side to the other. I put in ten dollars, mostly in change, and she passes me back a half-pint of no-brand vodka and a half-pint of no-brand whiskey. The woman's here every day, looking like a high school librarian, with horn-rimmed glasses, a lot of lipstick, and a dowdy kind of jumpsuit thing. Her face is creased and folded and withered and wrinkled like a dried piece of fruit.

She used to smile at me whenever I came in. Now she just stares at me with something like pity in her golden, black-spotted eyes—shaking her head—reluctant.

Obviously, she doesn't need to ID me anymore.

I stuff both bottles into my pants pockets, muttering "thank you" and then turning to get the hell out of there. The little bell rigged up to the door jingles behind me.

Fuck.

I guess I gotta start switching up liquor stores. That goddamn woman makes me feel as guilty as hell. And, I mean, who is she to judge?

Christ.

I find myself running back home just so I can drink some of the vodka before Russell comes by. The whiskey bottle I hide in the small space behind the TV so Sue Ellen can't find it. Doing this kind of shit, it's hard not to think back on all those twelve-step meetings I used to go to. I remember hearing people talk about how they would do shit like hide bottles around the house or sneak their empties into the neighbors' trash cans so the garbage people wouldn't know how much they were drinking. Actually, now that I think about it, I'm pretty sure I remember them talking about how they had to keep changing liquor stores 'cause they were too ashamed to face the same employees every day — or multiple times a day. But the difference between me and all those people at the meetings is that I'm aware of the signs, right? And I know how to catch myself before falling down too far. They talk about how their lives had become unmanageable, the way my life did when I was using hard drugs. But for now, drinking and smoking pot, I haven't had any negative consequences at all. So how could this be a problem? I mean, I keep telling myself it isn't.

For the first time in my life, I get to act like a normal twenty-something-year-old—carefree, going out to bars and having fun. Hell, even on my twenty-first birthday I was in a goddamn sober living. I've been totally robbed of all the experiences most kids my age get to have. Having to be sober was like being a forty-year-old trapped in a young adult's body. How could I relate to any of my peers? It was like I'd come from a totally different planet. And all because my goddamn parents were so overprotective and reactionary they forced me to go into rehab when I was eighteen. Can you believe that? I'd been doing crystal meth for, maybe, four or five months, that's it. But, of course, once I was in rehab, they brainwashed us all into thinking we have a disease, which is totally bullshit. I mean, cancer is a disease, HIV is a disease—addiction is so not. But they push that idea into our heads until we're so broken down we can't help but believe it. So, at that point, whenever I did use, of course I went all out. They'd programmed me to believe that was the only way I could do it. They created this self-fulfilling prophecy for me, and I just kept acting it out.

But that's all over now—the spell has been broken. I'm done with rehabs and twelve-steps and psych doctors and acupuncture and inner-child workshops and blah-fucking-blah-blah. I'm going crabbing with Russell. In Charleston, South Carolina. He picks me up a little after twelve thirty. Of all the celebrities and intellectuals and industry people and upper-crust New Yorkers and expensive doctors and whoever I've met in my life, I already have more respect for Russell than I've ever had for any of them. In LA, the first question everyone asks you is, "What do you do?" And how you're treated from that point on is completely dependent on your answer to the question. But down here it doesn't work like that. No one cares what you do. If anything, the way you're judged is on how you live your life, how you treat your friends — simple, not-very-glamorous shit like that. At least, that's the way Russell tells it. And, honestly, in my whole life, I can't say I've met more'n one or two people like that, ever. My friend Akira, in San Francisco, is one. And I can't even think of another.

Except this guy Russell. Already I admire him absolutely.

He knocks at the door, and I let him in really quickly to smoke a bowl before heading out.

The truck he's driving, he tells me, he borrowed from a friend, and there's a very shy, skittish black dog behind the front seat. It looks like some sort of lab mix.

"Oh," he says, "that's Carolyn's dog, Luna. She asked me to watch her for a couple days."

I don't know who Carolyn is, but whatever.

Driving out toward the beach, the live oaks with roots breaking through the pavement give way to stinking marshland with canals cutting through like line drawings on colored paper. We drive over bridges, past falling-apart gas stations advertising boiled peanuts, cold beer, fish and grits. For all the opulence and old-money wealth of downtown Charleston, the surrounding areas are desperately poor. Trailer parks, boarded-up houses, Piggly Wigglys, Wal-Marts, that's all there is. The heat makes the road shimmer.

"You'll like it down here," Russell tells me. "It'll do you good to slow down a little."

I nod, knowing that's the truth for sure. "Yeah," I say, my

eyes fixed on nothing out the side window. "I've never been too good at that."

"Well," he says, laughing a little, "I'm the champion of taking it easy, so you're in good hands."

He pulls the truck into a McDonald's parking lot, and we go over and wait in line idling at the drive-through.

"You want anything?"

"Nah," I say.

He orders a double Quarter Pounder with cheese and a large Coke, and then we drive 'round to the pickup window.

The woman behind the glass is heavy, with extensions braided tight to her head. She leans out toward us.

"You don't want no fries with that, honey?"

Russell smiles big, showing his square, white teeth. "No, ma'm. They tend to make me gassy."

She laughs and laughs, and I laugh, too.

Russell thanks her and we get the food and we go on and, uh, get.

The next stop we make is at a gas station, where Russell gets a twelve-pack of Budweiser and a net basket for crabbing, plus a pack of chicken necks for ninety-nine cents. I can't really help buy anything, 'cause I spent the last of my money this morning. He tells me not to worry about it.

"I worked on Wall Street, you know?" he says out of nowhere as we drive down the road, crossing bridges and passing strip malls. "Worked with a big firm playin' stocks and whatever. I lived in New York for two years and made a bundle of money. Hell, I ain't ever been more miserable in my whole life. There ain't nothin' worth workin' like that for, all shut up inside all day.

I'd rather be a little hard up and able to cook out, go walking on the beach, go crabbing with a fine gentleman like yerself."

"Ha," I say.

He veers the truck onto a side road, and suddenly we're driving with tall marsh grass on either side of us, making our way deeper and deeper into the swamp.

We park at the end of a splintering gray dock that stretches out into the murky channel of water reflecting sunlight.

Russell grabs the cooler and beer and the net. I get the chicken and try to keep Luna from running off into the mud and oyster shells.

We walk out all together onto the dock.

As it turns out, crabbing isn't really what I expected. I mean, it's not too exciting or anything. Basically, what you do is you take a chicken neck and kinda weave it into the bottom of the net so it doesn't fall out. Then you just lower the net into the water and wait. Then you wait some more. Then maybe ten or fifteen minutes go by and you pull up the net. If you're lucky, there might be a couple of crabs in there eating the chicken. So you dump the crabs into the cooler and drop the net back into the water. Of course, a lotta times there aren't any crabs at all, and you just gotta try again.

So we do.

I mean, we keep lowering the goddamn net and drinking beers while he tells me stories and I tell him mine.

"I've been through some dark times," he says. "Doin' coke and whatever else. Somehow, you just got to learn how to fall in love with life, you know? I mean, shit, man, just look around, right? How great is this? We ain't got shit to do but sit in the sun and maybe catch a few crabs, or maybe catch nothin' at all. It don't matter. And then we're gonna go back home and boil these fuckers up and melt some butter and talk some more, and maybe a game'll be on. That's it, man. That's fuckin' it."

There used to be this TV program in the '70s called *The Dick Cavett Show*. I have an old tape of one of Cavett's interviews with John Lennon and Yoko Ono. On the show, John talked about wishing he could be a fisherman—pulling his dinner from the sea, connected with the tides and the swells and whatever. He said he wished he coulda been that kinda person, instead of someone who needed to perform and question everything and be forever unsatisfied and wanting more.

Looking over at Russell, goddamn, I want to be a fisherman so badly.

I mean, why can't it ever be enough?

What is this craziness and pain in me that rips apart a beautiful day like this? The sun, the marsh, Luna hiding in the shade behind us. Why is there this restlessness that won't let me alone?

I look at Russell and I admire him completely.

He's figured out the greatest challenge for any of us: just being content.

So as the sun starts setting, we head back to his place. Then we cook up the crabs and eat them with melted butter and a big hunk of bread.

We sit in the living room smoking pot and drinking until both Kelly and Sue Ellen show up from work.

Russell and I get up and greet the girls. We decide to all go get some Mexican food.

I want so badly for this to just be enough, you know?

I smile and laugh and drink. But there's something in me that opens up and swallows all this and keeps demanding more. I can't be satisfied.

And I hate myself so much for that.

Ch.23

Is this really all there is—creating little tasks for myself to get me through the day—a schedule repeated in my head over and over so I never forget and never have to face a moment of stillness?

I write five pages. I make a cup of tea, smoke a cigarette, take a belt from the vodka bottle I have hidden under the back porch—eat something—write five more pages, smoke a cigarette, take another hit off the bottle—trying not to get too drunk but trying even harder not to get too sober. I listen to Syd Barrett, John Coltrane, Robert Johnson, Marc Bolan, the Yardbirds, Joy Division, Nick Drake. I put on my VHS copy of the Who's *Tommy* and let that play through while I keep working.

Five more pages.

Hit the bottle.

Smoke another cigarette.

Take a shower.

Brush my teeth three times to cover up the smell.

Rinse with mouthwash.

Get dressed.

I have to work a shorter, closing shift tonight—from three to eight.

It's important not to get too drunk.

It's important not to get too sober.

I'm working with that goddamn, super-uptight Elaina girl, so I definitely don't want to be any more sober than is absolutely necessary. And while I am fairly lucid at the moment, the alcohol's sure to pass out of my system before my shift is over, so a trip to the liquor store is beyond crucial. I mean, my life might just depend on it.

Unfortunately, however, I've already spent all of my last check, so I'm forced to rummage around through the jar of spare change Sue Ellen keeps on top of her dresser. The entire collection is a little under five dollars, but I guess that's just going to have to do now, right?

I take the money, the coins heavy and bulging in my pocket— jangling as I walk, like I'm some stupid cat with a bell tied around my neck.

The sky has blown clear again, the storm clouds like black floating mountains passing over the horizon. The rubber soles of my shoes are sticking to the sidewalk, and I find myself actually praying for the rain to come pouring down again— washing us clean. Though that's never how it works. Charleston is a swamp. When it rains, we're left floating in a clogged, piss-warmed toilet. The gutters overflow—the parks are all flooded—and the rats convene on the telephone wires, looking down on us and laughing, with fat, bloated bellies.

I go into the liquor store—cooled by the powerful air-conditioning unit.

I sigh real loudly, wiping the sweat off my forehead with my T-shirt and saying, "Goddamn, it's hot."

The woman behind the counter raises her eyes from the magazine she's reading—thick, Coke-bottle glasses perched on the tip of her pinched little nose.

"Hey, now, boy," she says, not smiling at all. "Don't you blaspheme in here. This is a Christian establishment. We don't need your kind comin' in here."

I wonder whether she means 'cause of my language or 'cause I'm white. That is, now that I think about it, I don't think I've ever seen any white folks at this liquor store. Still, it's not like I've ever been given a hard time before, so maybe I really just offended the ol' girl. Christ, a Christian establishment. Well, at least maybe she'll demonstrate a little Christian charity by having patience with me while I count out five dollars' worth of change on the plastic-sealed counter.

"I'm sorry, ma'm," I tell her, stacking the coins in little piles of nickels, dimes, quarters, and pennies.

"I didn't mean any disrespect," I continue, kinda stumbling over my words. "I just, uh...I'm sorry. It's been a rough day is all."

She eyes the mounting columns with one painted-on brow arched significantly higher than the other. "I can see that," she says. Her red-painted mouth is turned down at the corners, the dark-purple-colored lip liner like wax melted in the creases of her face. "You think you can hurry it up?"

She taps press-on nails against the counter surface—tap-tap, tap-tap. My hand shakes—fingers going all useless on me—the pile of coins toppling over so I lose the count completely.

"Man, fuck," I start to say, trying to cut off my words but not really succeeding—so instead I just kinda cover my mouth with both hands.

"I'm sorry," I stammer. "I...uh...I don't know what's wrong with me."

I stare down at the mess of coins, wondering if maybe I should forget about it and go try somewhere else.

In fact, I'm about to start shoving the change back in my pocket, when she startles the shit outta me by bursting out laughing—long and loud and deep. "Ah, hell," she says, cackling all over the place. "I'm just playin' with you. Boy, you shoulda seen your face. A Christian establishment! Ha. I really had you goin', didn't I?"

My head nods up and down—my mouth hanging open and my body kinda paralyzed there.

The woman laughs and laughs, wiping tears from her eyes and pausing to breathe every now and then, making a sort of "whoo" noise.

"Yeah, you definitely got me," I tell her, still kinda stunned.

She struggles to pull herself together, saying, "I did, didn't I? That sure was a good one."

I manage to laugh a little myself.

"Anyway," she carries on. "What can I get you, young man?

Looks like you got about five dollars goin' there now—ain't that about right?"

She starts dumping the coins into a cigar box, not counting 'em, and so I just ask for the cheapest bottle of whiskey she's willing to give me, which turns out to be a pint of Black Velvet. She also throws in three little airplane bottles of flavored Smirnoff, maybe as payment for making me feel like such an asshole.

"My name's Candace," she says, reaching a cold hand like crackling tissue paper out to shake mine.

"Nic," I tell her.

She says for me to come back anytime and, of course, I thank her, waving good-bye stupidly.

I walk out into the damp, clinging heat, rushing off down a side alley to take a couple more hits before work.

The black clouds have all disappeared—the sky perfectly clear and wide open.

"See," I say to myself, "it's gonna be okay."

I put the mouth of the bottle to my lips.

I drink.

By the time I get to work, I'd say I'm pretty well lit up, talking to everyone, messing around. The hours go by fast, and I maybe even start blacking out a little—my memory going. I can't keep track of most of the orders, and I end up burning a bunch of different shit. While I'm mopping, I knock over the bucket in the kitchen, and the gray water, slick with greasy sludge, soaks in behind all the appliances, and it takes me a good forty-five minutes to get the floor looking even half-assed decent. Then, as I'm taking out the heavy kitchen trash, the plastic bag rips when I'm just steps away from the back door—emptying out pounds of wet coffee grounds, discarded, no-longer-identifiable food products, and wadded-up napkins onto the freshly mopped tile floor.

Elaina, as you can probably imagine, isn't really speaking to me anymore, which is probably for the best, considering I must be practically sweating cheap whiskey at this point. I mean, the bottle's just about done. Not that I meant to drink it all. I was trying to keep it under control. Honestly, I'm not even sure what happened. It's like one minute I was opening the bottle, and the next, well, I'm where I'm at now: teetering, sloppy, throwing up in the bathroom sink. The world spins out of control—the floor dropping out from underneath me—my body pinned back against the wall—like I somehow stepped onto one of those rides at the carnival—centrifugal force—my stomach tightening like a fist.

I can't tell whether my words are slurred, but I know damn well that I won't ever come back here. If they called me out on my behavior, man, I just couldn't take it. I'm not gonna let them fire me. I mean, I get it, I fucked up—I drank too much. The hell if I'm gonna give them the chance to try 'n' tell me I have a problem. Besides, I hated this job, anyway. And it's the job's fault that I'm drinking like I am. If I wasn't so goddamn miserable working here, well, I wouldn't have to numb out like this. I've gotta get outta here. I can't stand it another minute.

My legs zigzag, stumbling their way up to Elaina behind the register. Believe it or not, I've got the goddamn hiccups.

"Hey," she says, putting down the rag and spray bottle she's been using to clean the pastry case. "I need you to take over for me while I go make a phone call. Why don't you start breaking down the espresso machine? Then you can do the mats when I get back."

I nod as she passes on by. Maybe I'm just fooling myself, but she doesn't seem to suspect anything. I mean, she's not treating me any differently than she normally does. It could be that I'm holding shit together better than I thought. I could even be getting away with it. 'Cause if Elaina thought I was drinking, I'm pretty damn sure she'd have called me out by now. Hell, that's the kinda thing that'd make her day. So, yeah, maybe she doesn't know.

But I still can't risk it. There's no way I'm gonna give these fuckers the satisfaction of firing me. I'd rather quit. That's the only way to go.

So I hiccup.

And even gulping water doesn't seem to help.

A customer comes up and orders a cappuccino—insisting on chatting me up, even though I'm hiccuping like a fool. He's nice enough about it, though, offering some advice about placing a spoon to the bridge of my nose while I drink water for ten seconds without taking a breath. He watches me struggling to complete his ridiculous little hiccup cure. It doesn't work. He goes on to tell me about a girl he saw on the *Today* show who'd had the hiccups for over three months straight.

I laugh. "Well, thanks anyway," I tell him, my words broken up by the goddamn hiccups.

It's all too goddamn embarrassing.

I mean, drinking isn't a problem for me, but I definitely

need to get my shit together a little more. As it is, I'm not even gonna be able to get my last paycheck. There's no way I can face coming in here.

So, with that as the only justification I really need, I quickly take two twenties out of the cash register — just enough to buy another eighth from Carmine.

I stuff the bills in my pocket and go to grab my bag from the office.

The hiccups haven't stopped.

I unscrew the bottle of whiskey and drain the last of it, immediately moving on to one of the little airplane bottles of raspberry vodka.

Everything's gonna be better now. I just need to quit this job, and then I'll be able to drink like a normal person again.

'Cause that's all I want.

To be normal.

And to drink.

Ch.24

Sue Ellen was pissed at me for quitting my coffee shop job—
especially since it's taken me over a month to finally find some
other work. But I did. I mean, I got a new job, and so far it
seems like a much better fit, for sure. Plus I'm making a ton
more money in cash, every day, which is good but, uh, hasn't
really helped me cut back on drinking at all. Not to mention
that the place I'm working, a barbecue joint called Dorothy's
that caters to Charleston's gay community, is equipped with a
full bar that I have ready access to throughout my shift. That is,
I usually have a vodka and Coke hidden away for whenever I
get thirsty—which, these days, is just about always.

Of course, I'm drinking at home, too—still trying to work
on my book during my free time—but always drunk, or, well,
not even drunk. I mean, I'm at the point where I barely even
feel the alcohol anymore.

But my body still craves it.

I wake up sick every morning, head pounding, hands shaking so badly I can barely get the bottle to my lips, forcing the liquor down till the tremors finally ease up some.

As far as she's letting on, it seems that Sue Ellen hasn't figured out what's going on. I keep bottles hidden all over the house, so I never actually have to drink in front of her. Plus, that way, if she does find a bottle and makes me dump it out, I'll still have more stashed around. 'Cause the thing is, I fucking need it. My body's developed a physical dependency. I mean, after all, I know what to look for. I've sat through thousands of twelve-step meetings and listened to thousands of drunks describing the exact same behavior I find myself doing now. They talked about hiding bottles, getting the shakes, shitting blood, watching their bellies swell. I'd never experienced any of that. They were alcoholics. I was a drug addict. But now, I guess, I'm not too sure.

We were visiting Sue Ellen's brother three hours away in Greenville, South Carolina, and I got so drunk before driving back that I had to keep one eye closed the whole way 'cause I was seeing everything double. And, of course, I couldn't ask Sue Ellen to drive, 'cause then she would've known something was up. I mean, I'd stolen a bottle of tequila from her brother's liquor cabinet and drunk the whole thing just before getting in the car. I remember the eye thing, but that's pretty much it. The rest is all lost to me.

My world has closed in around me. I can't hang out with Russell 'cause I'm too embarrassed for him to see me like this. I'm constantly terrified that the people at work are going to find out how much I drink. I'm lying to my editor in New York and my mom and dad on the phone. My body is weak and bloated. I'm slowly poisoning myself to death. And it's not like I haven't seen what this shit does to people. The most fucked-up detoxes I've ever seen are the people coming off alcohol. It's worse than heroin, worse than benzos, worse than anything. Alcohol can pickle your brain—leaving you helpless, like a child—infantilized—shitting in your pants—ranting madness—disoriented—angry—terrified.

But that's not gonna be me, I mean, it can't be. I may hate myself. I may fantasize about suicide. But I'm way too vain to let myself die an alcoholic death. There's nothing glamorous about alcoholism. You don't go out like Nic Cage in *Leaving Las Vegas*, with a gorgeous woman riding you till your heart stops. Alcoholism takes you down slow, robbing you of every last bit of dignity on your way down—leaving you bloated, paranoid, delusional.

There's no way I'm going out like that.

Not me. Not like that.

The only problem is, well, I can't stop.

Every night before I fall asleep, or pass out, or whatever, I promise myself I'm not gonna drink when I wake up. I set little goals, like not drinking till after I get off work, or drinking only beer and wine. But at this point, man, there's no way I can even go to work without at least a couple of shots of vodka in my belly. Without the alcohol, I can't even hold a conversation anymore—not to mention being all up and enthusiastic like you're supposed to be when you're waiting tables.

Every night is a performance. I put on my costume, smile

like an idiot, chat everyone up, all clever and funny and understanding. Honestly, it doesn't feel all that different from hustling. I mean, I've always been able to show people exactly what they want to see. And I become whatever it is they want me to be. And I flirt and tease and listen. The gay girls think I'm sweet. The gay men love me just like they always do, tipping big, leaving their phone numbers, business cards. And all I do is keep playin' it up, lying without thinking—a natural-born whore. The only differences now are that I'm not shooting drugs and I'm not actually sleeping with them. Instead, I drink and drink and wonder how much money it'll take to make me feel beautiful. The right offer will come. I'll fight to resist it, but it'll come just the same. And then I'll have another opportunity to show the world how weak I still am.

The right offer will come.

I mean, it does.

It just doesn't come the way I thought.

See, there's this new girl working tonight. She started a couple days ago, and it's not like we've even really talked or anything, but here she is, handing me a small baggy and whispering, "Here, quick, put this in your pocket before somebody sees."

The half-pint of vodka I drank on the way over here probably isn't helping my judgment any, but who am I kidding? I'm sure I woulda done what she told me anyway.

"Wh-what is it?" I whisper back, studying her round, cherubic face. She's a tiny little girl with brown ringlets in her hair like Shirley Temple or something. Actually, I'd say she looks a lot like Shirley Temple in general, with dimples and a goddamn perfect button nose. Her teeth are small and spaced apart like a child's. Her arms and hands are practically in miniature. Her voice is babyish, almost like it's been sped up on one of those old reel-to-reel machines.

Of course, I'd like to be able to say that her eyes betray something secret and sinister hiding beneath the surface, but as far as I can tell, they're just about as open and innocent as can be. As it is, I'm not even sure I hear her right when she says, "Come on, I know you party, don't you?"

I nod, even though I don't want it to be true anymore.

"Well," she says, quieter, her mouth pressed up close to my ear, "that's just a sample my husband wanted me to give out. He got a shipment of coke in the other day, and he's offering some really great deals. So you go ahead and try that, and let me know if you need to get in touch with him, okay?"

My chest feels all tight suddenly—my lungs contracted—the air knocked out of me, like I just jumped out a window and then splattered across the sidewalk.

Somehow, I have a small bag of coke in my pocket.

And the truth is, I'm fucking scared.

But I don't let on. I mean, I thank her, asking for her phone number and promising to call in the next couple of days.

That's what a stand-up guy I am.

Christ.

She goes off to check on her table, and me? I go straight to the goddamn bathroom.

Looking at the little ball of white packed powder, I can't help but laugh. I mean, as much as my drinking has gotten kind of out of control recently, I know damn well I'm a whole lot better off than I would be if I were using hard drugs again.

I know what hard drugs have done to my life. Hell, they're the reason I'm stuck in the goddamn South working at this goddamn restaurant. They've basically destroyed everything I've ever had. And I was totally cool staying away from them.

I mean, fuck. When I was using, there was no way some random person would come hand me a bag of coke. That would've been, like, the happiest day of my life.

So I guess it makes sense that now that I'm trying to stay clear of it, someone walks up and just stuffs it in my pocket. That really is the way this fucked-up world works, isn't it?

Obviously, what I should do is flush the shit right now.

What I do instead is open the bag to see if it smells like the real thing.

It does.

The chunk she gave me really isn't that big, but it'd be enough to make up a pretty strong shot if I had a needle.

My mind plays out possible scenarios for scoring needles.

Honestly, I can't think of any.

My eyes dart quickly over all the bathroom surfaces.

Nowhere to set up a line except for on the tank above the toilet, which is kinda gnarly, though I've definitely done it before.

Fuck it, I tell myself. The sooner I get rid of this shit, the sooner I don't have to think about it anymore.

I set up a line.

I don't hesitate.

I take the powder up my goddamn nose.

Ch.25

Sue Ellen leaves early for class.

The door slams shut, and I immediately pull myself up to a half-sitting position, my ears straining to hear the signs that she's really gone—the car engine firing, the wheels spinning against the gravel, the vague hint of music from the car stereo fading into the distance.

I listen till I'm sure. Though, of course, I still have to be careful. She could've forgotten something. Her class could be canceled. Or she could just randomly decide to come home early. Really, there's no way of knowing absolutely.

But after waiting all the rest of last night and then feigning sleep for the past hour after the alarm went off, I'm not sure I could hold back now, even if she were still here. As ridiculous as this sounds, it's almost as if there's some invisible person whispering in my ear, repeating the word over and over—

"cocaine, cocaine, cocaine." Like a haunting, beautiful woman caressing my throat with the tips of her fingers—stripping off her clothes—pressing the warm softness of her body up against mine so I can feel every nerve ending just screaming with arousal.

Cocaine.

My tongue swells.

Cocaine.

I can't speak any other word.

Cocaine.

I close my eyes and I see Zelda there, penetrating me with the needle in her hand, the thin trickle of blood running down the curve of my forearm. We kiss each other with desperate sadness and urgency, even as the cocaine explodes into the recesses of our minds—leaving us gasping—flooded with pleasure—our barrier of skin dissolved so our lungs and muscles and veins tangle together—the two of us one. Together—together—one—always.

Cocaine has brought her back to me.

Cocaine has brought me back to her.

And I am so disgusted with the choices I've made.

I mean, how could I have abandoned her the way I did?

How could I have settled for this rotting, stale half-life—drinking alcohol all day long so I don't have to face what I've become?

What I need is another line of coke.

So I steady myself, leaning against the doorframe while the first pulses of nausea convulse through my body. My head feels drained of all blood, like I might pass out any second. I have to keep hold of the counter surface while I struggle to pull the bottle of cheap-ass vodka out from where I've hidden it behind the refrigerator.

The first burning gulps of liquid make me gag, but I'm stronger already. I can feel the warmth in my belly fortifying my legs and arms so I can stand on my own again. I finish that bottle and then go to the front window, looking out to make sure Sue Ellen's car really is gone.

It is.

Having been replaced by a scraggly-looking bobtail cat lying contemptuously in the sun—flicking its tail—the sky pale blue and cloudless overhead.

Another bright, sunny day.

Christ.

I pull the blinds closed and check the locks on the door, making sure to secure the dead bolt so that if Sue Ellen comes home early, I'll have a little extra time to hide shit and whatever.

My mind plays over the possibilities of the day.

Mostly I just want to do the rest of the coke so I can get some really good writing done—especially since I'm pretty close to finishing the rough draft. The coke will give me a new perspective on what I've been working on and, I hope, help me figure out how to end the goddamn thing. I mean, I don't know, somehow writing the ending has been by far the hardest part. But the coke will give me the creativity I need to think up something really great. It'll help me see the truth. At least, that's what I keep telling myself.

Man, I remember when I was living with Zelda, we'd shoot coke in the bathroom and then I'd go out and write the dopest shit for just like hours and hours without stopping. I mean, I'm pretty sure it was the dopest shit—even if my editor kept telling me it made no sense and I needed to get into treatment. She probably just said that 'cause she knew I was relapsing. She was probably just trying to help me get clean. The writing was good. At least, I think it was. And I know this coke's gonna bring me back to that place—a place where I can write without any self-doubt or insecurity—a place of raw inspiration.

'Cause the thing is, even if the rest of my life is a total goddamn failure, as long as I'm writing, well, at least that's something to hold on to. And if I need coke to help me keep writing, then that's just the way it's gotta be. I'll use my tip money to buy a gram tomorrow. It's really not a problem.

So I put some music on the stereo.

David Bowie, of course.

Aladdin Sane.

I set up a line on the kitchen counter.

I wish I had a rig, but I don't.

I take the line up a rolled dollar bill.

The drip down my throat is bitter—putrid.

My jaw clenches, and this fierce sensuality rocks my body.

I imagine Sue Ellen coming home.

I could show her the dark sexuality in me she's never seen. We could make love the way I used to make love with Zelda.

But, no, Sue Ellen wouldn't want that. If anything, I'd be ashamed to expose her to it. I mean, she'd be terrified and overwhelmed, and I would only end up hurting her even more than she's already been hurt. I couldn't do that to her. There's almost a sick feeling in my stomach thinking about it. I'm suddenly repulsed by myself.

I mean, I love Sue Ellen. What I had with Zelda was dark and twisted and exciting, but it was all about death. Hell, everything in my life has been about death. This depression I have, this mania, this endless thirst. I have nothing positive to offer. I am a draining, sucking, using, consuming parasite. Sue Ellen doesn't deserve this. She deserves goodness. She deserves light. All I can offer her is destruction — death.

I'll kill her like I've killed everything else.

Unless I finally take myself away.

Away so that I can't keep hurting all the people I love.

Fuck.

I mean, what the hell is happening? I'm doing coke. This should be fun.

But suddenly all I want is to be normal again — normal like I was before — before I was getting high, before I was drinking.

I mean, back then there was a time when I was happy, wasn't there?

"Fuck," I say aloud, through my teeth all clenched tight. "Motherfucker."

I force my legs to take me over to the computer.

Writing will help. Writing will make it all worthwhile.

I light a cigarette, staring at the words on the monitor, trying to read over my last paragraph. My hands tremble against the keyboard. I write a few sentences — stopping and starting and stopping again — the words all jumbled — my mind refusing to listen to me—my mind repeating the same thing over and over.

My mind tells me to go into the bathroom.

My mind tells me to open the mirrored medicine cabinet.

My mind tells me to take the bottle of Tylenol PM into my hand.

I pop open the childproof cap, spilling out maybe twenty blue-and-white pills onto the counter.

Mix those with another bottle of vodka, I figure, and that should pretty well do it.

The tears come burning hot against my cheeks.

The breath is all stolen out of me, and I crouch against the tile floor, suddenly crying so hard it hurts to swallow.

I call out, just sort of trying to hear the sound of my voice.

It's time to end this shit.

I know that's the truth.

Hell, it should've been done a long time ago, before I had the chance to hurt so many people. And I swear I'm not being all self-pitying or anything—it's just a fact. The world would be better off without me. Sue Ellen would be better off. My family would be better off. They would all finally be able to stop worrying. I wouldn't be able to manipulate them anymore. I wouldn't be able to build them up with hope again, only to knock them down—like I always do.

A shivering cold contorts my body.

I tell myself to reach into my pocket. I make myself do it, pulling out the rest of the coke, tossing it quickly into the toilet—sickened—feeling the cold metal handle like a static shock against my fingers as I flush the drugs down.

Sweat soaks through my T-shirt so it is wet and clinging to my back.

I tell myself to grab a handful of the pills. I make myself do it, beginning to swallow them down one at a time—counting out loud—starting with one—moving on to two—then three.

My eyes are closed and open.

I throw my head back, dizzy with pain as it collides with the bathroom wall.

I try to remember things.

I try to remember Zelda's face.

I try to remember my father.

I remember his face.

I remember his brown-skinned hands pressing softly against my back. I remember the sound of his voice. I remember his features contorted in helpless crying. I remember seeing him weak and disoriented after the hemorrhage in his brain nearly killed him just a few years ago. I remember he is alive now. I remember he had a second chance.

And then I remember my little brother and sister. I remember the games we played and the stories we read together. I suddenly want to know so badly how they have changed over these last years. I want to know what they are like, what kind of people they are growing into. Fuck, man, if I could just take it all back. I can't build my life back up again, man, I just can't. I can't quit drinking. I can't make it better. I mean, hell, I just relapsed on fucking coke again. I am garbage. And the trash goes in the motherfucking trash can.

That actually gets a laugh out of me.

I look at the sleeping pills in my hand.

And then, suddenly, I have another idea. And this idea, well, it might actually work.

Maybe...maybe I can just sleep. I mean, maybe I can just lock myself in here and watch movies and sleep and, uh, yeah, it'll suck, but I think I might be able to do it. Sue Ellen will be supportive. And I'll stop drinking. And I'll finish my book. And maybe I'll even send my dad an e-mail and see if he might wanna start talking to me again.

My legs move beneath me.

I stand, putting the pills carefully back in their container. And then I walk, staggering, to the different hiding places around the house, gathering the bottles, emptying them one by one into the sink.

A blackness starts to close in at the corners of my eyes. The sleeping pills must be taking effect. My body slumps beneath the weight of the blackness coming down.

I make my way to the bed, stripping down to my underwear, my head filling with static—images cutting in and out.

I turn on the TV.

The sounds are all muffled and droning monotone—unintelligible—slowed to nearly stopping.

I nod and jerk awake.

I nod again.

The sleep presses in on me from every side.

I jerk awake.

Fuck.

I have to just let go.

I have to let go, but it's so hard.

My eyes close.

The sounds are a blur of color bars.
I have to let go.
I have to.
Let go.
Let go.
The sounds fade to nothing.
And I sleep.

Ch.26

Amazingly, well, it actually kinda worked.

For five days I slept and was sick and the cravings got so bad, but I didn't leave the apartment. I mean, hell, I barely left the bed. Sue Ellen was patient and brought me simple foods, and I slept and was sick and watched probably well over fifty different movies and then, finally, I don't know, I started to feel all right.

The cravings let up a good bit, and my body got stronger, and now, I mean, I'm all right—at least, relatively speaking. Hell, I've even started writing again, and I'd say I've got a pretty solid draft about ready to send out to my editor. That is, I figured out some sort of ending.

So, uh, yeah, things are better. And all I can really say about that is, well, I guess that's the cool thing about life, right? I mean, things change. One way or another, things always fucking change.

Unless I get dead.

If I get dead, then nothing'll ever change again. And there's this sort of numbness in me when I think about how close I came. 'Cause things really have changed. And they always do. I just wish I could remember that shit when the bad times come, you know? Hell, from now on I should just start locking myself in my room whenever I get too squirrelly. It's not a bad idea.

But, anyway, besides all that shit, I finally wrote an e-mail to my dad yesterday, and it was crazy 'cause when he responded, he didn't even sound angry at all. If anything, he just seemed grateful to hear from me. All this time I'd been thinking he was pretty much over having anything to do with me, and then, the first time I reach out to him, he writes me back, like, two seconds later saying he'd love to talk. We even set a time: tomorrow morning at eleven for me and eight for him. Honestly, I'm kinda dreading it. I mean, we're starting back at nothing. He doesn't trust me. My stepmom doesn't trust me. My little brother and sister don't trust me. It seems impossible to even try 'n' start building that shit back. Shame is like a whiplash drawing away blood and long strips of skin from my back and shoulders. The air is honed like a knifepoint. But it's not enough to stop me anymore. Fuck, man, I quit drinking on my own. I didn't need to go to rehab. I didn't need to lose everything again. I was able to get sober before shit got too bad this time. And I guess that's gotta be progress.

So I'll talk to my dad.

It's scary as hell, but I'm gonna do it.

At least, that's the plan.

I mean, he's calling tomorrow, so we'll see.

Otherwise, I've just been focusing on writing and watching movies—maybe going out for a coffee. I quit my job at Dorothy's, and I'm not really sure what I'm gonna do now. The boredom feels almost palpable. The time passes slowly. The sun sits motionless in the autumn sky. I am very lonely. I am all alone. But I can't go hang out with anybody 'cause I'm too afraid of drinking again. So I just sit with the loneliness. I search for small distractions. I wait for things to get better—whatever that even means.

But today, uh, I'm not really sure what to do or where to go. I drop off Sue Ellen at work, and it's a little after ten, so I decide to drive up to this coffee shop next to the dog park so I can maybe read a little. I got this book *We Have Always Lived in the Castle* by Shirley Jackson. Actually, I just picked it up 'cause I liked the cover and what I read on the back when I was at the downtown library. Seriously, it's like one of the most incredible books I've ever read. The writing is so haunting and beautiful—so strange and dark. I've almost finished the whole thing, and it's only been two days.

Anyway, I pull the car over on the narrow street in front of the coffee shop. The place is pretty new, from what I understand, hidden behind a tall white fence and a barrier of vines and laurels in the bottom floor of a converted Victorian town house. There is no sign in front, and the only way I even found it was 'cause I was checking out the run-down African-American bookstore across the street and I happened to see someone walking out with a paper cup in his hand. To the right of the little coffee shop/town house is a fenced-in dog park covered in wood chips and smelling of urine. I actually really love watching the dogs play and have even gone in a couple times to pet 'em and throw a ball or whatever.

Today, however, just as I'm opening the gate to go into the coffee shop, I hear someone calling out to me from the dog park, saying, "Boy, boy, hey."

Now, usually I try not to look over at someone who might be calling out to me, just 'cause I'm so used to all the crazies in San Francisco who'll start fucking screaming at you if you take the bait and even acknowledge 'em at all. But I acknowledge this woman—an overweight, kinda hippy-looking forty- or fifty-year-old—scraggly, long, thinning reddish hair—a face overwhelmed by coarse skin—her globular body draped in a flowy sort of dress. I squint my eyes and hold my hand up to try 'n' block out the unrelenting sun.

"Yeah?" I yell back.

She gestures with her head. "Come over here, quick."

For the first time I notice what her hands are busy doing, which is basically holding on to this grotesquely skinny, shivering little dog—some sort of hound, I guess—maybe a foxhound or a Walker hound or whatever. I mean, it basically looks like a beagle that's been all stretched out tall and is super underweight.

I walk over.

The woman speaks with gasping breaths, as though holding this meek, more-or-less stationary dog is a test of strength comparable to, maybe, wrestling an alligator or something.

"Hey," she manages to get out. "Hey, I just found this dog under a truck over there. She got scared and ran out, but I got her. You think you could help take her for me? I don't have a car here, but she needs to go to the Humane Society, I think. Maybe they can find out if she has an owner or if she's just a stray or what. Would you do that for me, honey? Look, she's a good dog. She'll make a great pet for someone."

I look down at the pathetic little thing. She's tricolored, with big, soft-looking ears. Her eyes are black and wide and terrified. Even from where I'm standing, I can make out a mass of ticks clinging to her neck. Fleas the size of sunflower seeds climb lazily along her legs and swollen stomach. Her nipples are large and extended like she might be pregnant.

"Yes, of course," I say, not taking my eyes off the little dog. "Of course I'll take her."

The woman smiles.

"Thank you, young man, that's very kind of you. Can you believe it, the one time I find a stray dog around here and there's not one person at the dog park. Thank God you came by."

I look over at the park and see that, like she said, there's nobody there. In fact, the entire block is deserted—no one on the street—no one anywhere.

"No, no...no problem," I say, crouching down to the dog's eye level. When I talk to the dog, I kind of use a soft, higher-pitched baby voice. "Hey, sweet girl. It's okay. You don't have to be afraid. I'm gonna help you."

The dog's eyes go all black, bulging out of her head, absolutely terrified-looking. I stare down at her swollen pink belly and rub one of her hanging-down, greasy ears, saying, "Damn, girl, you sure are a mess."

I take off my belt and loop it around the dog's scrawny neck so the woman can finally let go.

"You should think about adopting her yourself," she says, smiling—her mouth wide, exposing a mismatched jumble of crooked yellow teeth. "You two look good together."

I'm not quite sure how she means that or whether I should be offended, but what I say is, "Nah, I can't afford a dog. I'm barely getting by myself. Besides, I'm way too unstable."

Her smile doesn't wane or change or anything.

"I don't know," she sort of cackles. "I have a good feeling about you two. That's all I'm gonna say. Here, why don't you take my phone number so you can let me know what happens, okay?"

I agree, knowing full well I'm not ever going to call her.

I mean, I'm just no good on the phone. I practically have a goddamn phobia about it.

But, anyway, the woman pulls a scrap of paper out of her large, floral-patterned purse and writes her name and number down with a black permanent marker. Her name is Mary. I introduce myself and shake her plump little hand. "Good luck," she tells me, patting me on the shoulder as I start tugging at the belt to try 'n' get the dog moving. The dog doesn't move. She looks up at me confused and weak and totally scared outta her mind.

"She probably doesn't know how to walk on a leash," says Mary. "I wouldn't be surprised if she's never even been inside before. I bet she was bred for hunting out in the country somewhere and, for whatever reason, they must've abandoned her. She easily could have been living as a stray for a year or more. So it's going to take her some time to get used to, you know, normal dog things."

"Right," I tell her, bending down and lifting the poor, bony little dog in my arm—her eyes just about burstin' out of her head, she's so freaked out.

"Okay, well, thanks for your help," I say—kinda stupidly, I guess, considering I'm the one who got stuck with the damn dog. I carry her across the street and manage to toss her into the backseat of the car before turning to wave good-bye to Mary one more time. Only thing is, she's already gone—disappeared somewhere, even though that seems physically impossible.

Anyway, it doesn't matter.

I get in the car and start driving to the Humane Society, doing my best to remember where the hell the place is. In the back, the dog doesn't make a sound. Actually, she just cowers on the floor behind my seat, curled into a tight, tight little ball. My eyes catch my reflection in the rearview mirror. I try to tell myself it's not a big deal. The Humane Society will take her and get her adopted and that'll be the end of it. I mean, obviously I can't keep her myself. Not that I wouldn't want to keep her. I had dogs all my life growing up. I love dogs. Hell, I hope someday I'll be able to get one. But not now, man, there's no way. I can't be responsible for that shit. Christ, I can't even take care of myself.

Every time I come to a red light, though, I can't help but turn around and look at her. She's in a bad way, man, that's for sure. She's starving, sick, homeless, afraid. She's just like I used to be. I think back on how those friends of my family pulled me out of San Francisco when I was all strung out and homeless and stealing and turning tricks and sick and starving. They took me in off the streets like I was some damn dog—like this dog. And just like I was when they found me, she's too scared and freaked out and damaged to recognize when someone's trying to help her. But, anyway, like I said, the people at the Humane Society are gonna find her a good home, and that's gonna be the end of it. There's really no point in worrying. And there's really no point in thinkin' up names for her — even though I kind of am already. For example, Guitar Wolf would be kinda badass. But no, no. It's best just to call her "dog" for now. "Dog" is best.

When I get to the Humane Society, I have a pretty hard time getting the dog out of the back. However much I sweet-talk her and try to coax her out, she refuses to move from her little contorted ball. I glance around the parking lot quickly, but there's no one else outside.

After a couple more minutes of useless pleading with her, I finally decide just to try 'n' carry her again. I reach down awkwardly and struggle to get her free from the tight little space she's squeezed herself into. I hoist her up so she's kinda pressed against my chest, and start walking inside. Above the main entrance is a large painted mural of different animals with a circle of silhouetted children dancing around them. The phrase *Kids Love Animals* is written across the top.

I use my body to push open the swinging glass doors. My tennis shoes squeak as I walk across the wet linoleum that smells strongly of disinfectant.

The obese woman with the butch haircut sitting behind the reception counter smiles sweetly at me as I walk over.

"Hi there," she says, her accent real strong and twangy. "D'you find you that little doggy, did ya?"

"Yes, ma'm."

The dog fidgets in my arms, so I readjust her before continuing. "Yeah, uh, we found her right off Victory. I'm not sure if she's a stray or just got lost or what."

"Hmm, yup, she looks like a stray," the woman says. "I'd be real surprised if anyone's been looking for her, but I sure will check."

She wheels her tiny rolling office chair, which really doesn't seem like it should be able to support her, over to a big, blocky computer and starts click-clicking away at the keyboard with her plump, swollen fingers.

"Nope," she says after about a minute. "There ain't no dog in the computer here that fits her description. Why don't I scan her to see if she has a microchip at all?"

The woman scans the dog with what looks like a barcode scanner, but there's nothing there. She sighs and drops her shoulders and smiles.

"I'll tell you what, honey, we just ain't got no room here to take in another stray. We can't do it. The only option you really have is to take her to animal control, but if no one claims her in the next three days, well, they really can't keep her, either. You know what I mean?"

I nod. "Isn't there any other option?"

She moves her jaw around like maybe she's chewing on something, but I try not to think about what that could be.

"Would you be willing to foster her?" she finally asks. "We can put her on our website and try to get her adopted, if you'll just let her stay with you until then. Seems like she likes you already."

I glance down at the dog. Man, Sue Ellen's gonna kill me if I agree to this. But, uh, there's really no other choice, is there? I mean, I can't let 'em kill her.

"Sure," I tell her, my voice cracking a little. "Sure, I'll do that."

The woman tells me not to worry. She tells me it won't take long to find a good home for the dog. She tells me it's a great thing I'm doing. Then she scuttles off, saying she's gonna go get the vet. I guess they gotta do a physical and some kinda behavioral testing on the dog. So the two of us are left in the waiting room.

I put the dog down and try looping my belt around her neck again. I crouch down about three feet away from her, holding the end of the belt and saying in a high-pitched voice, "Come on, dog. Come on . . . come here . . . it's all right."

The dog doesn't move.

"Come on, dog. It's all right. I'm not gonna hurt you. Come on, dog. Come on, Guitar Wolf."

I say that last part just sort of joking, but then suddenly the dog wags her tail a click and walks the distance between us.

"Good dog," I say, way too enthusiastic—rubbing her long ears. "Good girl."

Walking another three feet away, I try it again.

Again she comes to me.

"Man," I say. "Guitar Wolf . . . I mean, dog, you are such a smart girl. Come on. . . ."

My hand pulls at the makeshift leash and then, amazingly—timidly—she starts walking with me. I mean, I've got her learning how to walk on a leash already. There's this feeling like endorphins flooding my brain. By the time the woman from the front and the vet come back, I'm smiling so much it's embarrassing.

On seeing the two of them, however, the dog immediately cowers behind my legs. Still, I'm able to lead her into the cold, sterile examining room, and the vet follows. At first the vet places a bowl of dog food in front of my dog. She starts eating immediately—frenzied—her eyes darting all around like maybe one of us is thinking about stealing it and she might have to take off a hand if someone so much as tries. She gulps the food down in record time and then goes on to drink a whole bowlful of water.

"Okay, now," the doctor says to me, his voice sounding very bored. "Why don't you lift her onto the table so I can take a look at her?"

I do what he tells me, and he starts poking and prodding the poor girl all over.

His first observation is that she's definitely pregnant. His second observation is that he thinks she probably has a few different kinds of worms. He pulls out a syringe and leans over to take her blood. That's when things really go wrong.

The dog starts growling deep and slow, lunging at his face very suddenly. Her lips curl back so her teeth look fucking savage as hell. Her eyes go black so they're almost glowing. Not really knowing what to do, I just grab hold of her and try 'n' keep her pinned down, and for some reason she doesn't bite me or turn on me or anything. But that doctor, man, she won't let that fucker anywhere near her. I mean, she will not back down.

The only way we can get her to finally calm down is for the

doctor to leave and let us alone. Then, immediately, she goes quiet again, even licking my cheek a couple times.

Christ.

Not surprisingly, that's the end of the Humane Society's willingness to help get her adopted. In fact, they tell me straight-out I need to have her put down. She's dangerous, they say, wild, untamable. Plus, she's pregnant. The right thing to do is to kill her.

To tell you the truth, man, I think about it. I mean, these people are professionals. And seeing her go psycho like that was pretty scary. Hell if I know how to handle some crazy-ass, vicious feral dog. But to kill her? Just like that? I don't know— I keep thinking about when I was on the streets. Maybe that's stupid, but I really was like a wild fucking dog back then. And, yeah, I definitely bit the hand that fed me a whole bunch of times. But, still, I mean, after all that, there were a few people who never gave up on me. Maybe this dog deserves someone to look after her like that. Christ, she really reminds me of myself, for some reason. Besides, there's gotta be another animal-rescue place that'll help me get her adopted. She deserves a good life, this dog. I don't know why. There's just something about her is all.

So I tell the Humane Society people to fuck off, even though they are literally screaming at me as I carry my dog outta there, telling me that I'm doing the wrong thing, that I'm being completely irresponsible.

As for me, well, all I can really do is laugh at that.

"It wouldn't be the first time," I call back, putting the dog in the front seat with me this time.

We drive off.

I look over at her, and she stares back curiously.

She stares and stares. She won't break eye contact.

I'm pretty sure I've heard that's a really bad sign.

Fuck.

Ch.27

Well, the dog hasn't turned on me or Sue Ellen yet, so I guess I'd say things are working out all right.

I managed to get her all washed down with this, like, heavy-duty flea-killer stuff, and she's starting to get used to being in the house, even if she does try to dig holes in the floor sometimes. Sue Ellen's family has taken an interest in the dog, so they help us get her an appointment with a new vet. She's this very strong, tall woman who thought to actually put a muzzle on the dog, which is totally what they should have done at the Humane Society. It also turned out that the dog is definitely not pregnant, and she's been given medicine to get rid of the hookworms and whatever that were making her stool all bloody and making her throw up all the time.

So the dog's doing good. And I finally settled on a name. See, Guitar Wolf is cool and all, but as Sue Ellen pointed out, if we're going to try to get her adopted, we need to come up with a more normal, nice-sounding name. Since I found her in Charleston, I figured she'd be well suited to a nice Southern name like Tallulah. So Tallulah she is. That is, Tallulah Guitar Wolf Jackson, because I couldn't give up on Guitar Wolf completely and Jackson is just the best last name ever. I'd say at this point Tallulah definitely knows her name pretty well, and I've been teaching her "come" in the fenced-in dog park.

Every day we walk and walk for hours, exploring all the different neighborhoods and hiking trails out by the beach. Thanks to her, I'm actually getting kinda healthy again and, well, I guess she could say the same thing about me.

It's interesting for me to watch her, 'cause in many ways I still see so much of myself in her — even if that's weird to say. I mean, like, when we're walking around the neighborhood, she is constantly scanning the ground for traces of food, often snatching up torn wrappers or chicken bones or whatever before I can stop her. When I was homeless, I used to walk around the city for hours, searching the streets and gutters for fallen money or food or drugs or cigarettes. And I would find shit — wallets, packs of cigarettes, leftovers. Hell, one time I found a barber's kit with $144 in it. But even after I got off the street, man, it was like I couldn't stop doing that shit. It had become so ingrained in me that every time I walked anywhere, I'd have my eyes fixed on the ground. Honestly, I still catch myself doing that shit sometimes.

And, yeah, with Tallulah it's like part of her knows she's safe now and she gets fed every day and whatever, but then there's this other part of her that can't let go of all the trauma she's lived through. Even now she's wary and aggressive toward most men she sees—especially big men. Christ, Russell can't go anywhere near her without her freaking out like she's about to be beaten.

But she's not. I mean, she's safe.

She's safe like I'm safe.

And she's actually building, like, a real life now—just like I am.

We keep each other safe.

Every night she comes and sleeps pressed up against me—snoring nonstop now—I guess 'cause she's finally able to really sleep, you know, without having to be afraid.

Of course, I can't keep her.

There's just no way.

First of all, I heard back from my editor about the pages I sent, and she was totally supportive. So, other than some minor revisions, it's finally all set. That is, it's going to be published. I can't fucking believe it.

And the other really awesome thing is that when I finally talked to my dad, it turns out he was able to finish his own book about his experience living with my addiction.

So the publishers want both of our books to come out around the same time, and they want us to go on this big-ass book tour thing. That'll mean we'll both have to be traveling for, like, a whole month. And since there's no way Sue Ellen would be able to take care of Tallulah, I'm gonna have to find her a permanent home before then.

Honestly, I really don't like to talk about it. I mean, it's gonna be impossible. But, whatever, I don't need to worry about that shit now. For now all I have to do is try 'n' find this six-mile trail Russell told me I needed to check out with Tallulah. Apparently, it winds along one of the inlets cutting in through the marshes. Russell says for him, coming out here is his way of going to church. We saw him last night for dinner — that's when he drew me this little map and wrote out directions. He also kicked me down about a gram of this really good weed that someone at work gave him. We smoked a good bit last night, but I'm saving it this morning till Tallulah and I get to the trail. Really, I love hiking when I'm stoned.

It's cool, you know, smoking weed feels so much better to me than drinking. Smoking weed is, like, positive and motivating for me. Plus, it won't make you so sick and desperate, like alcohol does. I mean, sure, it does set off that phenomenon of craving for me to a certain extent, but it's way less severe than anything else. Besides, it's not even around that much here, so there's no real danger of getting fucking hooked. I don't know, the day after, when I don't have any more weed, definitely sucks for sure. But I can ride it out. The important thing is, I'm not drinking and I'm not doing hard drugs. Weed's like nothing. I still consider myself sober, even though I do smoke sometimes. To me, seriously, it doesn't even count. Pot doesn't make anyone all fiendy. It just doesn't work like that.

But, anyway, yeah, I follow Russell's map to the trail entrance. There's a sort of dense, low-lying fog covering the marsh so that the tops of the trees are obscured completely, and a silvery light reflects off the gray, still water. As soon as I turn off the car, Tallulah is immediately scratching at the door and sort of half whining, half barking in excitement. I tell her "shh" and rub her ear until she kinda bites at my hand, giving me a look like "Don't you fucking touch me" and growling some to back it up. Fucking dog is a liability. But she definitely knows how to get what she wants — and I gotta respect her for that.

So I let her go on whining and scratching at the door while I take a couple of hits of the herb Russell gave me. Honestly, what they call good weed here doesn't even come close to the pot you get in California. The worst shit there is better than the best shit here — no joke. But, I mean, whatever — it still gets me high. My brain kinda clouds over, and I feel this rush of energy and weightlessness surging through my body. A warm sort of joy floods my mind. Colors and sounds become mysterious and fascinating. The world is wide open, and I watch it all unfold with the eyes of a child — everything new, exciting, beautiful, in a way I could never be aware of if I was sober. Every branch and grain of sand and insect fit together perfectly in this harmonious landscape of shared energy and molecular connections. We are all one, and nothing is a mistake. My life, the fact that I'm here right now with Tallulah — it's all exactly the way it's supposed to be. My entire existence has culminated in this moment, and I wouldn't change one thing. I'm just so grateful to be here now.

I open the car door.

Immediately Tallulah takes off down the trail, smelling frantically, chasing different scents out into the marsh, through the bramble, and then back onto the path. She barks and bays like a good hound dog should — yet she's always aware of where I am, following along with me as I walk. Occasionally she'll check in, and I'll give her water from my pack and pet her. When she's outside, she lets me pet her without being afraid at all—I guess maybe 'cause she knows she has an escape route. Anyway, I take what I can get, until she runs off again—the biggest, goofiest smile on her face you could possibly imagine.

It seems like she has a pretty good life now, and I'm so grateful to be able to give her that. Although she's totally given me the same thing. Everything is falling into place. I mean, goddamn, I'm going to have a book published. And honestly, I really gambled everything on the hope that it would happen—that I would make it happen. Dropping out of college, living the way I've lived, the one thing I had to believe in was my dream of writing a book and getting it published. Well, it's all happening now. It really feels like a miracle. And walking here, along the dusty dirt trail—tiny black crabs scattering with every step—the fog starting to break apart beneath the sun, revealing a massive metal cargo ship moving slowly up the waterway—Tallulah darting in every direction—I have to say, I feel content. My life is good. The world is good—beautiful, even. And for once I really don't wish I were someone else. I'm actually kind of cool with being me. It feels totally bizarre—but, uh, good, just the same.

For an instant I close my eyes and inhale, long and deep.

"Thank you," I whisper. "Thank you."

My eyes open.

And I scream it out.

"*Thank you!*"

Tallulah freezes in the distance and comes running back to me fast, like she thinks she's in trouble.

I tell her not to worry, that I wasn't talking to anyone.

Though I guess I could've been talking to a whole lot of people, huh?

There are tears now at the back of my eyes.

And I wonder why I'm such a pussy.

Part 3

Ch.28

So, apparently there's some couple a few hours south of here, in Jacksonville, who saw our posting of Tallulah on the Internet and have decided to adopt her. Actually, unless something goes wrong, we're planning on leaving her there with them today after we drive down.

I mean, it's not that I don't want the damn dog, because I do—obviously. It feels good taking care of another living thing—focusing on its needs and desires more than my own—trying to give it a good life—you know, the good life it deserves.

Have I been able to give that to Tallulah?

Yeah, to tell you the truth, I think I have. I think I've done a pretty all right job—way better than I would've expected. She's come a long way. And, well, I guess I have, too. I mean, she's definitely helped me as much as I've helped her.

But now it's time for her to find a permanent home—with a permanent family.

This really is for the best.

Or at least that's what I keep telling myself.

On the drive down to Jacksonville, Sue Ellen and I are pretty much quiet the whole time, and Tallulah stays in the back, curled up tight in a pathetic-looking little ball, almost as though she can sense what's about to happen.

I've never been to Florida before, so I guess that's something, but the drive is plain and ugly and depressing—miles and miles of strip malls; sick, half-dead palmetto trees; trailer parks; shapeless, colorless factory buildings; shapeless, colorless suburban tract homes. Jacksonville itself is gray and industrial and mostly empty.

As we get closer to the suburban community where the couple lives, Tallulah climbs up halfway into the front seat, balancing shakily on the center armrest. She leans her body over on mine, putting her front left paw up on my shoulder so I'm supporting a good bit of her weight. Her body trembles, and she makes these little whining, squeaking noises as she licks at my face kinda frantically. I'm driving and her breath is stank, but I don't try 'n' stop her, like I normally would.

All I do is to tell her, "I know, girl. It's okay."

I'm not sure if that's the truth or not anymore. But Sue Ellen has tears in her eyes now, too.

Fuck.

When we pull up to the house, it takes us both a good five minutes before we open our doors—securing Tallulah's leash and walking her up the redbrick front walkway.

Honestly, I think I was sort of hoping the place would be a shit-hole trailer or something, so I'd be let off the hook.

It's not, though.

I mean, it looks super nice—one those sort of '50s ranch-style single-story houses that stretch out real long on both sides—accented with fussy little flower beds and perfectly manicured grass. Palm trees line the driveway. Polished stones decorate the front entrance.

Sue Ellen's small hand reaches out to press the electronic doorbell, and almost immediately a flesh-colored blob appears blurred behind the etched, fleur-de-lis-shaped glass set into the stained-wood paneling.

The door opens—followed by a high-pitched series of shrieks and oohs and aahs.

"Isn't she precious," the rotund woman coos like her tongue's coming loose in her mouth. "Come here, baby, meet your new mama."

Tallulah pulls at her leash in the opposite direction, getting herself tangled behind my legs, but, thank God, not snarling yet.

"Sorry," I say weakly. "She has a hard time with strangers sometimes."

The woman straightens herself up, adjusting the narrow-framed glasses on her childishly sculpted Play-Doh face.

"Of course, I understand. Poor wittle doggy wog."

I bite the inside of my mouth. "Yeah, well, uh, anyway, sorry....I'm Nic and this is, uh, Sue Ellen and you must be, uh..."

"Pam," she says brightly. "I'm Pam. It's so nice to meet you both."

"It's nice to meet you, too," Sue Ellen tells her.

We all shake hands, and then Pam invites us in.

"Jock's finishing up on the grill out back, but I know he's just dying to set his eyes on little Tallulah, so if you don't mind, I'll give y'all a tour of the house after lunch. Y'all do eat meat, don't ya? I sure do hope so, though, I must say, I never know what crazy notions you kids'll take into yer heads next."

Sue Ellen fields that one. "No, don't worry, we eat meat. Ha-ha. No crazy notions here."

I put a hand on Sue Ellen's waist just to reassure her.

The inside of the house, from what I can see so far, is all very, um, precious. There're little glass trinkets and figurines all over the place, plus lots of superfluous, fragile decorations and pure-white carpets Tallulah would have no problem destroying in a matter of seconds. On the other hand, yeah, the backyard is giant. That's definitely not something I could ever give her. And even though I take her on all kinds of hikes and things, that's still not the same as having a big yard to run around in all day. Tallulah deserves a house like this. She deserves more than just a little studio apartment. She deserves someone who'll always be able to pay for her medical bills and dog treats. Hell, as it is, that Pam woman's already given Tallulah more treats in the last few minutes than I'd say I ever have in her whole god-damn life. Although, I think that might have to do with what a clever little manipulator Tallulah's turned out to be. After each treat she's received, Tallulah sits again, staring up at the woman with large, imploring, pitiful eyes.

"She won't ever stop," I say, laughing. "She'll keep eating 'em till she explodes."

The woman shakes her head. "No, no. The poor little thing's just hungry."

She gives up another treat.

I mean, what can I say? Tallulah's pimping the shit out of her right now.

Anyway, when we get out into the yard, the woman tells me I can let Tallulah off leash—so I do. No surprise the gluttonous little hound runs straight for the barbecue and the smell of cooking meat. She's actually just about to pounce on the plate of greasy, swollen hot dogs, when the seriously large man attending them, who somehow Tallulah didn't seem to notice, suddenly turns and surprises the shit out of her. Tallulah's tail tucks up tight between her legs, and she bolts off into the corner of the yard, cowering like she's just been beaten or something.

"Sorry," I say, rushing over. "She can be pretty wary of men. I mean, especially bigger men. She'll be all right, though. Come on, Tallulah," I call out.

Tallulah doesn't listen.

Then the big man takes a step toward her, and she immediately starts growling like she really means business.

"Sorry," I say again, this time directly to the man. "She's a big ol' scaredy-cat. Why don't we let her calm down for a minute? Is that okay?"

He kinda guffaws and slaps me on the back. "Aw, no problem, buddy. We understand, don't we, Pammy?"

Pammy says yes, and then the man sticks out his white, freckled hand to me, grinning and introducing himself as Jock.

I shake his hand and then he goes to shake Sue Ellen's hand and then we all know each other and everything's all good, except, of course, for Tallulah acting like some paranoid schizophrenic in the corner there.

We decide to leave her to her delusions of persecution while we all take our seats around the dining-room table—each one of us having been provided with our very own maritime-themed plastic placemat.

"You know," Pam says, through mouthfuls of potato chips, "I have to confess, the reason we decided to adopt Tallulah is because she looks exactly like the very first dog Jock and I ever had together. It's really quite something. It's like they came from the same litter, I'll tell you what. And I know you agree with me, Jock, that dog, Blue, was the best dog we ever had. He was so gentle and sweet and good-natured—not like the last dog we had. No, that was no good at all. Did the woman at the adoption agency tell y'all the story?"

Both Sue Ellen and I shake our heads.

"Well," she says, "she was a pit bull our daughter rescued down in Tampa, and of course we just couldn't say no . . . could we, Jock?"

"You couldn't!" he snorts, sitting up straighter in his chair.

She laughs sort of awkwardly at that, opening a second can of Diet Coke and gulping a good bit of it before continuing. "Now, now. That's not true. You agreed we'd give her a chance. And she really was a sweet little girl. But unfortunately, we both still work during the day, so any dog we get will have to be at home alone until a little after five each night. And while we've never had a problem with it in the past, Clementine—that's what we named her—must not've been used to being left alone, 'cause when we got home that first day . . . well . . . we . . ."

Her voice catches, and I see suddenly that her eyes have gone kinda red and glassy, like she's fighting off wanting to cry.

But it's Jock who goes ahead and completes her thought.

He shakes his head back and forth slowly. "It was like *The Texas Chainsaw Massacre* in here, that's what it was. Pammy had her four cats living here, and that dog, she got every last one. Little bits of cat was spread from one end of the house to the other. It was a darn shame."

Pam sniffles loudly, clutching her hand to her chest. "It was more than a shame, it was a tragedy. And the worse part of all was that we had to put that poor, sweet dog down. It was one of the worst days of my whole life. So you can see why adopting another dog means so much to me . . . to us."

Sue Ellen shoots a glance over my way.

"Wow," I say, really just trying to process the whole story. "That's so awful. I mean, that is so, so awful."

I pause to think for a few seconds before the question comes to me.

"But, uh, I don't understand. . . . Why'd you have to put the dog to sleep after that?"

The woman covers her face with her hands. "We had no choice," she sobs. "It was too dangerous to keep her after what happened."

I'm not sure I follow her logic on that, but thankfully I'm saved from having to respond, 'cause Tallulah is suddenly there at the sliding glass door, whining and pawing to come in.

"Oh," Pam sniffles, straightening up and making a big show out of wiping away tears that I don't think were ever really there. "Oh, heavens, just look at me. I'm so sorry. Here we are with a new doggy in the family, and I'm boo-hooing like a little girl. Why don't we let Tallulah in so she can get used to the house? Hon, you mind letting her in?"

That last bit was obviously addressed at her husband, who, in response, rises silently from his chair and goes directly to the door.

Sue Ellen kicks me under the table, but I don't have time to say anything before Jock's already got the screen pulled open and Tallulah is inside, running circles around the room with a frenzied look in her wide, glossy eyes. She pounces on the table and I yell at her to stop, and then she gets scared, so she runs and jumps onto the black, slightly purple leather sofa— spinning around several times before finally compacting herself into a tight little ball.

"Uh-oh. Uh-oh," Pam says, flustered.

Jock walks over to Tallulah in three strides, leaning directly over her.

"Tallulah, bad dog. No getting on the furniture," he sort of half yells at her.

I stand up quickly so I almost knock over my goddamn chair. "Wait," I call out. "Wait, I'll take care of it."

Jock's eyes shift back over in my direction. "No, no, it's all right. She's gonna have to learn to listen to me. I can handle it. I served four tours of duty in Vietnam. I'd like to think I can get a dog off of my couch without anybody's help."

He chuckles to himself, turning back to Tallulah.

"Honey, maybe you should let him do it," Pam tries, but Jock just snaps that he's got everything "under control."

I get myself ready all the same.

"Now," he says, kinda growling real low at her. "Tallulah, off the couch, right now."

She doesn't move. She just stays staring, staring up at him with her clouded eyes.

"Come on," he tries again. "Get off. Right now. I mean it."

His hairy hand inches closer, but still she doesn't move.

"*Tallulah!*" he suddenly yells, startling the whole lot of us. "*Off the couch! Now!*"

Tallulah doesn't like that one bit.

She lunges up at him so fast he barely has time to flinch.

Her barking is loud and vicious, and it's only by total luck that I'm able to jump and tackle her before she actually gets her teeth into him.

Of course, she yelps all over the place when I pin her down, but she doesn't try to bite me at all, so I'm able to get her leash back on and help calm her. She even finally licks my hand and I kiss the top of her head without really thinking. I mean, what can I say? She's a dog after my own heart.

But obviously I pretend to be really angry at her, and I am genuinely apologetic, and Jock and Pam try to be polite about the whole thing. I guess we're all trying to figure out how to get out of this without too much awkwardness. Sue Ellen makes some excuses for Tallulah's behavior, and we all agree that she's a dog that needs to be worked with a lot, and we theorize about how she ended up the way she is. The two of them never do actually tell us straight-out they don't want her, but we go ahead and load her back in the car anyway and say good-bye and get the hell out of there as fast as possible.

We drive in silence for a while—windows down, the cold purifying somehow. Tallulah has climbed up onto Sue Ellen's lap, and even though she's big and bony, Sue Ellen lets her stay. We're both petting her absently, and the cold is all around us.

I'm not sure how much time passes, but suddenly I look over at Sue Ellen and notice she's really crying hard. I mean, she's just crying and crying, and when I ask her what's wrong, she tells me she doesn't think she can stand letting Tallulah go to anyone else.

"No one will ever be good to her the way we are," she manages to get out through little gasps of breath. "No one will take the time to try 'n' understand her."

I glance down at the stupid fucking nutjob of a dog.

"Yeah," I say. "She's just kind of our dog, isn't she? I mean, she fits with us—and, uh, I don't think she'd really fit with anyone else."

Sue Ellen nods. "Nic, I don't mind taking care of her while you're on tour, okay? I know I said I did, but I promise you I don't. I wanna keep her, Nic. Is it okay if we keep her?"

I lean over and kiss both of them, even though I'm still driving.

"Yeah, we'll keep her," I say, focusing on the road again. "I don't think we ever had a choice."

Sue Ellen laughs at that. "No, we never did."

She reaches over and turns on the CD player.

I roll up the windows.

We all three of us drive home.

Ch.29

So, he's here, you know? Standing right next to me.

It's been such a long time, and yet, in a way, it's been no time at all. I take the warmth of his hand in mine. I put my arm around his shoulder. I lay my head against his chest. I am twenty-four years old. I am a little child. He is my dad. He's the one who raised me—the one who got me up for school in the morning, made my lunch, tied my shoes. He's the one who helped me with my homework, came to my sports games, plays, parent-teacher conferences. He's the one who was there—every day—every night—when I woke up screaming, terrified, calling out his name. He was the one.

And then, again, he was the one who was there when I came home strung out and crazy and sick and rambling. He was the one who answered my desperate phone calls. He was the one who drove me to rehab, visited me in rehab, had his stomach torn out every time I relapsed—and then relapsed again. He was the one who tried to find me, tried to help me, even when I threw the help back in his face. He was the one who didn't give up on me. He was the one who couldn't let me go.

But then what happened? It all got so tangled and frantic, and he couldn't let me figure things out on my own. He wanted to control me. He was too frightened not to. So I had to go away—show him that he didn't need to manage my life anymore—that I could do it on my own—that the words of a counselor at a rehab center weren't necessarily gospel. Because I really do believe that's how he came to feel. And it's not like I can blame him. He watched me fall and fall again. He watched me as I lived so close to dying that I barely even lived at all. He watched, powerless. He watched, waiting for some kind of answer—waiting for anything, anyone, who would promise to fix me. And that's what those rehabs promised—they promised to make me well. It was all he had to hold on to—the one hope, the one solution. Obviously he was gonna freak out when I decided to go against what the "experts" were telling me—you know, ditching out of that rehab in New Mexico and running off to the other side of the goddamn country. I totally get it. I understand. And, well, at this point, I just hope we can try 'n' put it all behind us, move forward, be friends again. 'Cause that's what we are—truly—friends. We've always been friends. And, man, it's great to be able to be here with him. It's amazing, really. I mean, I'm so thankful we're doing this together.

Being on book tour this winter is basically like the weirdest fucking thing ever. I feel like a fraud, like somehow I tricked all these people into thinking I have something to say. I feel like a fraud staying in nice hotels, ordering room service, having everything paid for when I barely even have enough money in my checking account to buy cigarettes. Professional drivers pick my dad and me up at the airport, take us to events, have complimentary bottles of water waiting for us. At bookstores people ask for our autographs. I mean, they actually want my signature. They want me to sign copies of the book that I wrote. It doesn't make sense. It's like somehow I stepped into someone else's life. It's like I'm a little kid playing dress-up — pretending to be an adult — pretending to know what the hell I'm doing when I've really got no clue at all. The concierge at the hotel calls me "sir" and "Mr. Sheff," and I just bust out laughing. It's a joke. I'm no "mister" or "sir" or whatever. All I am is a genuine, run-of-the-mill fuck up. I mean, hell, just look at me. I'm a fucking mess. I don't deserve any of this.

But, I mean, somehow I keep walking through it all. I go on photo shoots, get interviewed by magazines and newspapers, make TV and radio appearances — doing most of the big-time programs, including the Today show and Oprah and Terry Gross and, man, it's all so surreal I can't even believe it. I fly to New York. I fly to Chicago. I fly to Boston, Minneapolis, Toronto, St. Louis, Dallas, Portland, Seattle. And I'll tell you what, if I didn't have my dad here with me, I don't think I could do it. We support each other. We laugh about the craziness. We go out to movies at night when the hectic days are over. We talk about missing our respective families. We swim laps in the hotel pool. He holds my hand. I hold his. I rest my head on his shoulder. We stand at the podium together, addressing more than a thousand students from a high school in Boston somewhere.

To tell you the truth, this gig speaking at a high school scares me way more than anything else we've done so far. I'm not sure why that is, exactly. My dad has spoken first, like he almost always does, telling his own story briefly and laying the fundamental groundwork of our situation before introducing me. For the most part, I'd say the kids look skeptical. I watch them whispering to one another, rolling their eyes, goofing around. Not that I can blame them. When I was in high school, which really wasn't all that long ago, I remember being so totally annoyed anytime we had some stupid drug assembly. Mostly my friends and I would spend the whole time making fun of the speakers—picking them apart. I mean, seriously, you do not want to mess with a pack of surly teenagers. They're just about the meanest motherfuckers on the entire goddamn planet. Plus the people giving the drug talks were always such layups, you know, total squares—completely clueless. They were easy targets, and we showed no mercy, and as I look around the theater, I can tell my dad and I are getting the same goddamn treatment. Hell, in a lot of ways I feel like I'm right back in high school again, fighting desperately each day to avoid social annihilation. I can't even begin to tell you how much I hated high school. I dreaded every single minute of it. It was a nightmare. And for some stupid reason, when my dad calls me to the podium, that's actually the first thing that comes outta my mouth.

"Man," I say, voice trembling, acutely aware of the principal sitting there in the front row looking humorless. "Man, I know I probably shouldn't say this, but, uh, goddamn, am I thankful I'm not in high school anymore. I mean, high school really sucked hard."

The whole auditorium erupts in laughter and applause, and I make sure not to make eye contact with Mr. Principal Man.

"I don't know," I continue. "I'm not sure what to tell y'all, exactly. When I was in school, I sat through hundreds of stupid, you know, 'drugs are bad' assemblies, and obviously they never did a damn thing for me."

A bunch of the kids cheer at that, so I just keep talking, feeling like maybe some of them might actually be listening.

"I guess the truth is, I'm not antidrug at all. I'm not gonna stand here and tell you drugs are bad, 'cause I don't believe that. Drugs aren't bad. I mean, I'd say crystal meth and heroin and coke are all pretty gross, but it's not like they're inherently evil or anything. I was in a lot of pain, that's all. I always felt like I was some alien dropped off on this planet by mistake. I just couldn't relate to most people. I felt alone and scared and, I don't know, like a total freak or something. I think my biggest fear was that someone would see who I really was and then expose to the world the fact that I really was defective—no good—worthless, unlovable, a mistake. There was this despair in me that was just overpowering. I spent all my time waiting—either waiting for school to be over each day, or dreading having to go back. But, then again, being at home wasn't all that great, either. I guess I was waiting for something to come change my life—you know, take me away from it all. And when I was twelve years old, well, I found it. One of my friend's older brothers was a pot dealer, and so he brought some to school, and we went off into the bushes to go smoke, and it was like, yeah, instantly all that fear and self-loathing really just went away. Smoking pot was like the answer to all my problems. It felt like it was saving my life. And, I mean, I think it was . . . at least for a while."

Something catches in my throat, and I pause for a few seconds to take a drink of water. The entire audience is completely silent—staring up at me like . . . like they're fucking listening. And as I keep talking and, you know, keep telling my story, I look out into the crowd and, uh, yeah, the kids are paying attention. They're laughing and gasping, and it's just weird—I mean, they're not just blowing me off. It almost feels like some of 'em might be getting something from what I'm saying, even though I know that's probably stupid. Nothing anyone ever said to me made one bit of difference in terms of the decisions I made with my life. I was gonna do what I was gonna do, regardless. No one could've possibly changed anything for me. I had to make my own mistakes.

But, then again, there were a couple things people said that did stick with me. Not like they were gonna make me do a total one-eighty or anything, but they were still there, nonetheless—nagging at me—corroding the complex, nearly flawless infrastructure of denial and self-justification I'd constructed all around me. They fucked with my high. They held me back from losing myself so completely. Hell, they even say that about the twelve steps—something about how once you start going to meetings, you'll never be able to go back to getting high the way you used to. And it's the truth. Once I had some knowledge about alcoholism and addiction, it was impossible to go back to using all carefree and fun. The meetings and the things people told me had pierced the armor of my fantasy world. Somewhere inside I knew the truth. And, yeah, once it was there, I could never get rid of it completely. Even tweaked out of my brain, holed up in some apartment—even then a little twelve-step saying or whatever would come creeping into my consciousness, poisoning me with doubt and unwanted self-reflection. 'Cause, yeah, people definitely aren't lying when they say ignorance is bliss. The only problem is, well, in this case ignorance can kill you. And the bliss doesn't really last that long, anyway.

So, who knows, maybe these kids are hearing something that might stick with them, and maybe they aren't. Either way, they do seem fairly entertained, so at least that's something, right? They laugh at my dumb jokes and gasp at the brutal parts and stay quiet in the sad parts, and it feels good. I tell them my story, and I try not to swear, and I follow the fifteen-minute time limit as best I can.

When I finish, the crowd really applauds loud and long, and I'd say at this point I'm mostly just glad it's over. I mean, we still have, like, a ten-minute question-and-answer period left, but that's actually the part I like the most, anyway. I way prefer listening to other people's shares, rather than blabbering on about myself. So I ask the audience if they might have any questions, and surprisingly, like, twenty hands shoot up. In fact, each time someone asks a question or shares or whatever, more and more of the kids keep raising their hands and shouting things out and getting super excited about participating.

But after answering a question from a boy who asks what I

think he should say to his friend who recently started doing cocaine, I notice a young, slightly overweight girl with black ringlets raising her arm up very straight and still—crying silently, so her heavy black eyeliner is smudged and running down her sickly pale, translucent skin. Of course, I can't help but call on her. I mean, it definitely seems like there's something she wants to say real bad.

So, yeah, I call on her, and the entire auditorium goes quiet as she struggles to let her voice out.

"Th-thank you for sharing your story with us," she stammers, her still-childish voice wavering unsteadily. "It was very...uh...br-brave of you. And you...you've made me realize that I need to ask for help. I'm...I'm exactly like everything you said. I feel exactly the same way you did. You said it all perfectly. And...I...I don't know...I'm really scared. I need help. My...my mom and dad just got custody of me and my sisters back after seven years, but now they've started using meth again, and I know I'm not supposed to tell anyone, but they're really scaring me. And now I've started doing it, too... just a couple times, but, still, I had all the same feelings you had, and now I don't know what to do."

She cries hard and loud. There are a couple of her friends sitting next to her who take turns cradling her while she cries. Everyone else in the auditorium is beyond quiet.

"Man," I say stupidly into the microphone. "What you just did was so amazing and brave and totally inspirational, and I wish I could make everything better, you know? I wish I could tell you what the right thing to do is. But, I will say this, having just shared right now, like you did, is absolutely the first step. Everyone knows now. And I bet that's pretty scary, but it also means that now you'll be able to, hopefully, depend on the community here to give you the support you need—especially if you don't have that support at home. So all I can really tell you is just to keep being open about what's going on with you, and I'll totally give your principal here some contacts for professionals you might want to talk to and...and... shit, I don't know. I'm so impressed with how courageous you are. I wish more than anything I'd had that kind of bravery and insight when I was your age."

I see her nod as her friends continue to hold and rock her in their arms. The rest of us stay silent for a while—doing what? I don't know—just breathing, maybe. We are all here together, and I feel this intense closeness suddenly with every one of these kids. I mean, I have to admit, it's pretty amazing to realize that through getting honest about my own shit, I've allowed other people to maybe start doing the same thing in their own lives. It's weird. But, uh, cool, too. And being here, I do have this feeling like this could be something I truly want to do with my life, you know? Beyond writing, beyond TV shows and movie deals, it's this, right now, talking with these kids about addiction, that makes me excited about the future. I want to start working with other addicts. Hell, maybe down the road I could even open a sober living for young people or something—give back—try 'n' have some kind of impact—create something positive out of all the fucked-up shit I've done. It could happen. It totally could. At least, it's a little lovely dream to hold on to.

And I do.

I hold on to that dream.

But then one of the kids in the audience shouts out another question, and I don't even hear it 'cause I'm so lost in my head.

"I'm sorry, what?" I ask, looking over at the kinda wannabe gangsta kid standing toward the back. He takes off his Red Sox hat as if that'll make me hear any better, shouting, "What about weed? Do you smoke weed?"

My heart seems to freeze up for a second, but I recover quickly, laughing it off.

"Hey, man, I used to smoke weed, like, all day, every day, and, uh, you know, again, I wouldn't say there's anything wrong with the substance in particular. I mean, to me it's the same as drinking—I definitely don't see a difference. But the problem for me was that I started using all these different substances as a way of fixing myself. So instead of having to face any of my fears or issues or anything, I just got high. And because I was high all the time, I never actually learned how to cope with anything—I never matured—and, even still, I'm like a, no offense, but, uh, sixteen-year-old trapped in a twenty-four-year-old's body. I don't know how to have real relationships with anyone—either romantic or otherwise—and just in general I don't know how to live in the world. I can't hold a job. I've been in and out of institutions since I was eighteen. Does pot have anything to do with that? I mean, yeah, it does. I used pot—along with everything else—as an escape from reality, right? And now I barely know how to function in reality at all. It's super pathetic when you think about it. It's pathetic to need drugs to get through the day. It's embarrassing. I mean, I'm embarrassed about it. And the hell if I wanna have to keep living that way. So I choose not to today. But I can't do it on my own. I need help. And as much as I've totally fought against this idea, I am learning how to reach out and get humble and take suggestions. It's definitely a slow process, but at least I'm working in that direction. Does that make any sense at all?"

The kid kind of purses his lips, nodding his head and then smiling as he sits down.

His question is the last question.

Everyone applauds like crazy, and I spend a good long time talking to different kids who've formed a line waiting to ask me some more questions or whatever.

I try to answer as best I can and just to listen and be supportive and all, but I can't help but be distracted by this sense of guilt at my own hypocrisy, biting and scratching at my insides like a rat trying to escape its cage. Christ, I mean, I know I'm a phony—a goddamn liar. The worst part is, I completely agree with everything I told that kid. It is pathetic that I'm still smoking pot. It's pathetic that at twenty-four years old I still don't know how to face reality without getting high. All the things I love to do, I only love to do when I'm able to smoke first. I can't imagine my life without it—you know, watching movies, taking Tallulah on hikes, swimming laps at the community pool, hanging out with my friends, listening to music, drawing, any of it. I can't do it sober—I really can't. And pot's the only drug I have left. If I get rid of that, then I'll have gotten rid of everything. I'll be alone with myself. There'll be no more escape. I'll die like that. Fuck, man, it really feels that way.

But only I know the truth—the truth that back in Charleston

I have a fucking eighth of weed hidden over the refrigerator—the truth that for the past two years I haven't ever been really sober.

Nobody knows I'm straight lying my ass off.

These kids come up, one by one, telling me how great I am.

The teachers tell me the same thing.

Even the principal comes up. "Nic," he says, smiling finally. "I just wanted to tell you that in all the years I've been with this school, your talk was absolutely the most moving and, I'd say, important assembly we've ever had. Thank you so much for taking time from your busy schedule to come share with us."

I smile back at him.

I lie with my smile.

I lie with my eyes.

I lie with my words.

I am a liar.

It's not exactly news.

I've been a liar since as long as I can remember.

But standing here, right now, with all these kids actually taking time out of their lunch break to talk to me, lying doesn't really feel all that cool or clever. I mean, I used to respect good liars. I remember when Zelda and I first started hanging out, she was pressed up naked in bed with me, talking to her boyfriend on the phone, lying her ass off, while I kissed down her body at the same time. She seemed so above us all—so sophisticated and cunning. It was sexy then. I admired her for it. But then again, her lying did eventually tear us down till there was nothing left. Her lying was like an abscess spreading quickly beneath the skin. Her lying destroyed everything. And now I have a feeling that my lying is about to do the same.

Still, I don't let on.

I keep on smiling and lying and smiling.

I tell myself those familiar words, repeating them over and over in my head.

So far, so good.

So far, so good.

So far, so good.

The only problem is, well, things don't actually feel that good anymore.

The ground is coming up fast.

If I blink, I'll be there.

And my body will shatter.

And there'll be no one left to piece me back together.

Because I will have burned them all.

Ch.30

We've been traveling for over a month now, but as of today, well, it's finally over. It seems fitting, somehow, that the last city on our tour is San Francisco, the place where this all kinda started in the first place.

Of course, I'd like to say that I've returned here feeling triumphant — you know, having beaten the odds or whatever — getting a book published, being interviewed by NPR, appearing on live local news, having my meals and taxis and everything paid for. It's all pretty crazy. I mean, the last time I was here, I was eating out of garbage cans, breaking into people's houses. Now I have a swank hotel in Union Square where I can order room service and the people here call me "sir" and "mister."

But even more incredible than that is the fact that I haven't actually had to sleep at the hotel at all because my dad and stepmom and little brother and sister all decided they felt comfortable enough to let me stay at their house instead. That's really the biggest miracle of all. There was a time when I thought I'd never even see any of them again, let alone be allowed back in their home. So, yeah, being here, well, it is a triumph in a lot of ways. But for some reason I still don't feel all that triumphant. If anything, it's like I'm just being reminded again and again of all the fucked-up shit I put my family through. There are ghosts haunting every corner of this house. I shudder from remembering. And I know that as much as they all smile and tell me everything's all right, my family will never truly forgive me. I mean, how could they? My little brother and sister were given this totally perfect-seeming, protected childhood. Their parents stayed together. There was no fighting or belittling or weird sexual shit or anything. They were loved and encouraged and supported, no matter who they were or what they did. Everything seemed absolutely idyllic—and it would have been, too, if it weren't for me. I exposed them to all this terror and took their parents away from them and robbed them of the childhood they were supposed to have.

Although it's not like I ruined them or anything. I mean, they're totally not ruined. They both turned out uniquely wonderful and kind and sensitive and brilliant and, being here, I couldn't be prouder of them. We all play music together and draw together and take hikes out at the beach with their dog, Charles Wallace—who definitely makes me miss Tallulah. They tell me about school and their friends and their own feelings of isolation and uncertainty. They are beautiful, truly, and I'm so grateful to have them back in my life—in spite of the guilt I still feel. And, I don't know, being with them, it does give me hope that maybe I haven't fucked all this up beyond repair.

After all, I am here, aren't I? Lying curled in my sister's tiny bed, staring up at the drawings and paintings and collections of images torn from magazines taped on the wall above me.

It's early morning—my last day—the light gray and oddly bright through the slatted window.

The alarm on my phone goes off a second time, and I force myself to get up, supporting my weight on a wooden chest of drawers piled high with little sculptures and stones and dried flowers and hand-sewn dolls my sister made herself. I steady myself. A heavy, weighted sadness makes my arms and legs ache.

I don't want to leave.

I want to be part of this.

I want to belong.

I want to be my little brother and sister's real brother.

I want to be their age.

I don't want to have to go back to my own life.

I want to stay right here.

But I can't. I never could. I was always on the outside looking in, and that's never gonna change, so fuck it, right? I get dressed and walk out onto the heated concrete floor.

I make coffee and toast with jam and butter.

None of it matters.

I'm just fine.

It'll be all right.

I remind myself that there's an eighth of pretty decent weed stashed behind the refrigerator for me back in Charleston, so at least I have that. I mean, that's one thing I can rely on—one thing that's never let me down.

So I drink my coffee down fast.

The town car my publisher sent to drive me to the airport is already waiting outside and I feel bad, you know, holding 'em up.

I eat the toast and go to collect my things, just trying not to feel anything at this point.

I press the palm of my hand against the cold window.

I can't feel anything but cold.

There's nothing else there.

I grab my bag and hoist it onto my shoulder.

I'm ready to leave now.

But then I hear the door to my parents' room creak open, and my little sister comes walking softly up the stairs, followed by my dad. Her eyes swallow me up, absorbing everything and missing nothing. I give her a hug, and she hugs me back.

"It was really good to see you," I tell her.

She lets out a little noise like a laugh and nods. She hugs me again.

And then my dad tells me good-bye, and the sun is starting to burn through the thinning gray sky as I carry my bag out to the car.

I still feel nothing but the cold.

And everything is still.

Driving through the winding, twisted roads, there is nothing but stillness.

This past month has been so full and crazy.

But now I'm still.

If it wasn't for Tallulah and that eighth waiting for me, shit, man, I might just ask the driver to stop the car in the TL and never come back. That is the sort of comforting thing about San Francisco. It's the one city in the country where you can pretty much find any drug you want within ten minutes of looking for it. I don't know why that makes me feel so, you know, at home, or whatever.

Anyway, it doesn't matter. I don't tell the driver to stop. I go on to the airport and check my bag and wait to go through security and blah-blah-blah—take out my laptop, remove my shoes, make sure to show the security guy my stupid boarding pass.

It's the same everywhere.

Everywhere's the same.

I wander along the faded carpet until I come to my gate. The plane to Atlanta, my connecting city, isn't boarding for another twenty minutes or so. I go over to the magazine store and buy some flavored fruit drink thing, and then I head back—lying down right there on the ground next to the big, impossibly thick windows looking out onto the runway. I close my eyes and try to maybe sleep a little.

I'm not sure how much time passes.

I stay lying like that for a good long while.

Maybe I even fall asleep for a minute.

But then something jerks me awake very suddenly, and I open my eyes to see this girl staring straight down at me.

I sit up a little, trying to get some kind of read on her.

I'd guess she's probably around my age, with black hair cut

sort of jagged around her face and then hanging down long in back. She's small, with sharp, angular features and blue crystal eyes that shine bright. She wears a simple black cotton dress cut short to reveal sun-browned legs and burned shoulders.

"Hey," she says, laughing, her voice coming out reckless.

"Hey," I answer back—sort of startled or confused or something.

She leans in closer, still smiling, her eyes shimmering under the fluorescent light overhead.

"I'm sorry," she sort of giggles. "I don't know why, but I just had to come talk to you."

"Um," I say, sitting up a little more. "That's okay."

There's something very beautiful about her—pixieish—like she could vanish at any moment.

She drops down next to me, her legs pressed together, rocking back and forth, still giggling a little. She offers me a cashew.

I don't take it.

There's what feels like a very long silence before I think to offer her some of my fruit juice drink.

She laughs at that but then goes ahead and tries it, spilling some of the pink liquid on her wool sweater.

She says she doesn't like it very much.

I can't help but laugh along with her at that.

"So, uh, what'd you wanna talk to me about?" I ask, taking the bottle back from her and accidentally touching my hand against hers. The feel of her skin is very soft. A crackling of electricity surges through my head.

Her eyes stay focused on mine.

"I don't know," she says, not blinking or anything. "I felt like I had to. You're a great communicator. You have this power in you that is like nothing I've ever seen. You're going to do great things with your life. You're going to help so many people."

I laugh another laugh until I realize she's being serious.

That *Twilight Zone* music plays in my head, and I start looking around, not really focusing on anything, suddenly thinking I better find a way outta this.

"Come on," I tell her, smiling to try 'n' make a joke out of it. "What are you talking about? You don't even know me. I gotta say, you're sounding a little crazy."

She smiles big at that.

"Right? I know. It is totally crazy. But I just feel this, like, energy coming out of you. Are you an artist? Or, no, a writer. Isn't that it?"

I swallow something down in my throat. "Yeah," I say. "Well, I guess I am. Did you, uh, see me on TV or something?"

Her eyes just won't let go of mine.

"No, wow, you've been on TV? That's so cool. No I, uh, had a feeling I needed to come talk to you is all. What kind of stuff do you write?"

I can't help but look away, even though all the tension in my body seems to have drained out all at once. It's a feeling like giving in—like being wrapped in a thick comforter, finally letting sleep overtake me after years of restless wandering. I feel disarmed, wonderfully helpless. I tell her about my book and what's been going on with me. It's like the words just keep coming out before I can stop them. I know that's a cliché or whatever, but really, I mean, that's the way it is.

Anyway, when I'm done with my stupid monologue, I finally give her a chance to say something, and she goes on to tell me that she's leaving on this sort of mission thing to Nicaragua with a bunch of kids from her school—a ministry program out of northern California. They're going to pray over people there and shrink tumors and restore eyesight to the blind and hearing to the deaf and all that faith-healing bullshit. She's gonna bring God to them. She says all this to me super casually—like it's just assumed, or whatever.

And then she asks, you know, real simple-like, if she can pray over me.

I laugh.

It's all so totally ridiculous.

I mean, I figure, why the hell not?

It can't hurt.

Plus, she's beautiful, like I said.

So I tell her, "Sure."

Now, look, I've read stuff about the power of suggestion and mind control and whatever. After being involved in a very sort of extremist sect of a twelve-step program when I was younger, I'd become fascinated with the way desperate people are picked up by these groups, exploited and manipulated, and then tricked into having so-called religious experiences where they feel something they imagine to be God.

But, I mean, I don't really believe in any of that shit—I mean, not really.

Dostoyevsky wrote that man can find meaning wherever he looks for it. We can make any situation into whatever it is we desire it to be.

Still, you know, the thing is, with this girl, I really don't want the situation to be anything.

At least, I don't think I do.

So the girl prays over me.

I don't close my eyes. I just stare, sort of out of focus, at the ugly, frayed carpeting.

She puts her hand on my shoulder and begins to speak out loud—asking God to be with us—to show us his heart for us, whatever that means.

And then this crazy rush of energy comes like an electrical storm running through me. My breathing comes on me in great gasps, and I feel like the two of us are just floating here—her and me—me and her. It's like the world has faded out, leaving only her, this girl, ripped wide open, transparent, with light and energy and the most beautiful, shimmering voice speaking out of her core to me. I feel love and awe for her like I've never experienced in my whole life.

When I look up into the pale blue of her eyes, she seems almost as shocked as I am. My hands tremble.

"Do you feel that?" I ask, stupidly, I guess.

She nods, speechless, staring into my eyes. I swear it's everything I can do not to lean over and just kiss her mouth or hold her pressed against me.

We both just radiate out to each other, and I feel her all over me—like her skin is covering mine, and I know in that instant, I know that I love her. I can't help it. She's like the most beautiful thing I've ever seen, or felt, or been in the goddamn presence of. We move closer and closer together. There are tears burning my eyes.

I mean, what the fuck is happening?

I almost can't take it—the intensity is cutting into the very center of me.

I gasp, feeling her warmth and the pressure of her hand on me.

And then, suddenly, she jerks away.

Someone's calling her.

"Fallon, Fallon, it's time to go."

She looks shaken, and then she turns to face me again, and we both just start laughing and laughing so uncontrollably—like little children.

There's really nothing I can do.

Just sort of instinctively, I reach into my bag, handing over a copy of my book—the last one I have.

"Look," I say, "I wrote this. I mean, this is my life. You don't have to read it or anything. But, uh, I feel like I have to give it to you."

And then I write my e-mail address on the front page, only I can barely make it legible—my hands are shaking so god-damn badly.

"Hey," I tell her, my voice shaking along with my hands. "Write me if you want. I'm Nic, by the way."

Her eyes shine. "I'm Fallon."

She sprints away, obscured by the crowd.

I can't even watch her leave.

When I take my seat on the airplane, I fall instantly into this deep, almost delirious, sleep. I dream of Fallon. She is inside me. She is with me the entire flight.

I have to hurry to make my connecting plane to Charleston,

so I run across the airport without checking to see if she was connecting through the same airport.

But she is with me.

I can't shake her.

I don't even try.

Ch.31

I'd actually forgotten about the summer internship Sue Ellen applied for—mostly because I never really thought she had a shot at being selected for it. I mean, the woman she was trying to get the internship with is this super big-time artist—and really is one of Sue Ellen's idols and major influences. The woman's studio is in LA, of all places, and, uh, yeah, like I said, Sue Ellen kind of just applied on a whim, you know? Like, why the hell not?

But she got it. She actually got it.

Christ, it's practically her dream job.

In some ways I still can't believe it—and I don't think Sue Ellen can, either. I'd been back in Charleston only, like, three days when she got the phone call from the artist's assistant saying they wanted Sue Ellen out in LA by the following Monday.

So, uh, yeah we've basically been driving for three days straight across the whole damn country.

Thankfully, Sue Ellen's mom was able to rent us a little apartment in Mar Vista that allows dogs, since, of course, we brought Tallulah along. The whole internship is supposed to last three months, so it really is like we're moving here for a while.

Honestly, everything happened so fast and crazy I haven't had a lot of time to process coming back to LA and all. Plus, I pretty much drove the whole way myself, so I had to stay good and stoned as much as possible—which was, more or less, the entire time.

But now we're here. I mean, trying to set shit up as best we can in our new, temporary, tin can–sized apartment kind of near the beach in Mar Vista.

So far everything has just been bleeding out like ink running down wet paper—the hot summer drive, the dingy motel rooms, the rest stops and diners and whatever else. But now, back in Los Angeles, the blur of the road has transformed into a hyperfocused, high-definition reality. And I remember everything. I mean, besides the last year and a half in Charleston, I've basically been living here in LA since I was about nineteen or twenty—so that's, like, five years. Not to mention coming here when I was little to visit my mom over the summer and for holidays and whatever. I know this city—the back roads and secret little parks and cafés and theaters—all the places Zelda and I went together and all the places that remind me of her.

Because that's what this city really means to me. Zelda. She's still with me. Despite all this time with Sue Ellen. Despite that weird faith-healing, religious cult girl. Zelda is my one, you know? She always will be. And by some totally random coincidence, well, she just happened to have e-mailed me. I mean, I haven't heard from her in two years and now she's written me, asking where I am, telling me she's back in detox at a place called Las Encinas. She gets out in a week. I wrote to her that I'm here in LA, and now she wants to meet. It's all so random — or maybe not random at all. That cult girl would say otherwise. 'Cause, uh, yeah, she's been writing me, too. So I have two big-ass secrets I'm keeping from Sue Ellen. And I'm not sure why this is all happening right now.

In terms of Zelda, well, it's pretty obvious nothing's gonna come out of our seeing each other. I mean, as much as I'd want us to be together again like we were, I recognize that the way we were was pretty fucked up. And it doesn't seem possible to build something brand-new together after everything that's happened. I'd say too much damage's been done on both sides. But still, thinking about her, I feel this, like, racing crazy energy inside me, making my heart beat fast, like I'm on speed or something. Actually, I'd say that's pretty much the way I've been feeling in general. And, you know, while I do get like this sometimes — kind of hyped up and frantic inside, so I can't sleep at night and I just have to, like, go, go, go constantly — for some reason right now it feels like a hundred times worse.

I mean, like I said, not only am I talking to Zelda again but I've also been talking to that religious girl a whole lot — you know, more 'n' more every day.

At first it was just e-mails — the two of us writing back and forth. She said she'd been thinking about me the whole time she was in Nicaragua, and she'd finished my book, and she wrote me all about her time doing all that faith-healing stuff in the little villages there. Her writing was so effortless and whatever. It was like I could feel her with me through her words.

I learned about her childhood.

I learned about her life, you know, just day to day.

And the more I've learned, I mean, fuck, the more I've come to care about her. There's something so mysterious and seductive behind every word she writes to me.

In terms of all the crazy religious stuff—well, somehow I've managed to pretty much dismiss all that. I guess I've always been pretty good at compartmentalizing. Her religious babble is filed away in a place where it will be lost and forgotten. My head just discounts it all, somehow. I know there's nothing to it, and I'm not gonna hold that against her. The whole story is too perfect—her approaching me in the airport—the crazy, visceral attraction we both had for each other instantly. I can't just abandon it over a few e-mail references to Holy Ghost power or whatever.

Anyway, it was only a couple days ago that she gave me her phone number. After all we'd been through, it seemed sort of stupid that I was so nervous to call her. Maybe part of me was terrified that our connection wouldn't really exist if we were actually talking to each other.

Maybe part of me was terrified that it still would.

But her voice came through to me like the sweetest, most calming, positive, alive, beautiful, hopeful thing I'd ever heard.

It filled my whole body with heat and tingling and this intense fucking longing.

And then, on the phone, our voices echoing back and forth, I could suddenly feel her presence there next to me. She giggled and breathed, and I breathed, and we breathed together. And we had this love going back and forth. And it made no sense. And I couldn't explain it. And it scared the shit outta me. But it was. I mean, it was as real as anything.

Or, at least, that's how it felt.

And feels.

Now, of course, I can't talk about this shit with anyone. I mean, I know how fucked up this is — how crazy I'm acting — and what a shit I'm being to Sue Ellen. But it's almost as if I'm being controlled by some overpowering force outside myself — like invisible strings are manipulating my every thought and movement. There's a voice, something living in my head, commanding me in ways I still don't fully understand.

I mean, come on, how could this all be a coincidence? How could this just be some accident — some random whatever?

It can't be. There's no way. My book comes out, Sue Ellen gets this internship, we come to LA, Zelda contacts me, I meet this girl. Everything's working out exactly perfectly. It's all coming together. Life is beautiful. I feel beautiful.

Tallulah and I take a walk around Venice. She's getting better about not trying to bite everyone we pass. I've actually been making an effort to walk her through the most crowded areas, like down off the bike path where all the merchants and head shops are set up, walking her through the mass of tourists and street kids and performers and whoever, trying to get her used to being around people. We walk together for hours — through the day and the night and the day again.

I can't sleep anymore.

I don't need to sleep.

I walk with Tallulah.

And I talk on the phone. I talk to Fallon. All day and all night and all day again. Sue Ellen doesn't know.

I'm out walking with Tallulah.

I dial her number.

She answers on the third ring, her voice coming through sweet and beautiful. Lovely.

"I missed you," she says. "I know that's crazy, but I missed you. I want you to come be here with me. I want to just lie down next to you, that's all — just to be in your presence."

"I know," I say, softly — walking without sight or touch or hearing — that is, other than her gentle voice — her breathing. "I want to be with you, too. It feels like I'm existing in this in-between place — like both of our souls have left our bodies and have met together somewhere in the middle. It's like I'm not here at all anymore. You know what I mean?"

She giggles. "Yeah."

We go on talking like that — her pleading with me to come be with her.

"You'd love it up here," she says in a whisper. "This place will change your whole life. You'll come to know how big God's heart is for you. He loves you so much. He loves us both so much. That's why he's brought us together. That's why he's shown himself to us. He wants you to come find him here. I know that's what he wants. He is speaking to you. He has chosen you to do his work for him. But first you must come here to learn how to open yourself up to his light and his grace. They can teach you how to best serve God here. They can teach you how to interpret his word. And then you'll be able to go out into the world and accomplish everything that I know you're capable of."

"No," I say slowly, my eyes squinting to block out the setting sun.

For the first time I'm suddenly aware that it's almost night, so I should be getting back soon. But, still, I keep talking, pulling Tallulah away from a McDonald's wrapper she's busy licking off the sidewalk.

"No," I continue, my voice sounding oddly foreign. "No, I don't want to go out into the world. I just want to be with you."

She giggles again. "Well, I'll be with you of course, silly. I'll go anywhere with you."

I smile.

"I feel so much love for you," I tell her.

She answers without pausing or anything. "I feel so much love for you, too, silly."

We go on talking a little while as the sun falls lower and lower into the ocean, oranges and pinks and purples blossoming in rows like flower beds sprawling across the horizon.

I can see the world now.

It is coming through bright and sharp and clear.

It is a gift—all of it.

"Of course I'll come up," I tell her. "I'll rent a car and just say I'm going to go visit my family in San Francisco. I'll come this weekend. It'll be perfect. You'll be able to meet Tallulah."

She laughs/giggles/sighs.

"Yes, okay, perfect. I'll get someone to cover my shift on Sunday, and I can take you up to Mount Shasta with your dog. It'll be so beautiful."

I feel her body against mine.

We breathe together.

We go on talking about our plans.

We go on talking until the sun has disappeared over the water, and the fading glow is cold and colorless.

We could go on like this all night.

But then someone's calling my name, and I turn sort of instinctively, my stomach lurching into my throat like I've just been caught.

I look kind of frantically all around me.

"Nic, man...Nic Sheff, hey, man, where the hell you been?"

He's standing right in front of me now.

I breathe all the tightness out of me. I mean, it's no big deal. It's just John, this pot dealer/musician guy I haven't seen since I was dating Zelda.

"Hey, Fallon," I whisper into the phone. "Let me call you back, okay? I just ran into this old friend of mine."

I hang up, and then John gives me a kind of handshake-palm slap-finger snap thing.

"What's up, man?" he says, sounding as much like a surfer-stoner as ever. "You haven't been around in years. Where you been hiding, man, Reseda?"

I laugh, studying his sun-creased face and scraggly blond

beard and the large straw hat pulled down over his eyes. Honestly, I was never really that close with him or anything, but he definitely had a hookup for some of the best weed I'd ever had.

We talk shit for a couple minutes before I hint at the real reason I'm excited to have run into him.

He smiles real big when he's talking about herb. His bleached white teeth sparkle in the fading light.

"Ah, man, hell yeah, I can help you out. I get my shit from the dispensary now. Check it out, blueberry and mango, shit's far-out."

From his bag he pulls out two jars labeled like prescription bottles, handing 'em over to me one at a time.

"Smell 'em," he says.

He doesn't have to ask me twice.

"Man," I tell him, "that's crazy. It totally smells like blueberries."

And that's the truth, it totally does. The white crystals look like stardust sprinkled across the deep green and purple buds.

The other jar smells like mango.

And the shit looks so good. I mean, like it's not even comparable to that nasty-ass dirt weed I was getting in South Carolina.

"Hell, I'll take 'em both," I say. "You wanna come with me to an ATM?"

He agrees, and so we walk over there together, Tallulah growling at him whenever he tries to get too close to her.

I light a cigarette and hand one to John, not really listening to his stories about everything that's been going on with him.

Mostly I just keep thinking about how perfect it all is.

I mean, God is so good, right?

Mango and blueberry weed.

This beautiful, spiritual girl waiting for me up in Redding.

My life unfolding perfectly in front of me.

"Thank you, God," I whisper aloud. "Thank you so much."

John smiles back at me.

"That's right, man, that's right. It's about time you figured that shit out."

I smile back.

It's a good fucking life, for sure.

Ch.32

Zelda's text message told me to meet her at, as she jokingly put it, "the scene of the crime"—the Barnes & Noble on Westwood Boulevard where I used to come see her many, many years ago when we first met, the two of us hanging out after her outpatient group that was just around the corner. There's something that cuts deep into me about the way she said that. I guess it just reminded me of how goddamn clever and funny she is. I'd forgotten that. I mean, there was obviously a reason I fell so hard for her in the first place. And despite what the therapists and counselors tried to brainwash me into believing, I fell for her because of the person that she is—not 'cause of all the celebrity bullshit or whatever. Hell, I even remember the exact moment we knew we were in love with each other. We went to Point Dume Beach together. I went swimming, and we talked and talked and talked. That's the day she first told me she loved me. Of course, it was the same for me. I was in love with her because of who she is. Everything didn't get crazy till a long time after that.

Anyway, it's not like I had the slightest clue what I was doing. I was twenty-one years old. She was in her mid-thirties. There were a million things working against us being together. The fact that there actually was a time when we managed to make it work is a miracle—before we started using together—back when we spent the days and nights watching movies and making love and never leaving the queen-size bed in her little studio apartment.

Being with Sue Ellen was never like that. And as much as I want it to be with Fallon, well, I can see now that it doesn't even come close. Call me crazy or fucked up or whatever, but when I saw Zelda today, even after all the years that've gone by, the enchantment Fallon had been holding over me was gone in an instant. All that bullshit about God's plan for me and whatever. I realized right then it was all a lie—a lie I'd been telling myself because I wanted so badly for it to be true.

But it wasn't true—it isn't true.

There is no God.

It is all a fantasy—just like that love I thought I had with Fallon.

Zelda has shown me the truth without even meaning to.

Christ, man, I could never be with a girl like Fallon. I mean, not that there's anything wrong with her, but we're just completely opposite. Maybe I wish I was more like her. Maybe I wish I was positive and full of faith and could get so much pleasure out of such simple things.

But I'm not like her.

I'm like Zelda.

That's the truth of it.

Thank God the two of us met up today, 'cause I was about to make a big-ass mistake.

But it's over now. I swear it is.

Zelda came up behind me while I was ordering a coffee and grabbed me by the waist and said, "How weird is this, right? I recognized your voice from all the way downstairs."

I turned and hugged her frail body against mine for a long, long time.

And now here we are, sitting together on the outside patio, where we've sat together a hundred times before.

She looks older. I mean, I hate to say that, but it's true. She looks older and more scarred and lined, and she's super thin and sickly. Her green eyes are faded. Her upper lip is bruised from where she obviously must've just gotten Restylane injections or something—which is particularly sad, considering she got out of rehab yesterday.

But, of course, as always, her clothes are super cool, and she's got the newest iPhone, and she tells me about her BMW she's got parked in the garage. She shows me photos on her phone of different parties and things she's been going to and, of course, all these goddamn celebrities just happen to be making cameos in, like, every shot.

It's pathetic, really—pathetic and sad.

"I'll tell you what, Nic, I spent the last two months before going into treatment smoking meth with a bunch of drag queens downtown and, man, smoking that shit is such a better call for me than shooting it. Remember how fucking nutter butter I used to get—thinking you were hiding drugs all over the apartment and everything?"

I put my hand on her back, feeling the bones all sticking out there.

"Yeah," I say quietly. "Yeah, I remember."

She hangs her head down. "Nic, I really am so sorry about everything. I don't know how I can ask you to ever forgive me."

"Nah, come on, girl," I tell her. "You don't need to apologize. I mean, I'm sorry, too. We were both really fucked up is all."

"Yeah, but we were so much in love, too."

"We were in love," I say. "Hell, I've never stopped loving you."

I hold her tight against me, inhaling the smell of her.

"I love you, too," she tells me. "Even after all this time."

I breathe.

This is my future.

This is my life.

I can't believe she's here with me.

But she is.

And this is all I've ever wanted.

When I think about Fallon, I just wanna laugh at myself.

Zelda is my one. I've always known that.

"Do you wanna try this again?" I ask her. "We can do it right this time—I know we can."

She turns to me and smiles—leaning forward—kissing my hot forehead.

"Oh, honey, I don't know," she says, resting her chin on my shoulder. "This is all happening so fast. But, uh, I definitely think we should see each other again. And then, well, whatever happens will happen, right?"

I touch her neck gently, carefully, 'cause I remember how sensitive she is about that, considering her mom hung herself and everything. My fingers just barely caressing the line of her jugular. "Right," I tell her. "Right, that's right."

She pulls herself up to standing and then leans against the glass floor-to-ceiling window of the bookstore café—her breath coming out all raspy, so she has to get her inhaler out of her expensive-looking leather bag. I watch her sucking in the Albuterol, or whatever it is—laughing at herself for being such a dork.

"You look so fucking beautiful," I tell her.

She just laughs. "You're the beautiful one, my beauty. Hey, remember this." She pulls up her sleeve and shows me the tattoo she designed when we were together. I have the exact matching one on the same exact spot on my arm. It's pretty weird, I mean, to see it there on her like that.

"Look," I say. "Don't worry. Everything's gonna be all right. I'm gonna make everything all right."

Her eyes narrow. "Yeah, well, I hope so."

She squeezes my hand in hers.

And we go on and walk out of there together.

When I get back to our little apartment in Mar Vista, Tallulah just about licks my face off, she's so excited to see me. I put some water on to boil and listen to Dylan and load up a bowl of the superstrong blueberry chronic and smoke till my brain feels like it's been separated from my body. Honestly, since I met up with that John guy again, I don't think I've let myself get sober even once. As soon as I wake up, I make coffee and go smoke, and then I just keep smoking throughout the rest of the day. It's really, like, my lifeline right now. It's keeping me together. It's making all this possible.

I mean, can you believe it? Zelda and I might actually be together again.

It's what I've been fantasizing about for the last two years.

And now it's really happening.

I make tea and listen to music and try to just kinda sort everything out, you know.

I'm going to have to tell Fallon. I'm going to have to break it off.

And Sue Ellen — well, shit, man, I don't even know what to do about that.

So I guess for now I just won't do anything.

I put Tallulah's leash on and get ready to take her out.

I smoke another bowl.

That's the only answer I will ever need.

Ch.33

When I tell Fallon I'm not gonna be able to come see her and I probably need to cut off contact for a while, her reaction is surprisingly un-Christian. She tells me I'm an asshole and then hangs up. I can't say I blame her—or disagree at all.

I am an asshole.

And I feel so out of control.

This energy surging through me makes my hands tremble and my mind unfocused. I check my phone compulsively.

Zelda hasn't called or texted or anything. We were talking for a while there—building something, I thought—but then she disappeared completely. I've written and called and written, and still I haven't heard one thing back from her. I'm really getting kinda worried. I mean, as hot and cold as she can be, there's something that feels very wrong about this—like something serious must have happened. But, for whatever reason, she doesn't feel comfortable telling me about it, so I'm left just guessing, you know? Checking my phone every thirty seconds—making these lists in my head—repeating them over and over:

Wake up.

Make coffee.

Smoke a bowl.

Take Tallulah up to Los Liones Canyon—hike for a couple hours.

Come home.

Shower.

Eat cereal.

Smoke more.

Go get coffee and write.

Call my dad.

Call my mom.

Call John.

Go pick up more herb.

Go home.

Smoke more.

Take Tallulah to the dog park.

Come home.

Meet Sue Ellen.

Fight with her.

Do anything and everything to keep from thinking about Zelda.

I won't let her hurt me again. I'll shut her out completely. I mean, hell, at least this time I've got this chronic to smoke to make it all disappear. Because it does. Getting high takes it away. Getting high makes me strong. Getting high makes me not care.

So I just try 'n' stay high forever. 'Cause that's all I've got left. Even if I really do know it's only a matter of time till it stops working for me again—just like before.

And the time before that.

And the time before that.

And the time before that, too.

About Sue Ellen, well, I'm not sure if it's that she can sense me pulling away or what, but she keeps really tearing into me about every little thing. It's like she gets back from her internship, where they've been treating her like shit all day, and she doesn't know how to not take all her pent-up rage out on me.

Tonight, for some reason, she's been going on and on about my mom to the point that I actually get kinda angry with her. And, I mean, that really is saying something, 'cause I'm usually the first one to admit my mom's got, uh, issues. But, Christ, Sue Ellen just won't quit.

See, the thing is, after, like, twenty years of being married to this terrible man who I watched emotionally torture her, she finally got up the courage to leave him a couple months ago, and now she's living on her own in a house on the Venice Canals. Obviously, it's super weird to have my mom be suddenly single and free of that asshole I've been wanting her to get away from since I was little. I mean, it's frustrating that it's happening now, after all those years of me visiting my mom and stepdad only to be told over and over what a "weak, faggot" piece of shit I was by him. And not that my mom was a total angel or anything, either. Hell, it takes two, right? But I'm still proud of her for finding the strength to step out on her own, even if it did take more than two decades.

Honestly, I'm not totally sure why Sue Ellen is going on and on about my mom right now. I think maybe she's got it in her head that because I've been hanging out with my mom a lot more now that she's in this transitional stage and pretty lonely, somehow it's my mom who's been making me pull away from Sue Ellen.

"Ugh, she's just a sick woman," Sue Ellen says, her fists all clenched. "And you, you're just spineless. I mean, come on, she left you when you were practically a baby, and now you're gonna be all buddy-buddy with her. Uh-uh . . . that's not okay. I won't stand for it. She's vain and shallow and manipulative, and I don't want you seeing her anymore."

I light a cigarette and try to focus on the road, since we're driving up the PCH and it's dark and I'm not totally sure where we're going, exactly.

"Sue Ellen, man, you don't know what you're talking about. And, anyway, I don't know what makes you so holier than thou — we all make mistakes. Hell, if no one ever let me live down my past, there wouldn't be one goddamn person left who'd even speak to me. Besides, as flawed as she is, I respect what she's doing. It takes a lot of courage to get out of a bad relationship — especially when it's a whole lot safer to just keep putting up with it. And, I don't know, man, I kinda feel like I need to be there for her right now. Is that so wrong?"

She stamps her foot against the floor mat in front of her.

"Yes, it's wrong," she actually screams. "It's wrong because you're too much of a pussy to stand up for yourself. You're pathetic. You let everyone treat you like shit and you just keep being so polite and nice and you never say 'no' and it makes me sick. Ugh, you make me sick. Your mom doesn't deserve your attention. None of these awful people in your life deserve your attention. But you keep bending over backward for everyone and rolling over and never wanting to rock the boat. It's gross, Nic, it's really gross. And here we are going to this stupid party just so you can be Mr. Nice Guy to everyone and make everyone else happy and never once think about what would be best for you. I mean, why are we going to this party, anyway? Why isn't just being with me enough for you anymore? You never used to go out to parties. But now suddenly we come to LA and you turn into this little lapdog going around trying to please everyone. It's disgusting."

I drag long on my cigarette and then laugh.

I turn right up Topanga Canyon.

"Sue Ellen, man, I wanted to come to this party 'cause I thought it would be fun, that's all. Honestly, I thought you'd think it was fun, too. I mean, come on, they're having a full-moon séance in the woods. It's gonna be funny. This doesn't have anything to do with anything but that. I don't know why I'm not allowed to have a life just 'cause I'm dating you. Life's too short to waste it watching TV and sitting at home. These are the kinds of experiences we'll remember forever. You can't keep me caged up like your little pet hamster. You can't hold on to me like that. And, anyway, the reason I'm nice to people is because I actually really do like them. I like being around them. It's fun for me and, you know, actually fulfilling. That doesn't mean I don't love you or care about you. I mean, I want to do this stuff with you. But you can just be so negative and judgmental all the time, it's hard including you. That's why I go do things without you. But I'm really happy you came along tonight. Come on, let's not ruin it. Let's just try 'n' relax and have fun. The only way we're gonna make it is if we allow each other to build separate lives and, you know, share them together. I want to share this with you. Can't you just be a little open-minded right now?"

Her fingers have started twirling around in her hair, which is a bad sign.

She clenches her jaw tight when she speaks. "You're a jerk, Nic."

I honestly can't tell whether she's being rational or not. I mean, I know I have been a jerk to her. But, I don't know, I feel like I have been trying to make things better.

She just doesn't make sense is all. She gets her mind set on an idea, and then nothing I say or do can even begin to bring her back. I'm wasting my time trying to talk to her. But, then again, she'll get even more pissed off if I don't try. So, I mean, fuck, I just carry on like nothing's even happened.

I drop it.

Not that it's hard. At this point, denial is as much a part of me as breathing.

And I guess maybe that's part of what Sue Ellen was trying to say.

Anyway, it's not like it really matters. I can't change and she can't change and my mom can't change and my stepdad can't change.

No one really changes.

That's why I'm still here.

So I smoke a bowl in the car after we've pulled over near the gated-off fire lane. The directions John gave me have us cutting through the fences and following a narrow deer trail off to the left. There's a full moon. We don't need a flashlight.

"This is so fucking stupid," Sue Ellen says through gnashed teeth. "This is stupid and I'm scared and I want to go home right now."

The sound of cars in the distance echoes loudly through the canyon, like rain falling. Insects chirp and chatter in the dry brush. There are no people or signs of John's little séance thing anywhere. Still, I can't help being annoyed at Sue Ellen for making every single thing we do into something negative.

"Nic, I'm serious," she shouts at me, kicking her feet in the dirt. "I'm scared, let's go home."

I roll my eyes without really meaning to.

"Come on, Sue, what do you think's gonna happen?"

"I don't know," she yells, stamping her foot like a child. "I want to go home. I wish we'd never come here."

I inhale the sweet desert air through my flaring nostrils like a horse getting ready to charge.

"Where? Here, now, or just LA in general?"

"LA in general. Everything was fine before. I never should have let you come back here. I want to go home right now."

My fists are all clenched. "Fine, fine, whatever."

I start walking back toward the car without looking at her, but I can hear her footsteps and sobbing behind me. Suddenly she's crying really loudly.

"I'll tell you this, though," I say kind of under my breath.

"Things were not all okay before we came here. I've been so empty for such a long time. Why the hell do you think I drank so much? Why do you think I need to smoke pot every day?"

She lets out a shrill, shrill scream, and I turn around to see her all collapsed in the dirt, wailing her goddamn head off.

There's a sick, guilty feeling inside me, seeing her like this, and all at once I wish I'd never said anything.

"Fuck," I say, sighing—walking back over to her and crouching down on the balls of my feet. "Fuck, I'm sorry. I do love you. I'm not meaning to hurt you. It's just that I get frustrated with you being so negative all the time. It's like every time we try to have fun it becomes some big problem. And, honestly, I feel like you're constantly criticizing me. Like everything I want to do is stupid or something. But I don't want to be fighting like this. I don't want to fight at all. Let's just try 'n' have some fun together, okay? I know we can have fun together again."

She stands up, and I see her eyes go all narrow, and then she shoves me about as hard as she can.

"Goddamn you!" she screams. "God-fucking-damn you. How can you say that? You're the one who's been acting all different ever since we got here—wanting to go out all the time—making all these new friends. You're so pathetic. I was the one who was there for you when you had nothing. I was the only one who would even talk to you. And now you're too good for me. Fuck you. I'm done. I'm fucking done."

She stomps back toward the car, and I follow on after her, my head hung down.

"I know," I tell her, speaking all slow and soft. "I know,

you're right. I have been feeling different and, uh, I don't know why. It's like I can't help it. Something is going on with me. I don't know what it is. I'm not meaning to act like this."

She keeps walking and not looking back. "Bullshit. That's bullshit. You're just a pathetic human being. That's all it is. You're weak. Without me you'd have nothing. You need me, Nic. You need me."

My face goes flushed at that.

Tears burning.

Sickness in every part of me.

"I know I do," I whisper even more quietly. "I know I need you. I can't live on my own. I'm a total failure. You're right. Let's just go home now."

I jog up next to her and try to put my hand on her back, but she jerks away.

We walk the rest of the way in silence.

It's maybe twenty minutes later as we're driving back to the apartment that my phone starts vibrating like I've got a new text message. Of course, like the idiot that I am, I left my phone right in the center console, so Sue Ellen picks it up and flips it open and I can't say anything to stop her, 'cause I don't want to seem suspicious.

There's a full minute of absolute quiet before she suddenly erupts, throwing the phone forcefully onto the floor and screaming, "Let me out! Let me out right now!" She starts to open the door, even though I'm going, like, fifty miles per hour on the PCH, and pretends to try 'n' fling her body out. I swerve wildly, taking the bait, reaching over to grab her as if she were actually capable of doing it—which I know she isn't.

I do, though. I grab on to her and pull her toward me and straighten out the car and yell, "Fuck. Jesus Christ. Fuck."

She turns her attention to hitting the shit out of me.

"How could you? How could you be in contact with that pathetic, old, awful woman?"

"Who?" I ask stupidly.

"She says she 'loves you.' What the hell is that? How could you be talking to her again? Jesus, you are so pathetic."

"What?" I say. "What? What?"

"Zelda, you asshole. Zelda, Zelda. And look, what a surprise, she says here she relapsed again. What is she, forty years old now? You two deserve each other, you really do."

And then she starts crying again and then she starts hitting me and then she starts screaming and telling me over and over that she wants to go home.

So I drive her.

In a way, I feel almost relieved being caught like this. It forces my hand, you know? It forces me to act. I could've gone on forever taking it and taking it and never making a final decision. This is good...maybe...I don't know.

And more than anything else, I guess, I can't help thinking about Zelda.

She's relapsed.

Fuck.

Why is it we both can't get this shit?

She's relapsed, and I've been relapsing for the past two years. We're on these parallel paths of self-destruction. Sue Ellen is right. I am pathetic.

When we get back to the apartment, Sue Ellen is full of questions for me, of course. She paces back and forth across the imitation hardwood floor, shouting and demanding to know when and why I started talking to Zelda again, whether I've gone to see her, why I'm such a hopeless piece of shit.

"God, you are such a failure," she says. "You think you can make it without me? Ha. You can't make it without me. You and her are gonna start shooting up again, and then you'll OD and die, and the only people who'll come to your funeral are your mom and dad. No one else cares about you. They all think you're a selfish loser. You think Russell actually likes you? You think these people in LA give a shit about you? The only reason they invite you to stuff is because you got published. They aren't your real friends. They like you because you're a writer and you've been on TV. They are all whores just feeding off you. But then, you should know all about that, since you're a bigger whore than all of them put together. You call yourself a writer, but you and I both know that's a joke. Writers use their imagination to create stories. All you did was whore yourself out—like some circus freak show geek boy or something. You're a train wreck. People are interested in you 'cause they wanna see how far down you're gonna fall. It's entertaining for them. And they're rooting for you to keep ruining your life—which you obviously are."

I watch her face as it keeps turning deeper shades of red, like her whole head might pop off. Her voice is growing hoarse from yelling so much, but she still won't let up. My head pounds. Suddenly all I want is to go to sleep. I want to curl up and sleep forever—hidden away in a tight space somewhere, like between the bed and the wall. I could fall right asleep if she'd just let me.

But she won't and I don't. I stand up and walk into the tiny kitchen, taking out the new jar of that blueberry herb and packing a bowl. I hit it long and hard.

"Oh, sure, yeah, of course," she says, yelling through clenched teeth. "Just smoke more pot, that's really great. God, you're such a hypocrite, lying to everyone about what a little angel you are. I mean, Nic, you are not sober. Don't you get that? You smoke pot because you're a drug addict who's too much of a pussy to deal with real life. You lie and you lie and you lie to me and you lie to yourself. You are a liar, Nic, that's what you are. You lie so much you don't even know the difference anymore. This is the end, you got that? From now on you can't use my car, and I won't pay for anything. You're gonna stay right here all day when I'm at work, and then you're gonna spend every night with me until we get back to Charleston. I'm sick of your shit. Do you understand me?"

"Uh, yeah, I understand."

I take another hit and then stuff the herb and the pipe into my pocket. Immediately I go grab my suitcase and start packing it.

Sue Ellen screams and cries so horribly I'm actually scared. "No! No! You cannot go. Don't do this, please, Nic, please. You don't have to do this."

It takes me less than a minute to get a bag together. I hoist it onto my shoulder and put Tallulah on the leash.

"Wait a minute," she whines. "Wait."

I get the door open and then speak to her, very quiet and even. "Look. I'm gonna go to my mom's for a couple nights. I have that speaking thing in Washington this weekend, so let's just take this time apart. I'll call you when I get back on Sunday. But, listen, this really is the best thing for both of us. I agree with everything you said. I do. And I can see now that you'd be better off without me."

Tears come streaming down her face. "No," she says, gritting her teeth again. "That's fucking bullshit. And there's no way I'm letting you take Tallulah. I don't trust you with her. You're going down, Nic. It's obvious. And I don't want Tallulah around you and that crack whore."

I have to say, I do sort of panic at that. My breath catches, and I feel the muscles in my back and shoulders tighten.

"She's my dog," I say, my voice cracking like I might cry. "She's the only thing I've got. I would never, ever put her in danger. You know how much she means to me. I couldn't take not being with her. So you better not fight me for her. I said I'd call you on Sunday, and I will call you on Sunday. There's nothing more to discuss."

And so I walk out of there, with Tallulah pulling on the leash, both of us real happy to be outside.

It's just about a fifteen-minute walk to my mom's temporary place on the canals, so I call her on the way and basically tell her I'm coming over. She sounds excited, actually. I mean, I think she gets kind of lonely being on her own. She greets us at the door when we get there and tells me she's sorry, and I thank her over and over. It's pretty cool, you know, how my mom's really started being there for me, 'cause it definitely hasn't always been this way. But she's good to me and Tallulah, offering us food and making up the spare bed. She even stays up talking with me for about an hour, listening to my complaining and venting and whatever. She gives Tallulah treats and tells me everything's gonna be all right. I'm not sure I believe her, but I appreciate it just the same.

Eventually, though, she goes up to bed, and I go into the bathroom to brush my teeth while Tallulah waits outside the door.

Now, I swear, I had absolutely no intention of rummaging through my mom's stuff or anything. But I did realize I forgot to bring toothpaste, so I open a couple drawers, trying to find where the hell she might keep hers. And I do. I do find toothpaste. I find toothpaste and a bottle of Klonopin and a bottle of Darvocet.

"Oh, thank God," I say out loud, quickly popping one of the Klonopins and two of the Darvocets. It really is like a miracle to find that shit. My heart's been racing so fast for the last few hours I feel like it might explode at any second. So, yeah, I take the painkillers, of course, and pocket a few for tomorrow or whenever.

I go lie down in bed, and Tallulah curls up all pressed against me.

"Well," I whisper, looking up at the painted wood ceiling, "looks like it's just you and me now, girl. But don't worry, things are gonna be better from here on out, I promise. I'll figure everything out. You deserve a good life, Tallulah. And, hell, maybe I do, too. We deserve to be happy, right? I mean, everybody does."

My hand scratches absently at her ear as she drifts off to sleep and is immediately snoring loudly.

"We can do this," I tell her. "I know we can. I'm gonna get clean again and then we'll get our own place and we'll go to the beach all the time and go hiking and I'll actually make some friends and it'll be all right, you know? It'll be all right."

I close my eyes and hold them shut tight.

The pills are hitting me now.

They flood my brain with warmth and pleasure.

"Tallulah," I say again, "don't worry about a thing, girl, we're gonna be just fine."

I roll onto my side.

As the pills make it all better.

And for the first time I can remember, I actually believe everything I'm saying.

I believe I can do it on my own.

So long as I never have to come down.

Ch.34

The water is gray and still and clear—reflecting the sky and sun and fast-moving clouds in a perfect mirror image—like a parallel world—an upside-down reality. The approaching islands of dense evergreen forest existing both above and below. The ferryboat carrying us passengers in both this world and the other—each one of us replicated in the glassy water—as though we're inhabiting two separate dimensions at the same time.

Of course, I am here.

My dad is with me and we're standing on the deck.

While our reflected selves stand inverted in the water down below.

I wonder if maybe, living in that reality, somehow things are different. Maybe down in that world I haven't been taking

Klonopin for the last three days, almost completely depleting my mom's supply. Maybe I haven't been smoking weed this whole time. Maybe I never used Sue Ellen first as a way to distract myself from Zelda and then as a meal ticket, only to completely betray her now that I don't need her anymore. Maybe I never tried to get back together with Zelda even though I know I need to finally move forward with my life. Maybe I never lied to everyone during the whole book tour thing, saying I was sober when I so was not. Hell, maybe in that world I don't hate myself.

'Cause, I mean, isn't that what this is really all about? I hate myself. I truly hate myself. But, in the end, you know, fuck, I always end up right where I am now—powerless, strung out, crushed beneath the fallen wreckage of the people I've hurt and the damage I've caused. It's all so obvious, you know? But somehow when I'm in the middle of it, I can never see what the fuck I'm doing. I find myself like I am now, coming down off my last Klonopin, standing on the deck of a ferry with my dad on the way to go talk about sobriety to a bunch of kids at a rehab off the coast of British Columbia. It's the center's, like, twentieth anniversary or something. So besides all the kids in treatment there, we're also going to be speaking to all the donors and staff and alumni and, you know, other people who are paying big money to attend the event. And here I am, their little poster boy for recovery, who had to hit the bowl a couple times this morning just to wake up.

I stare down at the water and wish so hard I could just trade places somehow with myself in the reflection.

"You okay?" I ask him, putting my hand on his shoulders.

He turns to face me directly. "Yeah, I am," he says, looking at me sort of searchingly. "Are you?"

I tell him, "Yeah, I guess," though I can't quite look at him when I say it.

"You, uh, you know that if there's anything you need to talk about, I mean, anything at all, I'm here for you, okay? You don't have to worry about me judging you or getting mad at you or anything. I promise, you can tell me and I won't freak out."

I stare down at the sandpaper floor, smeared with dried salt and bird shit. "Did Sue Ellen call you?"

My dad puts his hands on my shoulders, holding tight. "I'm sorry, Nic, I didn't know whether to say anything or not. But I just figured, well, if someone called and told me you were carrying around a loaded gun, I wouldn't be able to forgive myself if I didn't try to do something. Of course, I wanted to hear your side of the story. I know Sue Ellen's in a really bad place right now, so I could see her trying to attack you in any way she can. Still, I just, well, when she told me, it seemed like it fit is all. I mean, it is true, isn't it? You have started smoking pot again?"

I still can't look at him. Shame almost drops me to my knees. I try to keep breathing. "Dad, I...it's not what you think. I... I've been smoking pot now and then for the last two years. But it doesn't seem like a problem anymore. I swear. I just do it occasionally with my friends and stuff. It was scary at first, you know, 'cause I thought maybe it would lead to hard drugs again, but it hasn't. I've been able to control it. That sounds like a cliché, maybe. I mean, I get that it's hard to believe. But, the

312

truth is, I don't seem to have a problem with it anymore. The only reason Sue Ellen's telling you now is 'cause she's trying to force me to come back to her. Do you understand?"

My eyes dart up for a second and, yeah, I mean, I can see he's crying now.

"I know that, Nic, I know that's why she called. But, still, you have to understand how scary this is for me."

I nod slowly. "Of course. I know. That's the reason I didn't tell you. I didn't want you to worry needlessly."

"I understand that, too," he says quietly. "I do. But it just seems like such a bad idea to me. I mean, even if it doesn't lead you to harder stuff, isn't that a risk that's really not worth taking? Think of how much you have to lose now. Think of Tallulah and having to give her up. I know how much she means to you."

I try to answer back something reassuring right away, but my voice cracks, and I'm tearing up suddenly. "It is worth it, though," I say through the blur of stinging teardrops. "It is worth it. I mean, everything is so hard. Pot's like the one thing that gets me through it. I feel so lost and out of control. I don't know what the hell to do. And I feel like the only answer anyone ever has for me is to, you know, go back to meetings — get a sponsor — work the steps. That shit doesn't work for me, Dad. I've tried and tried, but I just don't feel anything when I'm there. So then I'm left with no other option except to keep numbing out. You have to understand, I don't know what else to do."

My dad pulls me toward him, wrapping his arms around me and holding me tight like that. "I do understand, Nic. As much as any outsider ever will, I do understand. And I want you to know that I really do trust you to figure out whatever you think is best for you. I've tried controlling your decisions in the past, and I realize that was wrong. So I really am going to leave it up to you to decide what you need and don't need. For my part, I will help you in any way I can, if you need referrals for treatment options or psychiatrists. As it is, you're not seeing anyone right now, are you?"

I struggle to get my words out. "A psychiatrist? No. I haven't seen anyone since leaving Safe Passage Center."

"Nic, you're kidding. So you're not on any medication?"

"Uh, no. I mean, I didn't have any money, so I couldn't afford to go see anybody."

"Well, Nic, I don't mean to tell you your business, but weren't you diagnosed with bipolar disorder? Didn't you write about that in your book?"

"Yeah, but, uh, I didn't have any money to follow up on it."

"But you do now," he says, pushing my hair back out of my eyes for me. "And you've got insurance now, right? Well, don't you think that some of what you've been going through might have to do with the bipolar stuff? I mean, I feel like it has to be connected. The way you've been acting, it really seems very manic to me. And I know you go into some pretty intensely deep depressions, right?"

I pause for a moment just trying to remember — or think — or something.

God, I mean, could that really be it? I have been really manic recently — like there's a sports-car engine opened full throttle inside me.

The lows go so low, and the highs go so high.

And, man, I remember when I was diagnosed with bipolar the last time, the doctor talked to me about how people in a manic state can suffer delusions that they are in direct contact with God and are being given specific messages about what to do and where to go. Basically, it's exactly what's been happening to me this last month and a half. I've been totally delusional—practically hearing voices in my head—getting high off these delusions of grandeur—racking up an eight-hundred-dollar phone bill.

It's so obvious, and I feel so stupid. But I guess I really just didn't take the diagnosis seriously. I mean, I'm pretty disdainful of the way doctors seem to slap labels on practically everyone who walks in their doors. The last thing I wanted was to be playing right into the hands of the pharmaceutical companies, convinced I have all these disorders of which only their medication can cure me. Hell, I watch TV. I see how almost every other ad is for some new prescription drug designed to combat ailments I never even knew existed. Fucking bipolar disorder, narcissistic personality disorder, borderline personality disorder, restless legs syndrome, varying degrees of autism, ADD, ADHD, OCD. It's like doctors have gone fucking diagnosis simple these days. And there was no way I was gonna fall victim to that shit.

But the thing of it is, well, now that I've had some time to sit with the diagnosis—you know, just trying to evaluate whether it seems accurate, or whatever—I guess I've gotta say that the shoe pretty much fits. I mean, everything about my behavior is straight outta the goddamn DSM. I mean, not that it's any kind of excuse, or the answer to all my problems, but it does make a whole lot of sense. In fact, so much so that I suddenly can't help but burst out laughing.

My dad jumps back a little—startled, or frightened, or I don't know what. His face kind of freezes in what looks like total confusion. But I, uh, I can't stop laughing. I mean, I feel like I'm just about to split open, I'm laughing so hard.

I laugh and laugh and laugh, and then suddenly my dad is laughing, too, and we laugh together until finally he says, "What the hell are we laughing about?"

My body's all doubled over, and I'm gasping to try 'n' get a hold of myself.

"It's just...I...I can't believe I never put it together. I'm such a fucking idiot."

"Yeah, well," he says, laughing a little more. "I won't argue with you there. But, hey, now that you're in LA, maybe I can ask some of the researchers I interviewed at UCLA if they have a good doctor they can recommend. Do you want me to try that?"

I smile at him. "Oh, man, that would be so great." I pause for a minute. "You know, wouldn't it be awesome to find a doctor I actually really like? I mean, someone whose opinion I could respect. I've never once had any kind of connection with anyone I've ever worked with, so it's no wonder I never cared what they had to say. Maybe this time I'll wait till I find somebody I can be excited about working with. That seems like it might make a difference, don't you think?"

"Yeah, Nic, I do. I really do."

"And maybe I could even get into an outpatient program.

That'd be a really great way to start meeting people, plus I'd get drug-tested once a week."

My dad has tears in his eyes again, but in a different sort of way. "That would be wonderful. I think that's a great idea. I'll make some calls as soon as we get back."

I hug him and thank him and tell him how much I love him. For some reason, I actually feel pretty excited about everything. I'm excited to start getting better. I'm excited to move forward. I feel hopeful, suddenly. I'm not sure where that's coming from.

"Dad," I say, looking off at the horizon again, "I'm really sorry. I didn't mean to hurt you."

"No," he almost whispers. "No, I'm sorry. I'm sorry it's so hard. I'm sorry you keep having to go through this. I understand now, Nic, I really do. I hate that you have this illness. But I know it's an illness. I don't take it personally anymore. We all get it—Karen, the kids—all of us. We just want to help in any way we can."

"You are helping," I tell him. "I mean, you've just helped me so much. You did everything right. Man, you've really learned a lot from all this book stuff, huh?"

He laughs. "Well, so have you. I can't believe how easy this was. In the past you would have blown up at me and then totally shut off. You've made a ton of progress, Nic, whether you can see that or not. I mean, honestly, it might seem like you keep falling down again and again. But really, from the outside, I can see that when you fall now, you're really not falling anywhere near as far down as you used to. It's like you still make mistakes, but you're learning how not to make as bad mistakes — as often. You are getting better, Nic, I promise."

I laugh along with him at that. "Yeah, well, I guess that's something."

The ferry has slowed and stuttered, and when we look off to the side, I can see the harbor coming up fast. Above us the sun is obscured behind drifting clouds, and I notice that the reflection of the boat and the other world has vanished completely. The parallel reality is gone, and I'm stuck back here, trapped by the decisions I've made and the circumstances of my life. But as the ferry eases in to the dock and my dad puts an arm around my shoulder, I realize that, suddenly, this reality doesn't seem all that bad after all. I feel hope — you know, genuine hope. And I owe that entirely to my dad and all the hard work he's done trying to understand my alcoholism or addiction or whatever. It's kind of amazing, right?

So we walk together to the rental car, and I hold his hand, and I feel truly excited for the first time in...man, forever. As hard as it's gonna be, I actually feel like I can do it, and there's a weightlessness in me — a calm — a serenity. Even the fact that I'm about to have to lie my ass off in front of all these people at the rehab doesn't seem all that bad. I mean, I know it's fucked up, but the guilt isn't tearing me apart like it used to. Anyway, it's just one lie. And in a lifetime full of millions, I guess one isn't all that bad. At least I'm pretty damn used to it by now.

Ch.35

It took about ten phone calls, but I finally did find a psychiatrist here in LA who sounded pretty cool. I mean, all I had to go on was a brief phone conversation, but, uh, I don't know, this woman just seemed like a good fit is all. I can't totally explain it—other than to say that, uh, yeah, I got a good feeling from her. Plus, she's young and works specifically with addicts. And she's a she, which has always been more comfortable for me.

But, anyway, we met the other day and, man, she really is awesome. I just respect everything she says so completely, and she was totally cool about not pressuring me about twelve-step stuff at all—even going so far as to say that a lot of addicts in recovery don't relate to the program and I shouldn't feel bad or evil or doomed to failure. Hell, that's tantamount to heresy at every rehab I've ever been to, so I respect her not looking at everything as so goddamn black and white.

In terms of meds, well, she's starting me out on a kind of intimidating regimen of lithium, Lamictal, and Prozac. It's a lot of meds, for sure, but she definitely feels like I've been goin' around untreated way too long. So I'm going through the little sample packs of each medication, trying not to get my hopes up, but, you know, feeling hopeful just the same.

The whole medication thing is pretty fucking annoying, too, 'cause it's so hard to tell whether the shit's working or not. I mean, it's not like taking a hit of E, or whatever, where suddenly everything is all bright, shiny rainbows. It's subtle. It doesn't bring me up at all. If anything, it just makes the lows not as low as they would've been in the past. And the lithium, well, it really has started to even me out a whole lot. My obsessive racing thoughts have chilled way the fuck out. And these crazy, delusional fantasies compelling me to run off with cult girls or ex-girlfriends or all that shit have eased up as well. Not that it's perfect or anything. I'm still pretty nutter butter, as Zelda would say, but it's getting better . . . all the time.

Of course, I'd like to say that as soon as I got back from that speaking gig in BC, I took the rest of the medical marijuana I had and flushed it down the toilet or something, but that's just not the case. Instead, I basically smoked through the rest of it as fast as I could, telling myself it was kind of like saying good-bye or some bullshit—like I needed closure. So for about a day and a half, I was in a total stoned-out haze. I cried a lot and got pretty goddamn scared thinking about giving that shit up. But once it was gone, it was gone. I haven't gone to get more, and I'd like to think I'm not gonna.

I don't know, the way I look at it right now is that, no matter what, if I want to actually live a good life, someday I'm going to have to do this hard-ass fucking work of getting clean and figuring out all my shit. But the longer I wait, the more fucked-up shit I will have done, and the more damage I will've caused, so it'll just be that much more difficult to get clean and start all over again. I mean, the truth of it is, if I don't do it now, it's gonna keep getting worse and worse. So, uh, yeah, I might as well get it over with, right?

And I am.

I'm getting it over with as best as I can.

In fact, I'm even starting an outpatient program today, so, yeah, I really am trying this time. The group is run out of a place on Santa Monica Boulevard and, I gotta say, it sounds pretty all right. First of all, it meets only twice a week, so it's not too intense, and by some miracle, it isn't twelve-step-based at all. Not only that, but the other people in the group are right around my age, so hopefully we'll be able to relate all right.

There's a cool wind blowing off the ocean today as I ride up Santa Monica Boulevard on this old beach cruiser I got for fifty bucks. Actually, it's kind of ironic or whatever, 'cause the outpatient building is literally half a block from this pharmacy I used to go to 'cause they'd sell you syringes without a prescription or anything. And, even more ironic still, that pharmacy is literally two stores down from the Los Angeles twelve-step store where they sell all the twelve-step literature and medallions and cheesy bumper stickers and whatever. So between both personas I adopted when living in LA—the twelve-step zealot and the hopeless drug addict—it's pretty safe to say I'm more than familiar with this particular area. Plus, my mom's office building is just a couple of blocks over, on Wilshire.

So, anyway, yeah, I'm riding this shitty-ass bike up from Mar Vista, where I'm actually living back with Sue Ellen again. I don't know, the way I figure it, since obviously a lot of my behavior was a result of my untreated mental illness—and the fact that I was using—maybe our problems were just sort of a casualty of all that bullshit. I mean, it seems like it's worth trying it again—even if, well, it does kind of seem like too much damage has been done to ever go back. Already I've caught her going through my text messages and reading my e-mails. I don't have anything to hide at this point, but, uh, still—it carries over to the way she's treating me in general—suspicious, angry, pretty fucking mean, actually. I know she'd be better off moving on. But unfortunately she just doesn't see it that way. It's like, you know, she's really scared to try 'n' make it without me. And I guess I owe it to her to give her what she wants. I know I need to be there for her like she's been there for me. So, uh, here we are.

But I'm definitely looking forward to meeting some new people at outpatient. In a way I almost feel like I'm starting kindergarten for the first time—you know, excited and nervous—ready with my new set of crayons and Rainbow Brite lunch box. I lock my bike up to a NO PARKING sign and walk over to the front entrance.

The building is basically shaped like a square doughnut, with the hole in the middle being used as a kind of atrium with palm trees and wooden benches and ferns and other faux tropical plants and flowers. Dark wood paneling lines the walls and balconies, and everything is laid out long and horizontal, like the whole place was built as a set piece for *The Brady Bunch*. I'm practically expecting the different doctors and whoever is renting the little offices to come marching out in unison with their flared pants legs, singing "It's a Sunshine Day."

Which it is. I mean, sunshiney.

Anyway, I guess I'm maybe a little scared about going in right away or something, so I decide to smoke a cigarette really fast, even if that means coming in a minute or so late. But, uh, in LA—I mean, especially in West LA—anytime I smoke a goddamn cigarette, there's always someone who comes by deliberately coughing and acting all obnoxious, so I make my way around the side of the building to steer clear of any self-righteous yuppies coming back from their yoga classes with their chakras all aligned or whatever, ready to defend their precious, perfect lungs. So, yeah, I walk around to the side of the building and light a cigarette and then practically run right into this kid standing there smoking his own cigarette and looking like he's probably here for the same group as I am.

"Sorry, man," I tell him. "I'm kinda dazed out right now— and, uh, nervous. Are you here for the Matrix thing?"

He nods and smiles, taking off his black Wayfarer sunglasses and reaching out to shake my hand. "Yeah, I'm Justin," he says. "And I actually know who you are. My mom brought me to come see you and your dad speak at the Starbucks in Westwood. It was pretty cool. I enjoyed it, for sure."

I thank him and make some joke about how I'm sorry he had to sit through our stupid talk. Then we kinda just talk back and forth about whatever—how much clean time we both have—where we live—what we do for money—all that. Turns out he manages an apartment complex in East Hollywood—which is actually surprising to me, considering he looks pretty young—I mean, even younger than I am. But, still, I'm definitely intrigued by the fact that he might be able to help me find a place to live. That is, if I were to ever get to that point. Anyway, it's not like that's the only reason I keep talking to him. He really seems kind of amazing—even in just this short amount of time. He's supersweet and insightful and, I don't know, introspective...maybe even wise. Plus, he's, like, really into movies and books and music and stuff, so that's cool for me. He actually tells me that he's going to see a screening of that old '80s movie *The Lost Boys* at the Nuart after group, and he invites me to go along.

"Oh, man, totally," I say. "I'd fucking love that. I watched that movie, like, a thousand times when I was little."

"Yeah, me too. Anyway, I was gonna just go by myself, so that's awesome. Literally every single one of my friends is still using, so I don't really have anyone to hang out with anymore. Plus, I'm super awkward when I'm sober."

"Nah, you're not awkward at all," I tell him, stamping out my cigarette on the ground. "And I'm totally down to hang out with you. I'm trying to stay as far away from my girlfriend as possible right now, so it's perfect. And, besides, I don't know, I

get a really good feeling from you. I mean, I'm having an easier time talking to you than I have anyone in a long-ass time."

I smile and then feel kind of embarrassed suddenly that I
said that. Not that it's a lie, or anything. I do really like this kid
already, but I think I might be freaking him out a little.

"Yeah, you too," he says, smiling sweetly—playing sort of
absently with his long, sun-bleached hair. "For sure."

"All right, then, cool. Should we go up to group?"

He nods and I follow him inside, the two of us still talking
a whole lot while we climb a couple flights of concrete stairs to
the third floor. It's kinda far-out, you know—meeting this kid.
I mean, already I really like him—and that's definitely saying
something, since I suck at making friends when I'm sober—
especially with other guys. Anyway, it's a good start, right? And
a good way to start this whole outpatient thing, for sure.

Of course, we're late walking into the group, but they all
kinda stop for us 'cause I'm new and I have to introduce myself
and all. So I do that real quick, and everyone tells me "hey,"
and then I finally look around for the first time.

The group leader is a very striking, tall, thin, blond, Eastern
European–looking woman who sits very straight and talks like
she's narrating one of those guided-meditation tapes. The rest
of the people are all, like I said, right around my age—more
girls than guys—which is definitely fine by me. There's actually this one girl here who says she relapsed this weekend on
heroin but has cleaned up again and is asking for the group's
support—which is totally surprising to me, since every other
outpatient I've ever been to will kick you out immediately if
you relapse. But the way they see it here is that relapse does

happen, and they just want people to pull themselves out of it as fast as they can. So, basically, the group is here to help them no matter what, not to penalize or whatever. It's pretty great. I mean, I've definitely been in positions where I've relapsed and wanted to get help, but I knew it was too late and I was already gonna get kicked out, so I just decided to go all the way. Hearing this girl tell her story and watching the group leader and the rest of the group doing their best to support her is really inspiring. And, you know, again, just like meeting Justin, this definitely seems like a good start to the whole outpatient thing.

I don't know, it's like things just seem to be making sense suddenly—like I'm on the right path or whatever. And, I mean, it's gonna be slow, for sure, but somehow that seems like the only way this is ever gonna work. My whole life I've been looking for the easy way out. It's like I've been wearing those little plastic water wings, pretending that I could swim but never actually taking the time to learn how. So here I am, twenty-four years old, and I can't even swim. The water wings are gone, and I'm sinking—I'm going down and I'm gonna die if I can't get someone to teach me how to swim. In the past, of course, I'd be too damn ashamed or proud to ask for help. Instead, I'd just keep going back for the water wings 'cause I couldn't survive without them. But now, man—now I'm finally asking for help. And I really do believe that this psychiatrist I'm working with and this outpatient program are the right ones to teach me how to swim—genuinely—with no shortcuts or hidden flotation devices. I think it's gonna work—I know it will.

I'm moving on.

I sit in group, listening and sharing—talking a lot to that girl who just relapsed last weekend. At the break I bring up Justin's whole *Lost Boys* idea, and there're actually a bunch of kids interested in coming with us.

"Man," says Justin, talking kinda secretively to me. "I don't know how you're able to talk to everyone like you do. I'm way too shy to just open up like you do."

I laugh. "Are you kidding? I'm super shy and, anyway, you talked to me just fine. But, uh, no, I'm terrified talking to people. Do you mind me inviting 'em?"

He shakes his head. "No, it'll be fun."

"It will be fun," I say.

We head back inside, but I'm quiet now, just thinking about what Justin said. It is true that I feel more comfortable being around people—more comfortable than I ever have in my whole life. And, honestly, I couldn't tell you why. It's almost as if everything I've been through these past few years has actually left me with a sense of confidence about myself. It's almost like I'm not really minding being me anymore. I feel kinda good about who I am. I mean, it's freakin' me out. I don't feel afraid. And I'm not even sure what the hell to do with that.

Ch.36

Well, it's almost over. I mean, it's hard to believe. Three months have gone by, and Sue Ellen's internship is over, so we're supposed to be going back to Charleston on Monday — an idea that really terrifies me. I'm not sure what it is, exactly, except to say that for me, going back to Charleston feels like going back to shooting heroin. Of course, it would be the easiest thing to do. I wouldn't have to worry about being alone or running out of money or outpatient groups and random UAs. I'd be able to start using again, and no one would have to know or try 'n' stop me. John Lennon says that "living is easy with eyes closed." Well, going back to Charleston would be like stapling my goddamn eyes shut. And it would be easy — safe and easy.

But, honestly, I'm not sure that's what I want anymore. As much of a fucking pain in the ass both therapy and outpatient are, I still can't help believing that staying committed to the work will really help me learn how to live without needing to get high. I believe they're teaching me to love myself and to love other people. Already I feel like I've become super close to almost all the people there—especially Justin and that girl who'd just come back from relapsing—Dylan is her name. Not only that, but I have this awesome connection with my psychiatrist, and I feel a whole lot more stabled out from all the meds. So, yeah, as much as I'm afraid not to go back to Charleston with Sue Ellen, I almost feel like I'm even more afraid not to stay here. I mean, I think I'm really changing. Or, at least, I think I'm finally ready to change.

And today, driving back on the PCH with Tallulah—the churning green and blue ocean on our right and the dry, cracking canyons on our left—I can't help but think how miserable it will be for Tallulah to have to go back to the South. She loves the beach so much. And she loves hiking up in the mountains. She loves the dog parks here. She's gotten so much better about strangers and other dogs since being here. Charleston is a dirty swamp. There are almost no places to take her off leash, and there are crazy bloodsucking flies and fleas and ticks everywhere. She's so much better off now. This is really a great life for her.

But, of course, it's not just about Tallulah. This is a great place for me, too. I'm building a life. I'm taking direction. I'm doing it right this time—starting with a solid foundation and working up little by little. I feel alive, you know? Whereas before I was just drifting in this sort of half sleep—numbing everything out with drugs and TV and endless daydreaming about the way things could be or should be. I spent my whole life just killing time—waiting and waiting—waiting for something to change, even though I had absolutely no idea what that might be. I waited for the day to end. I waited in fear for the next day to begin. I waited and waited and waited and lied to myself that magically it would be all right.

But now I'm not waiting anymore. I'm not putting it off or pretending it's not there. I'm not trusting in some deity that it'll all work out. I'm not relying on some prescribed set of rules that promises me stupid platitudes if I unquestioningly shout "How high?" every time I'm told to jump. No, this time I am doing it my own way. I'm following the steps that seem right for me and I, well, I feel good about that. My life seems, uh, full. I'm excited about things again. I have real friendships. I don't want these days to end. I want to go on like this—building and growing. It seems so beautiful to me. And it's kinda life or death at this point, anyway—living or dying—standing at the dividing line.

Fuck.

Charleston or LA.

Sue Ellen or my new friends here.

I hate that it's come down to this. But it fucking has. And either way I lose.

"What the hell do we do?" I ask Tallulah, wiping away some crusted sand and salt water from her eye.

She smiles kinda goofy at me and licks my face. Her breath smells like rotted fish.

"Ugh," I say, and she goes in to lick me again. This time I block her.

When we get back to the apartment, I really don't have time

to do more than chuck Tallulah inside, 'cause I have my last therapy appointment in, like, twenty minutes, and I'm totally running late.

The drive from Mar Vista to Westwood should be real quick, but of course it never is, 'cause of all the traffic and everything. I'm listening to the Velvet Underground's self-titled album, and I'm sweating like crazy, even though the air-conditioning's going full blast.

I smoke another cigarette, listening to Lou Reed singing, "I'm beginning to see the light."

And I sing right along, walking through the crowded UCLA campus to the medical building where I have my appointment.

Dr. Cooper's actually super nice to me about being late and all—which is a lot cooler than some therapists I've had in the past. She leads me back to her little office and sits down cross-legged opposite me in her uncomfortable-looking computer chair. I have the choice of a couch or a kind of plush armchair, so I go for the couch and cross my own legs and breathe out loud.

She adjusts her wire-frame glasses, asking me the same question I've been asking myself all day. "So, how are you feeling about going back to Charleston?"

I sit up straighter, and then I go over everything—repeating all the reasons I feel obligated to go back with Sue Ellen and all the reasons I don't want to.

"The fact is," I say, trying to make eye contact as best I can with her, "she was there for me when I needed her. So whether I'm in love with her or not, I need to be there for her now. That's the right thing to do. I mean, I really do owe my life to her. That's how it works, right?"

Dr. Cooper actually laughs some. She tucks a strand of blond hair behind her surprisingly tiny ear, and I notice for the first time how long and thin her fingers are.

"Look," she tells me, acting kind of mock exasperated, or something. "Don't kid yourself, all right? What she did for you was not some selfless, saintly act. She's no Mother Teresa. She acted on her own self-interests just as much as you did. I mean, let's face it, you both used each other, right? The decisions she made were based on her own needs and desires. So, I promise you, one hundred percent, you don't owe her anything. Obviously, it'd be great if you could end the relationship in a straightforward and kind manner, but even that you don't actually *owe* to her. And I gotta say, Nic, without trying to tell you what to do at all, you really do have a lot to gain by staying in LA. The work you're doing here is already paying off in a big way, but, honestly, you're still in the very beginning of the building process. Now, I'm not saying you can't continue this work in Charleston—and, obviously, I'd be happy to keep up appointments with you over the phone—but the support system you've built here just seems to be working so well for you. I'd hate for you to have to lose that."

"No, I know, me too," I start to say, but she cuts me off, apologizing.

"Sorry, Nic, I just want to say one more thing. You talk a lot about how you're not in love with Sue Ellen, but I think there's a big part of you that feels like the reason you don't have that love for her is because you are comparing her with Zelda. I'd even go so far as to make up that you don't think anyone could ever possibly compare to Zelda, so there's no point in even trying. But the truth is, Nic, the only reason you don't feel Sue Ellen compares with Zelda is that you very simply don't have a real connection with her. There are girls out there who will compare with Zelda, though, I promise you that. There are girls out there who will even far surpass her. What you have to do is be patient until you find that girl. Because she really is out there. And, Nic, you deserve that. And, honestly, that girl, whoever she is, deserves you, too. But Sue Ellen is not that girl. I know you know that. I'm just trying to help clarify things for you."

My voice gets all choked up when I try to respond too quickly. Tears are coming down. "So I don't have to sacrifice myself for her?"

Dr. Cooper laughs, but just to emphasize her point. "Of course not, Nic. I mean, this isn't the Middle Ages. We don't need martyrs anymore."

I laugh, even though I'm still crying.

"Look," she continues. "You don't need to hold yourself to such ridiculous standards. I can tell you honestly that you've made just so much progress. You're allowed to be happy, Nic. You deserve that. You deserve to live for yourself and, yeah, to love yourself. I give you permission, okay? And that actually means something because I'm a doctor, right?"

We both laugh together at that, and then I just close my eyes and sit silent for about a minute, breathing.

"Yes," I finally say. "Okay, yes, you're right. I deserve to be fulfilled. I mean, why not? Everyone else deserves it, so why not me? I deserve to find some sort of happiness and, yeah, I believe I can. I believe doing this work here and in outpatient and with my friends and all really will give me the foundation I need. I believe in the life I'm building. So I'll stay. I'll figure it out and I'll stay. Hell, maybe I'll call that kid Justin and see if any of the apartments he manages are open. That'd be perfect."

"It would," she tells me. "That would be just great. But I do want to say one more thing. If you do this, which I absolutely support, it'll be the first time you haven't been in a relationship in . . . what, five years? Is that right?"

I think for a minute before nodding. "Yes."

"Well, that's going to be a major transition, so wherever you go, I'd suggest you try and find something where you can be around other people who can help you through this. If that means living with your friend Justin, then that would be perfect. But I really do think that is something you should definitely be aware of."

My head keeps nodding.

"And, Nic," she says, her words coming out slow and deliberate. "Since we're on the subject, how would you feel about abstaining from relationships for at least six months?"

She smiles slyly, but, uh, surprisingly, my stomach doesn't drop out or anything. I mean, I get it and, uh, for once, I totally agree.

I thank her a whole bunch of times before leaving the office. We make an appointment for next week—when Sue Ellen will be gone and I'll still be here.

I have to admit I'm pretty fucking scared.

But, then again, I mean, what the fuck else is new?

I smoke another cigarette.

I dial Justin's number.

It rings twice before he answers.

I've always been awkward as hell on the phone, but, uh, here goes.

"Hey, man, it's Nic. What's going on?"

"Nothing, man, nothing. I'm just hanging out with my dad. What's up with you?"

"Nothing."

My hand's shaking some, but I don't tell him that. What I say is, "Hey, man, I don't think I'm gonna be going back to Charleston with Sue Ellen anymore. I mean, I think I need to stay here. So, uh, I was gonna just go stay with my mom, but I was wondering if maybe one of the apartments you manage might be open or something. I'd pay rent, of course. I just thought it'd be cool to live where you do."

There's a good long silence.

"Well," he finally says, "there is this one place where I used to live. It's a tiny little space, but it backs up to an old abandoned barbershop. I've been thinking about taking the wall down between them and making it into a livable space for two people. You could stay there if you want. There's no hot water, but all we have to do is install a heater, and then the gas company can come set up an account. It needs a lot of work, for sure. The kitchen needs a new ceiling, and there's no stove or anything. But it'd be great to have you come live here. And, I mean, of course I wouldn't charge you anything. Would you be down with that?"

"Are you kidding?" I tell him, smiling all over the place. "That would be awesome. I'd love to work on fixing the place up with you. That'd be such a cool project."

"Yeah, it'd be pretty ironic, right? Fixing up that broke-down place while we're fixing up our broke-ass lives."

We both laugh together.

"When can I come by?" I ask.

He tells me to come as soon as I can.

"All right, then," I say, my voice coming out light and excited. "I'm gonna go get Tallulah and my stuff, and then I'll drive out. It's gonna be World War Seven when I try to leave, but, uh, I'll figure it out."

He laughs again. "Oh, shit, you mean Sue Ellen doesn't know? Man, I'm sorry, that's gonna be so hard. How 'bout this, then: As soon as you get out here, I'll buy you a milk shake at the most awesome ice cream place."

I smile big at that. "Thanks, man. That'd be perfect. And, look, Justin, I really appreciate this. You're a really great friend to me. I mean, I really love you."

"I love you, too, man," he says. "And don't worry about it. I'm happy to have you here. So, uh, just call me when you're heading over, okay?"

I tell him I will.

We both hang up.

The cigarette's burned down close to my hand, and I can feel the heat of it smoldering.

I walk back to the car, humming that same Velvet Underground song.

Because it's true now — I am.

Beginning to see the light.

All I have to do is take Tallulah and go.

Ch.37

The wall came down today.

With a plaster cutter and a couple of sledgehammers, we broke through the dividing wall from the little one-room apartment to the abandoned barbershop in front. Of course, it's not an ideal space. The only windows in the front shop are boarded up and broken, and it doesn't really make a whole lotta sense fixing 'em up, 'cause the street we live on is kinda dodgy and it seems wise not to advertise our presence too much. Hell, the day I was moving my stuff in, these teenage kids got into a gun battle about ten feet in front of us. It was a miracle no one got shot.

Not only that, but twice a week some Christian organization hands out food in front of the building, so there's a line that wraps around the block from, like, ten to three, and we wouldn't be able to really use that entrance anyway.

Still, it's actually kind of a great neighborhood. The Hispanic bakery on the corner is ridiculously cheap, and all the people who live right around us are super nice. Plus, it takes me, like, five minutes to drive to Griffith Park, so Tallulah and I have been going on hikes there every morning, exploring all the different trails, me watching while Tallulah harasses tourists at the observatory. We go on hikes in the morning, and then I come back and take a cold shower (since there's still no hot water). I feed Tallulah and I feed myself, and then I write for a while until Justin comes over. We work on the apartment for most of the day, taking a break to go drink coffee at this super-great café in Silver Lake. At night we go to outpatient or to dinner or we go see a movie or watch a movie on the old TV we got for the apartment. Sometimes we fall asleep during the day and nap for a couple hours. Sometimes we drive out to Malibu to take Tallulah to the beach. Sometimes we hang out with kids from outpatient. We've even gone to a couple of twelve-step meetings.

It's kinda funny, you know, 'cause as much as I can get sort of turned off by twelve-step meetings, Justin really can't stand them. He doesn't understand it at all, and I can see how visibly annoyed and frustrated he always gets. Still, I keep making him come along with me every now and then. I mean, for me, it just seems like a cool way to meet some other sober people, you know? It's nice to feel like there's this community out there that'll always be available for me, no matter what. There's something super great about that. In terms of the actual content of the steps and everything, well, I guess I really try not to think about it too much. I'm grateful the meetings are there. And for me — for now — that is enough.

But mostly, I mean, we just work on the apartment, like I said, talking and laughing and listening to music and really working hard — rebuilding the broken-down structure — rebuilding our broken-down selves.

'Cause Justin was right, you know? We're not just working to fix this place up together — we're working to fix up our lives — together. We're both going to therapy. We're both trying to get on the right medications. We're both going to outpatient. We're both trying to learn how to make friends in sobriety — how to be a friend in sobriety — how to fucking love ourselves, sober. And the truth is, even if I can't see the changes in myself, I can see the changes in Justin. He's opened up so much. He's become so much stronger, so much more authentic. And, genuinely, I can see him learning how to love again. It's pretty fucking rad. He's growing up, you know? I feel proud of him. That probably sounds stupid, but I don't even care. I love him.

As for myself, well, I think I have started changing, for sure, but that doesn't mean I've, like, stopped making mistakes altogether. After breaking it off with Sue Ellen and dealing with her subsequent screaming "Fuck you!" yelling fits and the barrage of really angry e-mails, I guess I was feeling pretty fucking scared and insecure, 'cause I did end up sleeping with that Dylan girl from outpatient. And, I mean, she was super great, and it wasn't like she was looking for anything other than sex from me, either. Still, I know I was just using her not to have to feel everything that was going on with me and, whether or not that was right for her, it was wrong for me. Plus, she has a boyfriend, so, uh, yeah—exactly. I might be changing, but I sure as hell haven't become a better person overnight. Still, after making that one mistake, I was able to call it off and apologize, and we're still really good friends and all, so that is some sort of progress.

I don't know, it almost seems like that's as good as it's gonna get for me. I mean, I'm always gonna make mistakes, right? The trick now is to make less bad mistakes, less often. And I think it might actually be working. My mistakes aren't as bad—and they're definitely a whole lot fewer and farther between. That might sound like a cop-out, but it really isn't. I'm learning and growing, man—I am. Problem is, I'm just a whole lot dumber than most folks. It's taken me a hell of a lot longer than it does normal people. But I am doing it—at my own pace—putting one goddamn foot in front of the other. And things, at least for now, are slowly getting better. I have friends today. I have people in my life I genuinely care about. I have a pretty awesome dog. I have a great place to live. I have an amazing support system. I have a life, you know? A full life. And it's getting better all the time.

The wall came down today.

We broke through to the other side.

Justin and I.

Tallulah.

Dr. Cooper.

My outpatient group.

My family.

Justin hands me a cigarette as we sit down in the pile of rubble we've left on the floor.

The random playlist on my computer has landed on a Syd Barrett song—his monotone voice half singing, half talking. "Isn't it good to be lost in the wood. Isn't it bad so quiet there, in the wood."

I light my cigarette.

Justin lights his.

"Well," I say, exhaling loudly, "we did it, huh? We made it through."

Justin laughs, punching my shoulder. "Yeah, man, we did. But, uh, let's not go congratulating ourselves too much. We still have a long way to go. Knocking it down's the easy part. I mean, it's building it back up that's the fucking bitch."

I go on and laugh along with him.

Hell, it's the truth.

But somehow, at this moment, it doesn't seem so bad.

I guess I just know we can do it.

I know we can.

I do.

EPILOGUE

The truth of it is, well, nothing ever works out like I plan.

And yet, somehow, it all seems to work out all right.

I've been sober a year and six months today.

Tallulah's lying on the couch in the living room, and Quimby, the new dog I adopted, is curled at the foot of the chair I'm sitting in.

I'm finishing up my second book right now — which, by all accounts, is a total fucking miracle. Whether it's any good or not, well, I guess I'm not sure about that. But, I mean, hell, just to have the opportunity to write another book is such a fucking blessing. When I first talked to my new editor the day I found out the publisher was accepting my proposal, I totally started bawling my fucking head off. I'm so fucking grateful. And I really live most of my days like that — you know, in gratitude. 'Cause, well, Christ, man, everything worked out. I never thought it would, but it actually did, and way better than I ever could have imagined. Even just writing about it makes me wanna start crying. I . . . I have such a good life. It's humbling, man, it really is. I mean, I just kept trying and trying and trying and failing and failing, but then suddenly everything changed. I'm all right today. And I wouldn't trade my life for anything — my quiet, simple life.

In terms of Dr. Cooper, well, we still talk once a week, and she's monitoring my meds super closely, and I really fucking respect her and I call her when I'm panicking, and she's there for me — absolutely always. And the meds, uh, they seem to be working pretty okay. I mean, I still get super depressed and anxious and crazy, but it's like the meds just turn down the volume on it all — however slightly. Anyway, I'll take what I can get.

Of course, I'm not doing outpatient anymore 'cause my insurance ran out on it a while ago, but I do still talk to most of the kids there — Justin most of all. He's doing super well and is actually about to start at a law school here in LA, which is totally amazing. So, yeah, it's kind of all a fucking miracle. I really can't explain it. I mean, I'm not even sure what's different this time, exactly, but it does feel different. We live this really simple, beautiful life, you know? I take Tallulah and Quimby on runs in the morning. I write all day. I'm trying to figure out what the hell I'm gonna do now that I've finished this book.

But I don't know, man, it's all okay.

I watch a lot of movies and read a lot of books.

I feel pretty, well, you know, content.

I mean, not that I don't get intensely lonely or get so depressed I start fantasizing about suicide again, or smell someone smoking a joint on the street and feel some pretty fucking serious cravings. There are a lot of times when I still hate everything—you know, most of all myself. And in those moments, well, using can seem like an all right idea. But, fuck, man, the thing is, those moments are only moments. I've been through 'em enough times to know that they will pass—that is, unless I get high. If I get high, I will lose everything all over again. But if I can fucking wait it out—you know, just hold on—I mean, it will get better. At least, it always has so far. So what I do is, man, I hide out in bed. I watch a movie. I lie on the floor with little Quimby and pet him and cry and wait. 'Cause it passes. A day goes by, or two, or a whole fucking week, but then it's over and I can see the truth again. The truth is: It's a beautiful life.

I've just got to hold on, is all.

I've gotta hold on.

'Cause it'll be all right.

And we can keep moving forward like that.

No matter how many times we stumble.

No matter how many times we all fall down.

If we keep holding on, man, we will make it through.

I just know we will.

ACKNOWLEDGMENTS

All right, well, Christ, I don't know what to say. Of course I want to thank, again, my mom and my stepmom and my dad. I love y'all . . . even if I don't always call.

Jasper and Daisy, I'm really proud of both of you. I mean, you two are really some of my favorite people and my best friends, and I love you and respect you and care for you so much.

Thank you to:

The St. John Coltrane African Orthodox Church

Mark and Jenny and Bear and Becca and Steve and Mark and Susan and Lucy and Nancy and Don and Joan and Sumner.

And Adam (I love you).

And Max (I love you, too).

Even if I don't always call.

And Binky, thank you so much. You're incredibly wonderful to me.

And Elizabeth, this has been so awesome. Thank you for everything. I think you're totally amazing and cool.

Even if I don't always call.

And Jeremy Kleiner, I really admire you a whole lot.

And Ron Bernstein, I admire you, too.

And Cameron, you've been so great to me.

And Dr. Mooney, thank you, thank you, thank you.

Thank you all very much.

Love.

Me.

FOR MORE INFORMATION

Al-Anon and Alateen
www.al-anon.org
www.al-anon.org/alateen

Alcoholics Anonymous
www.aa.org

Nar-Anon
www.nar-anon.org

Narcotics Anonymous
www.na.org

National Association for Children of Alcoholics (NACoA)
www.nacoa.org

National Institute on Drug Abuse for Teens
teens.drugabuse.gov

The Partnership at Drugfree.org
www.drugfree.org